Crash Course in Library Budgeting and Finance

Recent Titles in Libraries Unlimited
Crash Course Series

Crash Course in Library Budgeting and Finance

Glen E. Holt and Leslie Edmonds Holt

Crash Course

 LIBRARIES
UNLIMITED™

An Imprint of ABC-CLIO, LLC

Santa Barbara, California • Denver, Colorado

Library of Congress Cataloging-in-Publication Data

Crash Course in Library Budgeting and Finance
Library of Congress Cataloging in Publication Control Number: 2016013107

ISBN: 978-1-4408-3474-5
EISBN: 978-1-4408-3475-2

20 19 18 17 16   1 2 3 4 5

This book is also available as an eBook.

Libraries Unlimited
An Imprint of ABC-CLIO, LLC

ABC-CLIO, LLC
130 Cremona Drive, P.O. Box 1911
Santa Barbara, California 93116-1911
www.abc-clio.com

This book is printed on acid-free paper ∞

Manufactured in the United States of America

CONTENTS

Section VII: Assessment and Evaluation

Section VIII: Communication about Money

ILLUSTRATIONS

FIGURES

TABLE

SECTION I

Introduction

CHAPTER 1

Introduction to Library Money

Money is in some respects like fire. It is a very excellent servant but a terrible master.
—P. T. Barnum[1]

This book is a practical guide to library finance and budgeting. It is written by two library practitioners for other library practitioners. The best way for you to study the material in this book is to ask yourself what you want to do in library work.

We begin with a question:

WHAT ARE YOUR PROFESSIONAL GOALS?

Are you currently trying to be an effective library financial manager?

Are you attempting to move up from line staff to middle and upper management where you will have to handle budgeting and financial issues if you have not done so already?

Are you a beginning librarian who needs to make good decisions about collections, programs, services, or staff, that is, do you have to work within a budget allocation and spend for impact?

If you are a library practitioner professional (or an aspiring practitioner), then we have tried to organize this book for you. Knowledge of library budgets and finance will help you make the library's work effective and at the same time help you individually do your job better no matter what your position title or type of library.

ADAPTATION ALWAYS INVOLVES FINANCIAL CHANGE—AND MONEY

To sum up, this is a book about how professionals use money to shape all kinds of libraries not with occasional projects, but as a process of continual adaptation to changing community needs and fluctuations in financial support. Two different library historians, Matthew Battles[2] and Alberto Manguel,[3] write that adaptation always involves change. And, change always involves money. If change is to bring improvement, it must be organized and managed for impact. And, the paramount element in change management is money, whether the application of financial resources involves addition or diminution.

This need for adaptation, including rethinking finances, is especially critical just now, since it follows an extended period of budget cuts for all kinds of libraries. Lauren Barak, contributing editor of *School Library Journal*, reported the December 2013–January 2014 survey of school librarians and media center professionals under the theme of how school librarians were "doing more with less."[4] This notion continues to be anathema to all kinds of library professionals. A whole bevy of them, operating independently, have risen both previously and after the Newman article to tell the profession that the more correct version of the financial story ought to be how library staff during budget cuts "did less with less."[5]

In 1993, librarian Lesley S. J. Farmer in her book, *When Your Library Budget Is Almost Zero*, also emphasized the significance of necessary adaptation. She told her readers that a lack of funds and staff need not stop library changes. She encouraged school librarians, small library administrators, library school staff, and large library administrators to use her book to find ideas about how to make changes in mission, evaluation, management, operations, public relations, and fundraising. In other words, Farmer is saying that librarians, particularly school librarians, need to continue adapting and changing their institutions even in bad financial times.[6]

Librarian Elizabeth Doucett concurs with Farmer. In her 2011 book, *What They Don't Teach You in Library School*, she points out that (1) change and adaptation have to be constant in libraries even when the budget declines and that (2) library professional education has neglected budgeting and spending.[7]

Within those contextual features, Doucett says that the modern professional needs to be capable of demonstrating the librarian's worth by measurement of benefits and positive impacts and its growing dependence on the technology of data and information. The ability to demonstrate benefits and impact, Doucett asserts, can be accomplished only after librarians have learned as much as possible about budgeting and finance. Doucett concludes:[8]

Sadly, for those of us who are number phobes, data is an important part of our jobs as librarians today. The objective of this . . . [study of finances] isn't to teach you to love budgeting, numbers, statistics, data, and other quantified information, but rather to demonstrate how to use them effectively and accurately when necessary in your job, and to help you lose your fear and avoidance.

Doucett's quote is a perfect rationale for this book. You might not like finance and budgeting as well as you love reading your favorite novel genre, but you need to know how to make the best decisions when you and your work peers discuss financial priorities on the way to making decisions about budgeting and finance and you need to be able to make sense of the benefits and impacts of library spending.

This crash course book should help you drive along that road. And, if you master the main points in the volume, you will learn a lot about how financial resources fuel (and help you steer) library juggernauts in good times and bad.

ACTION ISSUE FOCUS

Part of becoming familiar with the language of institutional finance is learning that even when the amount of money is deemed small, spending it is a more complex process than balancing a personal checkbook or making sure not to spend too much on personal credit cards. Librarians always work with other people's money, whether in the public or private sector. That's why librarians need to learn about audits, because library funds are audited to ensure that they have been spent according to legal requirements, agency regulations, and professional and institutional standards. To keep you out of trouble, library funds require greater protection than you give to your own spending.

After a basic text on how our library finances came to be where they are now and an introduction to how computers are changing finance, we present library finance under the major categories of national and library financial life that form the progression of the annual budget cycle in both publicly financed and corporate libraries. We draw on basic works by Daubert[9] and Gross et al.[10] for this organizational construct. These categories are dynamic: their duration and application is set by the professionals who manage the library's conceptual and service life.

We have arranged what you need to know into 10 sections. To paraphrase promoter and circus impresario P.T. Barnum, our explicit goal is to help you make money the library's servant rather than its master. To use library money in that way, financially effective librarians need to know these elements:

MAKING MONEY THE LIBRARY'S SERVANT

1. **Financial Context**: Far too many books on finance, whether for librarians or staff in other professions, treat money as if it were nothing more than accounting. Library money is a lot more, including having a legal and policy-making context and where you can turn for help when you hit a financial problem that you can't handle. We regard the context chapters in Section 1, including this chapter, as containing material that will help you manage the remainder of the book. So don't try to handle this material too quickly.
2. **Electronic Communication Impact**: How electronic communication and the Internet have affected library finances.
3. **Financial Planning**: Includes general goals and specific objectives, plus timing and training of staff and program connections.
4. **The Budget and the Audit**: How library budgets get made, what's in a budget, and how it changes its legal status as it is approved.
5. **Income**: Sources of funding, controllable or adjustable, including use of reserves, anticipated or promised income from fundraising, public funding of all kinds, and earned revenue.

6. **Purchasing and Expenses**: Expense. Anticipated spending on all budgeted activities to accomplish planned goals.

7. **Special Categories of Expenses:**
   a. **Staff Budget**
   b. **Collections Budget**
   c. **Capital Budget**
   d. **Special Projects**: Implementation. The larger the institution and/or the more problematical the income/revenue mix, the more articulate policy makers need to be about how the organization and timing of activity levels. There is considerable focus just now on data-driven library activity. Connecting data and activities in implementation is part of this equation.
   e. **Control**: Controls are legal, including the formal requests for spending (e.g., purchase orders and accounts receivable and payable, the annual audit of financial transactions) along with feedback between policy makers, governance officials, and operations staff.

8. **Results**: Focusing on measurements tells institutional staff if they accomplished what they set out to do.
   a. **Assessment**
   b. **Outcomes**
   c. **Benefits**
   d. **Impact**

9. **Communicating Effectively about Library Finance**: How to communicate effectively about your library's budget generally and specifically with users, tax payers, and governance officials. Communication includes both internal and external, by those who make policy and oversee operations for the library with staff and with constituents, both users and (if separate) those who pay for the operation of the service organization. A library's financial communication, at its best, builds the library's financial case. The best communication is both responsible and celebratory. Such communications add to your and your library's positive reputation among your staff, within the greater library community, and among the library's users and funding constituents. Even if your library does not need new revenues now, the communication ought to suggest the solid results that library funding brings to those whom it serves.

10. **Glossary of Financial Terms Used Heavily by Libraries**: Some people learn better when they can get comfortable with the new language that the class or major or profession is going to introduce. Our glossary is just such an introduction to the language of library finance and accounting. It is our way of saying that you still have to know the language of librarianship, but if you're going to play a significant role in your institutional work home, you're going to have to learn that language as well. For those who learn languages by picking them up in the context of their study, we believe we have provided the necessary definitions within the chapters that constitute this crash course book.

These 10 points represent the subject-learning goals of this book. Each point represents one section, with each section containing one or more chapters. Taken together, all these points are about the money involved in institutional change. Without such adaptation, libraries quickly become mausoleums, whether for books, archives, and electronic equipment or places for staff to retire as ineffective servants of those whom they are paid to help.

CONNECT ACCOUNTING LANGUAGE TO LIBRARY FINANCE AND WORK

Running through the first nine sections and summarized in the glossary in Section 10 is the language of accounting. We have made a special effort to instruct you in the meaning and library work context of this accounting language. In other words, when you finish, you should know some of the library nuances of basic financial terms.

In addition, we have tried hard to provide specific accounting information highly beneficial to librarians, many of whom lack formal training in accounting. To paraphrase Rachel A Kirk, who has written a very fine book on library accounting for Libraries Unlimited, we want to enable librarians to develop their "inner accountant" by "capitalizing on the professional abilities they have acquired through their careers."[11]

What we hope that our book on basic money matters suggests is that, in institutions, money is connected to everything. Externally, it is connected to how civic leaders, policy makers, and citizens view the library. Internally, it is the fuel supply that determines much about the shaping of policy, implementation, and the quickness of results. As one of the authors of this volume wrote over a decade ago, institutional money is not just "about economics but about politics, board relations, community relations, human resources, and how to keep one's balance and sense of humor even when chaos seems to reign all around."[12]

As you use this book, you will quickly recognize that we have attempted to make the volume self-teaching. As mentioned earlier in this chapter, all the accounting terms introduced in this volume are found in the glossary. The endnotes that accompany the text connect to easily accessible sources, many of which are available on the Internet, sometimes suggesting other sources as well.

As you use the volume, we hope you will find that it carries out its author-mandated assignment of providing a crash course in library finance. And, in the process, like the real world of library management, it helps you see how money is the major connecting tissue for all library activities.

NOTES

1. Barnum P. T. (n.d.). *BrainyQuote.com*. Retrieved on July 25, 2015, from BrainyQuote.com website: http://www.brainyquote.com/quotes/quotes/p/ptbarnum177789.html.
2. Battles, Matthew. *Library: An Unquiet History*. Reprint Ed. New York: Norton, 2004.
3. Manguel, Alberto. *The Library at Night*. Cambridge, MA: Yale University Press, 2009; Battles, Ibid.
4. Barak, Lauren. "SLJ's 2014 Spending Survey: Savvy Librarians Are Doing More with Less," *School Library Journal*, April 15, 2014. Retrieved on July 26, 2015, from http://www.slj.com/2014/04/budgets-funding/sljs-2014-spending-survey-savvy-librarians-are-doing-more-with-less/#_.
5. Newman, Bobbi. "You Can Not Do More with Less—Less for Libraries Means Less for Our Communities and They Deserve More," *Librarian by Day*, July 18, 2012. Retrieved on July 26, 2015, from http://librarianbyday.net/2012/07/18/less-for-libraries-means-less-for-our-communities-and-they-deserve-more/.
6. Farmer, Lesley S. J. *When Your Library Budget Is Almost Zero*. Santa Barbara, CA: Libraries Unlimited, 1993.
7. Doucett, Elizabeth. *What They Don't Teach You in Library School*. Chicago: ALA, 2011, p. 134.

8. Doucett, Ibid.
9. Daubert, Madeline J. "Fundamentals of Accounting," in *Financial Management for Small and Medium-Sized Libraries*. Chicago: ALA, 1993, pp. 36–52. (Available as pdf on course website.)
10. Gross, Malvern, John H. McCarthy, and Nancy E. Shelmon. *Financial and Accounting Guide for Not-for-Profit Organizations*, especially Chapter 23.
11. Kirk, Rachel A. *Balancing the Books: Accounting for Librarians*. Santa Barbara, CA: Libraries Unlimited, 2011, p. XX.
12. Holt, Glen E. "Ten Years in the Director's Chair: A Guide to Management Longevity," *Bottom Line*, 10:3 (1997), pp. 133–36.

CHAPTER 2

Financial Literacy in the United States

A wise man should have money in his head, but not in his heart.

—Jonathan Swift[1]

Library finance is a lot more than accounting terms mumbled like a rote prayer over a few rows of statistics about income and expenses.

Library finance begins with an implicit set of values on money and finance held by Americans, generally. That relationship is the reason for this chapter.

No matter what kind of library it is, if that organization operates in a community that is slow to provide appropriate income of every kind, especially its educational agencies, the library will have trouble being anything except a chimera, which in Greek mythology is a fire-breathing female monster with a lion's head, a goat's body, and a serpent's tail. And in spite of the chimera's notable appearance, its chief character point is that it represents a thing that is hoped or wished for, but in fact is illusory or impossible to achieve. Its synonyms are "illusion, fantasy, delusion, dream, figment of imagination, castle in the air or mirage."[2]

A library without substantial and appropriate funding is a chimera—a make-do bastion filled with overpromising and a lack of quality execution, in spite of being clothed in an idealized purpose statement.

This chapter and Chapter 3 as well are about the context of financial meaning or, more specifically, the financial knowledge system in which libraries (and all other American public service organizations) have to operate. We begin with this chapter because we believe the old adage "What you don't know can hurt you!" And America's lack of accurate financial knowledge is a great burden for all public institutions.

AMERICAN MONEY KNOWLEDGE

Decades ago, Maurice Hunt and Lawrence Metcalf explored economics as one of the "closed areas of American thought." Their contention was that the U.S. population generally did not know very much about economics, budgeting, and finance at either the policy-making or personal level.

Hunt and Metcalf, after reviewing lots of social science research, noted that Americans did not want to talk about economic issues with their families, their friends, and certainly not with people, that is, the poor, who were not successful members of the broad "middle class" like they were.[3]

In spite of the decades since Hunt and Metcalf made their observations, budgeting and finance continue to involve a set of "value issues," which have all sorts of troublesome ethical and policy crosscurrents for Americans. These issues pervade the professions, where members always seem to be worried about the probable controversies and acrimony in money discussions. It is easier, for example, to complain about library budgets than learn how they work and how to use budgeting authority to operate a better institution that delivers the best possible services that institutional funding provides.

The Federal Government officially recognized the need for more personal economic knowledge among citizens when, as a response to the Great Recession of 2007–2008, President George W. Bush used his executive authority to create an Advisory Council on Financial Literacy.

Under the guidance of its chair, Charles Schwab, founder of the huge investment company that bears his name, accepted Bush's charge "to improve financial literacy of all Americans." The projected definition of personal financial literacy was "the ability to use knowledge and skills to manage financial resources effectively for a lifetime of financial well-being."[4] This is a reasonable institutional and professional goal for librarians as well as for individuals.

After the initial burst of activity, the Council, put under different leadership and with different members, changed its name at least twice and talked a great deal about what the group should do. The main outcome of the Bush initiative was to speed the work of the Federal Government to set up its electronic information systems to answer citizen questions about monetary issues. The most visible and best known of these efforts were often used websites like www.treasury.gov; www.benefits.gov; and www.consumer finance.gov.

Unfortunately, there are no such sites to explain library finance.

LIMITED KNOWLEDGE OF FINANCIAL ISSUES

Citizen knowledge about financial issues, meanwhile, remains as emaciated as ever. In April 2014, writer Sophia Bera recounted the lack of financial knowledge among the American population.[5] Assimilating survey and research data from many sources, she wrote:

Only 40 percent of adults keep a budget and track their spending. Three-fourths of American families say they live paycheck to paycheck. More than one-fourth of American families have no savings at all . . . Collectively, American consumers owe $11.52 trillion to lenders and creditors. . . . Only 50 percent of American families have more than three months' worth of expenses saved. Nearly as many—43 percent—are concerned that their savings won't be enough to cover unexpected costs or emergencies. . . . Americans feel uncertain about their ability to retire. For those [aged] 45 to 54, the median saved was only $101,000. It's no wonder that 38 percent of adults are concerned about being able to retire on time if they'll be able to retire at all.

Summarizing much more of Bera's work, most adults wish they had financial course-work. Only 5 percent say they were taught about money by a teacher, and 40 percent say they would give themselves C's, D's, and F's on their grasp of personal finance concepts. A full 85 percent of American parents believe that financial education courses should be a requirement for high school graduation. And 52 percent of teenagers want to learn more about money, and they're most interested in budgeting, saving, and investing.

So consistent is this financial illiteracy that economics professor Annamaria Lusardi of the George Washington University School of Business has become a full-time distinguished researcher on this cultural phenomenon. In mid-2015, she wrote a post on her blog titled *Financial Literacy and Ignorance*, in which she discusses American lack of knowledge about financial matters. She wrote:[6]

To gain an understanding of the level of financial literacy in the population, Olivia S. Mitchell [a professor of economics at the Wharton School at University of Pennsylvania] and I designed and fielded three key questions which have now been used in a large number of national and international surveys. We have also administered the survey to a variety of employees at large companies, to see exactly what they know—and don't know.

Try the quiz yourself (right answers are in bold)

1. The Interest Rate question (Numeracy)
   Suppose you had $100 in a savings account and the interest rate was 2% per year. After 5 years, how much do you think you would have in the account if you left the money to grow?

   More than $102
   Exactly $102
   Less than $102
   Do not know
   Refuse to answer

2. The Inflation question
   Imagine that the interest rate on your savings account was 1% per year and inflation was 2% per year. After 1 year, how much would you be able to buy with the money in this account?

   More than today
   Exactly the same
   Less than today
   Do not know
   Refuse to answer

3. The Risk Diversification question
    Please tell me whether this statement is true or false: "Buying a single company's stock usually provides a safer return than a stock mutual fund."

    True
    False
    Do not know
    Refuse to answer

Our findings in the US and around the world proved to be shocking! Only one-third of Americans can answer all three questions correctly.

And while one might expect that the more experienced would be substantially more financial literate, this is not the case. In fact, older adults are not much savvier than the young, despite their having had to make many financial decisions including about retirement savings.

We also find that financial illiteracy is particularly severe among certain demographic groups, such as the low paid, women, and young adults.

Moreover, when we take our financial literacy survey abroad, the results are not much better! Respondents in Australia and Germany do perform better, while thus far we see respondents in Eastern Europe and Russia are the least financially savvy.

But all of us have a long way to go.

And for librarians trying to make their organizations outstanding in the services they are charged with delivering and the new ones they are trying to deliver, American financial illiteracy is a huge problem for many different reasons. To paraphrase Jonathan Swift, a major problem for library finance is that too few American taxpayers and donors have financial knowledge in their heads, even though they have a great love of money in their hearts.

NOTES

1. *Brainy Quote*. Retrieved on April 20, 2015, from http://www.brainyquote.com/quotes/topics/topic_money.html#1ZjsaDatW8cG3qOo.99.
2. Google, Chimera. Retrieved on July 30, 2015, from https://www.google.com/webhp?sourceid=chrome-instant&rlz=1C1QJDB_enUS595US596&ion=1&espv=2&ie=UTF-8#q=define%20chimera.
3. Hunt, Maurice P. and Lawrence E. Metcalf. *Teaching High School Social Studies: Problems in Reflective Thinking and Social Understanding*. Second Ed. New York: Harper & Row, 1968.
4. U.S. Department of Treasury. *Annual Report to the President, 2008. Executive Summary*. Washington, DC: Treasury Department, 2008.
5. Sophia Bera. *The Scary State of Financial Literacy in America*. Posted April 18, 2014. Retrieved on January 5, 2015, from http://www.dailyfinance.com/2014/04/18/the-scary-state-of-financial-literacy-in-america/.
6. Lusardi, Annamaria. *Financial Savvy Key to a Secure Retirement. Financial Literacy and Ignorance*. Retrieved on July 28, 2015, from http://annalusardi.blogspot.com/. This article also is on her *Forbes* blog at http://www.forbes.com/sites/pensionresearch council/2015/04/17/financial-savvy-key-to-a-secure-retirement/. Paragraph breaks have been inserted to make easier the recognition of the separate findings.

CHAPTER 3

Financial Aliteracy of Librarians

What you don't know can hurt you!
—Dr. Cynthia K. S. Reed, Organizational Psychiatrist[1]

Chapter 2 discusses the amount of financial illiteracy that exists among Americans. Every profession has to deal with this American lack of financial knowledge. We have no reason to believe that financial illiteracy is any worse in librarianship than any other profession. We do know from what librarians say and what they have written that there is a good deal of financial illiteracy in the profession.

WHAT LIBRARIANS SAY THEY DON'T KNOW ABOUT FINANCE

Like other professional groups, librarians have had to adjust to social and financial change. And they were no better prepared for the shifts than any other group of U.S. professionals without specific education in money and accounting.

When they talk among themselves, librarians admit how much about finance they don't know and wish they knew. One such discussion occurred on *The Annoyed Librarian Blog* site in 2011. Here is a summary of the issues that librarians raised in their responses to a blog posting about their deficiencies in financial knowledge.[2]

- A lack of practical budgeting information about both income and expense.
- No financial overview available, because library [financial] discussion is usually piecemeal.

- Actual library change involving finance is often sudden and unanticipated.
- Library professionals often go into their work settings with misinformation about library economics, including about the job market.
- An information split on financial information exists between managers/leaders and all levels of staff. There is poor communication about money up and down within the organization.
- Librarians are not sure what they need to know or how to find out about library finance.
- Most new librarians lack practical workplace experience, including specifics of how budgets and work intersect.
- Many librarians recognize the importance and methodology of evaluation but lack training in qualitative and quantitative assessments and evaluation.
- Many library professionals lack training in constituent relationship building, which is at the heart of fundraising.

LIBRARIAN SCHOLARS AGREE WITH THESE SELF-PERCEPTIONS

Several librarian scholars who have examined aspects of library finance agree that professional librarians lack knowledge about the language and documents concerning library finance:

- Earnest T. Stringer's Fourth Edition of his *Action Research* devotes just a little over two pages to "financial planning." In this brief account, however, he provides insight on why institutional finance is so much ignored—and/or so little explained. One of Stringer's paragraphs notes:[3]

  Finances are often the most contentious part of a process because of most people's experiences with bureaucratic organizational settings, where power and authority are invested in those delegated to control the finances. . . . In working through these controversial issues and the negotiation of sometimes conflicting demands, a group [of stakeholders] can establish feelings of purpose and unity. When people in positions of power make forced decisions, divisions and antagonism often result.

- Mary Krautter has done an excellent job of summarizing some basic issues about conflict in libraries. She suggests that conflict can be cleansing, but not if it is mishandled. The main issue in good handling of conflict is the leader's skill in handling controversial issues.[4] Financial discussions tend to be implicitly contentious. Good leadership can overcome this issue.
- Arlita Hallam and Theresa Dalston (2005), who have written the most widely used textbook on library finance, say that this absence of professional money knowledge is about accounting language, financial report forms, RFPs, and proposal documents.[5]
- Another knowledgeable librarian scholar, Elizabeth Doucett, in *What They Don't Teach You in Library School* (2011), points out the great holes in money knowledge that librarians take to their first jobs. Things as simple as knowing the difference between a P&L statement (a short-term projection of income sources and how money will be spent) and a balance sheet (a complete snapshot of a library's financial situation) or how to find

out if your project idea was turned down because of a lack of funding or some other reason are not common intellectual perspectives brought from an MLS education.[6]

- Another brief complication of statistics on library literacy comes from a 2010 survey of five Wisconsin public library systems. Among the respondents, 66 percent had an MLS (professional degree). Most of the staff had at least 4 years of experience, 63 percent interacted with public, and 24 percent were library directors. Of the survey respondents, less than 10 percent had any financial literacy training and only 5 percent had library school training related to financial information.[7]
- Last but certainly not least, there is the comment about librarians' lack of knowledge about financial matters in C. Trimpey's Amazon.com review of Anne M. Turner's 2007 book, *Managing Money: A Guide for Librarians.*[8] Her acerbic review concludes, "Want to learn how to manage money? Talk to an accountant, not a librarian."[9]

There are some course options where new librarians can learn about this important subject. But genre studies have a bigger bibliography than library finance literature. Far and away, the best book is *Balancing the Books: Accounting for Librarians* (Libraries Unlimited, 2011) by Rachel Kirk. G. Stevenson Smith's volume *Cost Control for Nonprofits in Crisis* (2011), in spite of its more general title, is a (2011) publication of the American Library Association and a recent addition to a succession of books helping librarians to learn more about finance and accounting.[10] Then, there is the Hallam and Dalston book, already cited in this chapter. The eighth edition of the Evans, Saponaro, Christie, and Sinwell book on *Library Programs and Services* (2015) has an excellent summary of "Fiscal Concerns" in its next-to-last chapter.[11] And in its specific attention to financial issues, it follows the eighth edition of LIS text by Moran, Stueart, and Morner on *Library and Information Center Management* published in 2013, which contains two specific chapters on finance—one on Fiscal Responsibility and Control and another on Library Development and Fund Raising.[12]

On the other hand, it is striking how many recent monographs addressed to improved library practice lack any coverage of financial matters. As recent examples illustrate, the index of Priscille Dando's *Say It with Data* (ALA, 2014) contains no references to the terms "budget," "finance," or "money."[13] Neither does Jeannette Woodward's *Transformed Library* (ALA, 2013).[14] These are significant books about big changes that move a library toward a new future, but without inclusion of substantial discussions about financial resources raised for or spent on various innovations. Such writing seems oddly out of touch with the heavy financial issues floating around in LIS.

As he often has done, Michael Gorman is a good transitional figure at this point when he writes in his revision of *The Value of Libraries* (2015), "The time has gone, if it ever was, when we could be confident that our libraries and their funding would be supported without question. . . . We will have to work in formal and informal ways to increase and maintain support for libraries among as many people and groups as we can."[15] This is a good, current message for everyone in the library community.

WHY LIBRARIANS NEED TO BE FINANCIALLY LITERATE

In Chapter 2, we cited the professional outlook of some economists who regard the vast majority of Americans as "financially illiterate." Like most academics, their analysis is better than their remedy for a massive problem.

The question is whether or not library professionals are financially illiterate or financially aliterate. The difference is profound. Here is the nice summary of the difference between the two words from *Wikipedia*:

> Aliteracy (sometimes spelled alliteracy) is the state of being able to read but being uninterested in doing so. This phenomenon has been reported on as a problem occurring separately from illiteracy, which is more common in the developing world, while aliteracy is primarily a problem in the developed world.

Incorporating that definition into this chapter, individuals and groups usually are considered illiterate because they have never had an opportunity to become literate. An individual or group is aliterate because they have chosen to remain so. Their choice has been not to learn something which they can learn. In this sense, librarians are financially aliterate in the areas of library statistics and budgets because they have chosen to be aliterate.

Overcoming financial aliteracy is not difficult. As we have suggested in Chapters 1 and 2 and in this chapter, it takes no special intellectual prowess to become financially literate. If you can read and write, add, subtract, and multiply and divide, you can become financially literate in library economics.

Quite simply, financial literacy requires some study. And for persons who already hold MLIS degrees, obviously they already are literate. So, they are financially aliterate *only* because that is what they are willing to be.

We think that library professionals ought to become financially literate. And, they ought to do so because it is in their personal and professional interest to do so. Here are some reasons:

First, they need to be able to deal knowledgeably with the financial rationale for the library's existence. It is hard to construct a factual rationale without a sense of useful facts. Writing about U.K. research libraries, Rick Anderson points out that the academic budget makers for higher education libraries are asking what is the library's purpose: to support the institution's purpose, especially its educational effort, or to support scholarship which has sometimes ephemeral purposes that go well beyond institutional boundaries.[16] Librarians have a stake in the outcome of that purpose debate. It would be well if they understood their personal, professional, and institutional financial stakes in the outcome of that discussion.

The struggles over U.S. school libraries have nuances of this British academic budget battle. In Ohio, for example, a major budget battle has played out in the public schools over how involved libraries and librarians should be in the education of public school children. This uphill struggle for librarians is over how teachers and libraries should be involved in meeting their constituents' needs. The State of Ohio, a library-friendly state by nearly any professional standard, in the past 10 years has reduced the number of librarians or full-time equivalents in the state's public schools by 43 percent, from 1,628. In the 2004–05 school year to 923 in the 2013–14 year, according to the Ohio Department of Education.[17] That is a profound statement by Ohio State officials about the lack of importance of school librarians in growing and sustaining basic literacy and intellectual success of children.

Second, librarians are being called on increasingly to calculate and explain the benefits and impact of their work. The greatest legal push for accountability and quantifying outcomes for all libraries comes from a specific federal law. In 1993, the federal government passed the Government Performance and Results Act (GPRA).[18] The Institute for Museums and Library Services (IMLS) interpretation of the statute noted that the federal mandate was a significant point that library grantees had to meet. The document also pointed out that "a similar emphasis on accountability is being incorporated into funding guidelines for most major foundations."[19]

Library consultant Joe Matthews over a decade ago did a wonderful job of explaining numerical literacy of all kinds in his *Measuring for Results.*[20] The year before, Matthews did the same thing for special libraries and information centers.[21] Matthews's message in these two volumes is a simple as it is profound: Libraries need to be known among their stakeholders for their effectiveness and efficiency in service delivery against funding rather than the simplistic assertion that they do good. Chapter 24 is on the subject of measuring impact and benefits.

DEARTH IN FINANCIAL TRAINING FOR LIBRARIANS

Third, there is the profound issue of the critical services that library constituents need. In much of the writing and speaking that both of this book's authors have done, we have made the point over and over that our constituents have certain basic needs. When their users' jobs disappear or change dramatically, as they are doing now, people look to libraries for solid information on how to deal with their personal and family issues. Librarians who do not know very much about finances—that is, those financially aliterate—are not going to be able to provide quality educational reference or develop needed courses on personal and family finances for their constituents.

Carol Smallwood takes a step in helping improve this knowledge in her *Complete Guide to Using Google in Libraries* (2015), when she encourages librarians to use Google Finance to help answer users' financial questions. She writes:[22]

> Google Finance is a financial website intended, and best suited for, use as an informational source. . . . [It shouldn't be used for stock and bond trading but it] *is (Emphasis in original.)* a tool even librarians should not overlook when it comes to providing a great breadth of information and plentiful instructional opportunities [on the finance of companies].

Like other knowledge areas, the more that user knows about finance, the more that person will gain from using Google Finance. Until schools and education experience major reforms, many, many individuals, families, and immigrant groups are going to be looking for study options to learn about finance and economics. If professional librarians become more knowledgeable about finance, they will be helping their institutions and the constituents they serve.

Along with Library and Information Science degree programs, library administrators are going to have to play an increasing role to overcome the dearth of training about institutional money, both as a requirement of professional education and as a major aspect of in-service training. Part of a professional's job as a library practitioner—and part of the work tasks of every library professional—is to bring an end to library financial knowledge as a lacuna. Finance needs to be brought out of its dark closet and worked through in decision making as part of annual policy making and ongoing operational change. This is no easy task, but it is one that librarians should find worth doing. Certainly it is a task that needs doing.

NOTES

1. Reed, Cynthia K. S. *What You Don't Know Can Hurt You.* National Business Research Institute, Inc. (US). Retrieved on July 28, 2015, from https://www.nbrii.com/customer-survey-white-papers/what-you-dont-know-can-hurt-you/.
2. *Annoyed Librarian,* Learning That Can't Be Taught, Posted December 5, 2011. Retrieved on January 9, 2015, from http://lj.libraryjou0rnal.com/blogs/annoyedlibrarian/2011/12/05/learning-what-cant-be-taught/.
3. Stringer, Earnest T. *Action Research.* Fourth Ed. New York: Sage, 2007, p. 156.
4. Krautter, Mary. "Advocating for the Devil: Transforming Conflict in Libraries." *ACRL,* April 10–13, 2013, pp. 9–15.
5. Hallam, Arlita W., and Teresa R. Dalston. *Managing Budgets and Finances. A How-to-Do-It Manual for Librarians, Number 138.* New York: Neal Schuman Publishers, 2005, p. xv.
6. Doucett, Elizabeth. *What They Don't Teach You in Library School.* Chicago: ALA, 2011, pp. 118, 140.
7. Smith, Arnott, and Kristin R. Eschenfelder *Public Libraries as Financial Literacy Supports.* The School of Library and Information Studies, University of Wisconsin, Madison, December 2011, Center for Financial Security, Family Financial Security Webinar Series, December 13, 2011. Sponsored by a grant from the UW-Madison School of Human Ecology Beckner Endowment. Retrieved on July 27, 2015, from http://cfs.wisc.edu/presentations/Eschenfelder2011_PublicWebinarPR.pdf.
8. Turner, Anne M. *Managing Money: A Guide for Librarians.* Jefferson, NC: McFarland, 2007.
9. The "C. Crimpey" review appears at http://www.amazon.com/Managing-Money-A-Guide-Librarians/dp/0786430524.
10. Smith, G. Stevenson. *Cost Control for Nonprofits in Crisis.* Chicago: ALA, 2011.
11. Evans, G. Edward, Margaret Zarnosky Saponaro, Holland Christie, and Carol Sinwell. *Library Programs and Services. The Fundamentals.* Santa Barbara, CA: Libraries Unlimited, 2015, Chapter 18.
12. Moran, Barbara B., Robert D. Stueart, and Claudia J. Morner. *Library and Information Center Management.* Eighth Ed. Library and Information Science Text Series. Santa Barbara, CA: Libraries Unlimited, 2013.
13. Dando, Priscille. *Say It with Data. A Concise Guide to Making Your Case and Getting Results.* Chicago: ALA Editions, 2014.
14. Woodward, Jeanette. *Transformed Library: E-Books, Expertise, and Evolution.* Chicago: ALA, 2013.
15. Gorman, Michael. *Our Enduring Values Revisited. Librarianship in an Ever-Changing World.* Chicago: ALA, 2015, p. 53.
16. Anderson, Rick. "A Quiet Culture War in Research Libraries—And What It Means for Librarians, Researchers, and Publishers," *Insights: The UKSG Journal,* July 7, 2015. Retrieved on July 31, 2015, from http://insights.uksg.org/articles/10.1629/uksg.230/.
17. Thebault, Reis. "School Districts in Ohio Cutting Librarians," *Columbus Dispatch,* July 27, 2015. Retrieved on July 28, 2015, from http://www.dispatch.com/content/stories/local/2015/07/27/downsizing-librarians.html.
18. GPRA has its own website at https://www.whitehouse.gov/omb/mgmt-gpra/index-gpra and a number of related websites explaining its impact, many of which are available

by simply inserting the law's acronym. Perspectives on Outcome Based Evaluation for Museums and Libraries.

19. Retrieved on August 1, 2015, from http://www.imls.gov/assets/1/assetmanager/per spectivesOBE.pdf. The quote is from an earlier document of the same name written by Beverly Sheppard, which is less wordy and which we have in our possession.
20. Matthews, Joseph R. *Measuring for Results: The Dimension of Public Library Effectiveness.* Santa Barbara, CA: Libraries Unlimited, 2003.
21. Matthews, Joseph R. *The Bottom Line: Measuring the Value of the Special Library or Information Center.* Englewood, CO: Libraries Unlimited, 2002.
22. Smallwood, Carol. *The Complete Guide to Using Google in Libraries: Research, User Applications, and Networking.* Vol. 2. Lanham, England, and Plymouth, UK: Rowman and Littlefield, 2015, p. 264.

CHAPTER 4

The National Economy and Library Continuity

The more things change, the more they are the same.

—Alphonse Karr[1]

A key to understanding our own financial times is recognizing the impact of economic trends over time. A good starting point is the end of World War II in the mid-1940s.

When the war ended, the United States reigned supreme. The nation was out of the Great Depression. The economy was booming. America's cities and towns—unlike those in many cities and villages in Europe and Asia—remained unbombed, and therefore not only intact but expansive. Federal veterans' benefits were enabling tens of thousands of GIs to go to college. And jobs were plentiful for those who finished high school or courses in technical training and for those who achieved a college degree in nearly any subject.

The prosperity signs were everywhere: New capital goods like refrigerators and housewares, new automobiles and televisions, massive suburbanization, new expressways, and highway-and-street fix-up programs—and throughout, there was the expectation that individuals and families could use the education and information available to them to improve their lives.[2]

No nation had ever experienced the kind of prosperity that the United States had between 1945 and 1960. Gross national product, a measure of all goods and services produced in the United States, jumped from about $200,000 million in 1940 to $300,000 million in 1950, to more than $500,000 million in 1960.[3]

Economic historians Andrew Graham and Anthony Seldon (1991) captured the mood of the historic time. One review of their book notes:

> The chance to begin anew seldom occurs. Yet the nearly complete breakdown of the world economy between 1939 and 1945, together with the dominant position of the United States at the end of the war, provided just this opportunity. A new international economic order was built on the ruins of the old.[4]

LIBRARY DEVELOPMENT, 1929–1960s

During the Great Depression and World War II, library economic fortunes varied. Through the depression, many libraries had to cut both services and staff salaries. In general, however, like all population-serving institutions maintained through the depression and war, libraries had gotten good at delivering library services on the cheap. Along with the development of a tradition of being able to work effectively without gigantic funding, American libraries in the depression and war built a reputation as institutions that provided enormous help in individual, family, and community economic development.[5]

Libraries exited from the war with limited economic resources to help Americans build bright postwar futures. Post–World War II prosperity kicked off many reform movements. The Women's Movement, the Civil Rights Movement, and President Lyndon Johnson's War on Poverty all reflected the expansive quality of thought about what the United States ought to do for its own people, whether explicitly or implicitly. David Halberstrom calls the 1950s the crucible decade in which the rest of the century was formed in just a few years.[6] Libraries reflected that periodicity, with all the major reform movements impacting one or another library type in some major way.

FEDERAL GRANTS FOR LIBRARIES

In its new prosperous mood, the Federal Government got involved with funding for libraries in a new monetary way—passing the Library Services Act (LSA) in 1956. The avowed purpose was to bring isolated rural communities into modernity by planting or upgrading libraries. LSA was amended in 1964, The Library Services and Construction Act (LSCA), adding funding for library construction and rehabilitation in urban as well as rural places. And that was followed by the Library Services and Technology Act (LSTA) of 1996, helping libraries fund new technology to match the rapid changes in a new age dominated by technology.[7]

NEW FUNDING: GATES FOUNDATION GRANTS AND E-RATE

This federal largesse produced a new, higher funding tide for libraries, making their leaders much more responsive to equity issues like rural isolation, discrimination, poverty, and physical and mental handicaps. With the passage of LSCA and LSTA, along with the Gates Foundation's millions of dollars in grants to libraries begun in 1995. The Gates

Foundation's program accomplished in conjunction with the American Library Association was designed to spur technology development in low income communities. That program, plus the incentive funding from Federal E-Rates, which began in 1996, floated a good deal of discretionary money into library hands.[8] Much of library technology complexes for their professional staff and their users were developed from the grants issued in this period and from E-Rate funds.

PUBLIC LIBRARY INQUIRY

Along with new funding came the need for proving impact of externally funded projects as well as for local support library services. The profession took cognizance of this situation early on. A group of library professionals initiated and led the effort called the Public Library Inquiry which operated between 1947 and 1952. In the data-based and often scholarly inquiry were many visions of a bright future if libraries were improved with better funding.[9]

DEMAND FOR EVALUATION (MEASURABLE OUTCOMES)

With federal funding came the incentive for evaluation. The Government Performance and Results Act of 1993 required libraries to measure the impact from their expenditure of federal funds.[10] This change meant that library professionals who historically had focused on "outputs," now had to pay attention to "outcomes," "impacts," and "benefits."

More attention to outcomes meant that many library staff members became more attentive to income, expense, and performance results that would withstand formal audits by outside accountants. In the process, it became increasingly difficult for library professionals and institutional leaders to avoid sophisticated, long-term involvement with financial issues.[11]

We began this brief history chapter with Alphonse Karr's quote, "The more things change, the more they are the same." That certainly is true of library history and library finance since World War II. The major theme of that history is the continuity that exists in library development, especially library finance.

CONTINUITY IN LIBRARY FINANCES

With the major upheavals in the national economy in recent decades, library financial problems appear to have remained the same year after year, in good times and bad, even when technology seems to be changing the whole field. Here is a discussion of basic issues that continue through the period to the present.

- *More staff wanted.* There never seems to be enough money to fund all the activities that library managers and staff want to see their work units do with more employees plus different collections and more time (the latter also a declaration for more staff). The complaint for more staff is legion in the profession. Other than for recruiting volunteers, the only way to obtain more workers is to hire them, and that means more money from the budget. The great problem is what happens to the institutional budget when staff is increased greatly. If the salary line, including benefits, costs only 50 percent of the total budget, money is relatively flexible. If total staff salaries absorb 60–70 percent or 80–90 percent, then other budget needs will have to be minimized. There are other pressures on staff demand: Technology, clerical work, materials sorting, delivery, and adding new non-librarian specialists to staff—all are affecting staff composition and staff costs. An interviewee sounded the problematical nature of the staffing theme when she/he noted, "We need more staff to do anything at all. Innovations are exciting, but few and far between in terms of having the staff or budget to implement any. We love the self-service and automation options, but can't implement them at our price point."[12]

- *Collection priorities.* The shift from speculative (just in case) demand is driving collection development to just in time acquisitions. Larger public libraries and research libraries generally can enjoy substantial money savings by putting collections in place only when patrons request them versus libraries that anticipate, collect, and hold every item they can for possible patron use at some future time.[13] That, of course, biases library collecting toward electronic items, a decision that can mean a great difference in the budget total spent on collections.

- *Nature of collections and sharing changing.* The gap is widening between the universe of published output and collection budgets. As the Great Recession of 2007–09 continued, prices for medical and science journals escalated even as library budgets tightened.[14] As this book manuscript is being prepared, the demand for eBooks and electronic data bases has increased dramatically and continues to increase. And many vendors, both established and remarkably new, are shifting the sorting formulae and costs of distribution to individuals and libraries. Netflix and Amazon Prime are two huge "category killers" that already are affecting library demand.

- *Service demand shifts.* Rapidly changing demand for library services is an ongoing reality for many libraries. Many new users want to download books and articles on their tablets and smartphones. And the increase in eBook demand is driving use statistics for many public, academic, and school libraries. Chris Buckley's excellent summary article on Pittsburgh illustrates this conclusion nicely.[15]

- *Library space use changing.* In his examination of Charlotte's ImaginOn Library design, one of this book's coauthors has shown just how far away from book storage that public library design already has moved.[16] And Carl Grant shows conceptually the huge change that libraries are going to have to make through the 21st century. In essence, he says that libraries and library work has shifted dramatically, and buildings need to catch up.[17]

- *User assistance needs shifting.* Libraries are witnessing a high demand for free or very cheap but high quality job-preparation courses, especially as jobs move from the manufacturing sector to information/knowledge sector.[18] See a typical public library response from Fairfield Public Library, Fairfield, CT, which advertises one-on-one meetings with a job counselor, lectures on various aspects of getting a job, pod casts on similar issues, coaching on how to do well in an interview, and a job search boot camp, plus many other kinds of employment help and programs.[19]

- *Accountability demands.* Increased scrutiny of library budgets and demands for accountability currently are a growing part of the library budget process. When money gets tight, institutional leaders often turn to the language of accountability as a way to put the library pressure of increased scrutiny and possible public exposure on budget officers. It is only a matter of how much time before all library professionals will build accountability measures into operations to make short-term assessments in quality of operations and long-term evaluations of benefits or impact of particular programs.[20]

- *Cuts in funding. Budget sequestration and zeroing out library budgets.* Big cuts in federal and state funding put more pressure on local and single library funding. Sequestration was a federal budget tactic imposed in 2013. It is the imposing of automatic government spending reductions by withholding appropriations by a fixed percentage that applies uniformly to all government programs, except those exempted. When the federal budget sequestration of 2013 was announced, Kathleen Hanselmann, chief librarian at the Defense Language Institute Foreign Language Center in Monterey, California, noted a whole litany of losses. Cuts included the furloughing of 260 librarians and 800 technicians for 11 days each through the current fiscal year on those who worked in various units of the Department of Defense Libraries. Hanselmann noted that the loss was not only an imposition on workers, but also a reduction in service to those who used DOD libraries.[21] Zero budgeting is a favorite tactic of "liberal" presidents like Clinton and Obama, who zeroed out library appropriation budget lines to get their draft budgets balanced, relying on self-interest of elected officials in the house and senate to put money for libraries and museums back into the federal budget.[22]
- *Schools hardest hit.* For decades, Philadelphia's public institutions and schools have contended with severe budget cuts. The results can be seen in school library positions. "In 1991, there were 176 certified librarians in city schools. Now there are 11—for 218 schools." Such budgeting may create the illusion of librarianship but it is hardly a fair representation of what effective library services could bring to the city's school children.[23]

You'll learn more about specific budget basics in the next sections on budget, income, expenses, and controls and evaluation.

NOTES

1. *Brainy Quotes*. Retrieved on April 27, 2015, from http://www.brainyquote.com/quotes/quotes/a/alphonseka125474.html.
2. A helpful summary of the 1950s can be found in *Wikipedia*. "United States in the 1950s." Retrieved on January 12, 2015, from http://en.wikipedia.org/wiki/United_States_in_the_1950s.
3. *About.com*. "The US Economy, 1945–1960." Retrieved on January 12, 2015, from http://economics.about.com/od/useconomichistory/a/post_war.html.
4. Graham, Andrew, and Anthony Seldon. *Government and Economies in the Postwar World: Economic Policies and Comparative Performance, 1945–85*. London: Routledge, 1991. The quote is from the Amazon.com introduction to the contents of the book. Retrieved on January 6, 2015, from http://www.amazon.com/Government-Economies-Postwar-World-Comparative/dp/0415072883/ref=sr_1_23?ie=UTF8&qid=1420587686&sr=8–23&keywords=US+economy%2C+1945–1960.
5. McCook, Kathryn de la Pena. *Introduction to Public Librarianship*. Second Ed. New York: Neal Schumann, 2011, pp. 49–53.
6. Halberstrom, David. *The Fifties*. New York: Ballantine Books, 1994.

7. McCook, pp. 53–57; *Wikipedia*. Library Services and Construction Act. Retrieved on January 9, 2015, from http://en.wikipedia.org/wiki/Library_Services_and_Construction_Act.

8. *Wikipedia*. "E Rate." Retrieved on January 9, 2014, from http://en.wikipedia.org/wiki/E-Rate.

9. Raber, Douglas. *Librarianship and Legitimacy: The Ideology of the Public Library Inquiry*. Westport, CT: Greenwood Press, 1997.

10. U.S., White House, Office of Management and Budget. *The Government Performance and Results Act of 1993*. Retrieved on January 10, 2015, from http://www.whitehouse.gov/omb/mgmt-gpra/gplaw2m.

11. Dresang, Eliza T., Melissa Gross, and Leslie Edmonds Holt. *Dynamic Youth Services through Outcome-Based Planning and Evaluation*. Chicago: ALA, 2006, p. 8–21.

12. Zickuhr, Kathryn, Lee Rainie, and Kristen Purcell. *Library Services in the Digital Age. Part 5. The Present and Future of Libraries. Pew Internet and American Life Project*. January 22, 2013. Retrieved on August 1, 2015, from http://libraries.pewinternet.org/2013/01/22/part-5-the-present-and-future-of-libraries/.

13. Entlich slides. Mangles, Andrew. "Collection Development: Just in Case vs Just in Time." *PLA Blog*. April 4, 2009. Retrieved on February 10, 2015, at http://plablog.org/2009/04/collection-development-just-in-case-v-just-in-time.html

14. Entlich slides. Bosch, Stephen, and Katie Henderson. "Winds of Change: Periodicals Price Survey, 2013". *Library Journal*. April 25, 2013. Retrieved on January 10, 2015, at http://lj.libraryjournal.com/2013/04/publishing/the-winds-of-change-periodicals-price-survey-2013/#.

15. Buckley, Chris. "Financial Problems Plague Local Libraries." *Trib Total Media*. February 24, 2014. Retrieved on January 9, 2014, from http://triblive.com/neighborhoods/yourmonvalley/yourmonvalleymore/5626793-74/library-libraries-ambrose#axzz3RH2NBDub. Also see Besen, Stanley M., and Kirby, Sheila Nataraj. *E-books and Libraries: An Economic Perspective—Report to the American Library Association—September 2012*. Retrieved on February 10, 2015, from http://www.ala.org/transforminglibraries/sites/ala.org.transforminglibraries/files/content/final%20economic%20report%20sept2012.pdf.

16. Holt, Glen E. ImaginOn, "The First 21st Century Public Library Building in the US." *Public Library Quarterly,* 27:2 (2008), pp. 174–91.

17. Grant, Carl. "It's Time to Define a New Brand for Libraries. Let's Make Sure It Leaves People Soaring, Not Snoring." *Public Library Quarterly*, 34:2 (2015), pp. 99–106.

18. Buckley, Pittsburgh, loc. cit.

19. Fairfield Public Library. *Job and Career Resources*. Retrieved on February 10, 2015, from http://fairfieldpubliclibrary.org/classes-and-events/job-and-career-resources/.

20. Entlich slides. Entlich, Richard. "Strategic Use of Circulation Data. Moving Beyond the Basics." Charleston Conference, November 6, 2011. Retrieved on February 6, 2013, from http://www.slideshare.net/rge1/strategic-use-ofcirculationdatacharleston2011entlich. See, for example, *New Directions for Higher Education. Special Issue: Strategic Financial Challenges for Higher Education: How to Achieve Quality, Accountability, and Innovation*. Winter 2007. San Francisco, CA: Jossey-Bass, 2008.

21. Buckley, Pittsburgh, and Kathleen Hanselmann. "Under Sequester: How Military Libraries are handling Budget Cuts." *American Libraries Online*. Posted August 20,

2013. Retrieved on February 10, 2015 from http://www.americanlibrariesmagazine
.org/article/military-libraries-and-sequestration-0.

22. "President Obama's Budget Strips FY2012 Library Funding." *American Libraries*,
42:3/4 (March/April 2011), p. 8.

23. Graham, Kristin A. "School Cuts have decimated Librarians." Posted at *Philly.com*
on February 2, 2015. Retrieved on February 11, 2015, from http://articles.philly
.com/2015-02-02/news/58679838_1_school-library-librarian-philadelphia-school-
district.

SECTION II

Building Financial Infrastructure
for Your Library

CHAPTER 5

Electronic Communications: How Computers Are Changing Library Finance

I do not fear computers. I fear the lack of them.

—Isaac Asimov[1]

PAPER AND COMPUTERS

Not long ago, a visit to a library finance office was like entering a paper maze. Every table and desk surface was piled high with stacks of papers: audit documents, requests for payment, staff time sheets, purchase orders for office supplies, and orders for paper-based and electronic books.

How could a "modern" library organization be burdened with so much paper related to financial transactions? Why did these financial operations look like a badly run 19th-century office? Some otherwise modern libraries still run their finances this way, but most have embraced computing tools to work better and faster (and more neatly).

That observation seems especially relevant given the conclusion of George Stachokas in his 2014 volume, *After the Book.*[2] *Information Services for the 21st Century* (Amsterdam, Boston, and London: Chandos, 2014). Stachokas writes, "Electronic resources pose a fundamental challenge to libraries. New skill sets, different organizational structures and different approaches to work are required to manage electronic resources."

The shift will occur in all libraries, because technological progress occurs at different rates across different libraries. As part of their change, libraries will have to move from a local to a global strategy with new services, organizational structures, and new improved management. And, along with all that other change, Stachokas says is the greatest library-related change of all—the need to reform the Library and Information Science (LIS) education system. Through it, meanwhile, all library professionals will have to break away from their professional work to focus on print.[3] That means a major reorganization of work, not just in style but in the character of the tasks that have to be accomplished.

Part of that dramatic shift will be a big change in library budgeting and finance. Here's the way a basic book on accounting describes the impact:[4]

> Computer technology permits companies to employ **continuous or perpetual budgets** (Emphasis added). These budgets may be constantly updated to relate to the next 12 months or next 4 quarters, etc. As one period is completed, another is added to the forward-looking budgetary information. This approach provides for continuous monitoring and planning and allows managers more insight and reaction time to adapt to changing conditions.

This computer advantage in finance is huge: The new technology helps organizational planners to consider and to project future revenue and spending in more far-reaching terms, a great advantage in all public service institutions no matter how they are funded.

A bigger advantage, however, is that the general public has embraced electronic banking and even use of library computers for financial transactions. In a 2010 survey, 92 percent of library computer users utilized the institution's Internet machines to make commercial transactions; 42 percent of these users said they did not have access to any other computer than those at their library; 62 percent said they did online banking; 53 percent said they used them to make online purchases; and roughly 50 percent reported they used them to pay bills.[5]

The ability for library customers to utilize all kinds of electronic devices to carry out financial tasks means that libraries have the potential to create not only online reserves and checkouts, but also to do anticipatory marketing to individuals and groups, to create special search environments, and search-related purchase options on library websites. Suggestions of this kind of activity are included at Innovative Interfaces website under the heading they provide called "The Open Library Experience."[6]

The new computer environment also suggests opportunities for breaking out of the limits of such heavy dependence on the staff that work in a single building or single system, whether they operate in reference or finance. Computer communication has made shopping and services ubiquitous, and collaboration and outsourced work with other agencies will increasingly become part of the library way of professional work.[7] Many of these options will appear in more detail in the budgeting, income, and expense chapters that follow this section.

The point of this short chapter introduction is to advise that if your library is still trying to do all its financial operations without a computer, it is time for a change. Library financial record keeping has gone electronic, and it is difficult to articulate a valid exception to this current records-keeping practice. Buffalo and Erie County Public Library, for example, issues an electronic monthly financial report to its constituents.[8]

Within that context, we know that on some occasions Information Technology (IT) staff has disagreed with those overseeing library financial records over the prospect of keeping the organization's financial records "in the cloud." That issue can and should be resolved, even if it becomes necessary to bring in an outside financial records specialist from an area bank, accountancy, or auditor to provide expert advice.

RECORDS MANAGEMENT

In the context of record keeping for finance, whether you are reading this book for an LIS class or are making the effort to learn about the subject on your own, we want you to know that modern library finance no longer needs desktops and storeroom shelves stacked high with "official" accounting reports no matter how small the library or how weighted down in paper traditions the library finance office has been in the past. Some paper is still required as a matter of obeying financial laws. However, the ability to make exact (and unchangeable) copies of former paper documents and the desire for a smoothly operated electronic records system has lessened the need for more and more paper records. The head of your finance operation and/or the attorney who advises you on institutional financial matters should be able to define record groups that need to be saved and those that can be shredded and recycled.

A good place to start is with the Foundation Center's Grant Space, which offers a nice summary document on which business-related records that not-for-profits ought to save and for how long.[9] The Internal Revenue Service is aware of the records issues faced by not-for-profit organizations and has established guidelines about what paper records you can save and what you can throw away.[10] Remember that the Patriot Act also has an impact.[11] Consult the previous three endnotes for the electronic sources. If you fall into a different category of library, the guidelines we have cited will give you a place to start.

Sorting out which accounting and finance software that either can be loaded on institutional computers or made accessible from the cloud from desktop computers, tablets, and telephones owned by the library or by individual staff members with appropriate security access is a challenge, but there is nearly endless writing on this topic and a huge number of consultants ready to help you make a decision.

However, remember that modern electronic Integrated Library Services (ILS) may require some programming to be connected to accounting software that the library wants or needs to run. Staff needs to be trained to use financial software, and realistically the library will need on-going technical support to keep the financial software not only operational, but current as well.

Simply stated, even small libraries should go electronic when it comes to budget and finance with some technical support.

AGILE COMPUTING IN LIBRARY FINANCE

In libraries big and small, there are four historic power centers built into the organization. The first is the executive management section, including oversight and supervision of all library work units. The second is technology services centered on computers and IT. The third is finance, whether that authority is in a single bookkeeper or in a Finance

Office staff. And in North American libraries with large collections along with significant reference and research collections, the fourth power center is the cataloging individual or group that orders and processes materials making them shelf ready and/or recording their presence in the electronic catalog, plus eliminating them from the collections records when they are weeded.

With these four groups articulating their varied purposes, it is difficult to get everyone to agree on any institutional computer system, much less one that establishes an "agile computing environment" especially for finance. In the progressing era of big data, however, agile computing systems are increasingly needed.

Robert Kugel, CFO and director of business research at Ventana Research based in San Ramon (California), provides this overview of agile computing. He says that an agile library electronic environment has these characteristics[12]:

> Emerging in-memory systems will fundamentally change the way finance organizations handle planning, budgeting, forecasting and analysis. They can help finance be more agile and able to shift its focus from the traditional "rear-view mirror" orientation of historical accounting data to a forward-looking approach that emphasizes analytics-based contingency planning to identify a company's best course of action.

According to Kugel, not many computer systems in the professions are agile. Kugel says the first characteristic of big data operated in the cloud is that you don't wait to make analysis on old data. For example, the budgets that the American Library Association issues to its members currently are not months but years old, and the forecasting for future policies and operation is done on past data and not current data modified by future projections. To sum up, users now ought to have access to much larger data sets and computer software that allows not only speed and accuracy, but also interactive calculations about the present and future using complex data models.[13]

As with all changes in complex organizations, such shifts do not take place easily. A comprehensive 2007 survey on issues of agile computing in business noted the low levels of adoption of agile features in business finance.[14] Research on businesses with at least 100 employees found

> that just 13% of midsize or larger companies . . . can explore every relevant scenario and examine the implications of each to any degree of detail across the entire company. Another 37% can assess the full implications for a limited number of scenarios, while the remaining half cannot gauge the impact of possible actions to any significant degree.

It is likely small libraries need the same agility as larger libraries, and because of diseconomies of small scale, they are less likely to have it than larger and more amply funded systems.

One author suggests that the characteristics of an agile computer system would include the following:[15]

> Tailor information sources selected to targeted users.
> Employ representations familiar to targeted users.
> Provide aid to enhance information seeking and use.
> Manage the process that information is intended to support.
> Glean insights from the information sought and used.

Epitomize excellent ease of learning and use.
Adapt all of the above to evolving intentions of targeted users.

The authors of this book recognize that computerized communication and analysis is reshaping finance, including library finance. Thus, while this book still uses the generic language of accounting (a purchase order is a purchase order, whether paper or electronic), we try to acknowledge the significance of computerized communication in the way that libraries can operate their financial management operations. Going one step further, we try to make computerized communication integral to the process of library finances, because that's the way it is or is becoming in the vast majority of libraries in North America.

One important way we accomplish this latter goal is to not include library-specific forms as illustrations. Instead, we use a few simple, general forms. If you want to see a specific type of financial form, it is always available on the Internet, usually as a Federal or State Document or a working document from a library system similar to yours. Carrying out this goal, therefore, results in a shorter book, which we believe should be characteristic of the titles in this series of Crash Course volumes.

The point, then, is to remind those trying to learn more about library finance that shifting electronic communications are changing financial management just like they are changing all other aspects of library operations.

In the marketplace, the cliché phrase most often articulated is "Caveat Emptor"—"Let the Buyer Beware." If you have any ambitions about doing a great job of financial management as a library staff member, even one in which you are moving up in position rather than from one institution to another, then your guardian phrase ought to be "Bibliothecarius Emptor Pecuniarius Inscientia" or "Librarian Beware Financial Ignorance."

In conclusion of this chapter, we want to point out that small libraries need to become self-conscious about agile computing and that there are financial systems that make such effort possible.

TechSoup is one vender to consider in this category. Like other organizations, TechSoup offers computers fitted out with accounting software for libraries. According to the company's advertisements, the payments for such software is low, perhaps 5–20 percent of the retail cost of what a hardware-software system might cost on the retail market. The software offers include AccountEdge Pro or QuickBooks for both MACs and Windows.[16] The TechSoup offer is made in association with IdealWare.

Users quickly find distinct advantages. Unlike EXCEL, it is hard to delete entries accidentally. Moreover, a single entry can be entered into multiple reporting environments. Next, the software allows quick assembly of varying reports, including cash flow summaries and information to help fill out the Federal 990 declaration for tax-free institutions. And finally, the financial operation can be run in the cloud or discretely on a single library computer.[17]

Larger library systems will find all kinds of electronic financial accounting systems available, both those that already operate in tight conjunction with the library's ILS system and those that will require connection. University, corporate, and special libraries will likely be part of an organization-wide financial system that may or may not be easily adapted to library functions. It is important that librarians in these settings use the organization financial computing systems fully and advocate that the systems be adapted for library use as necessary.

To carry through on that idea suggests a new kind of library, one used both by Stachokas in the opening of this chapter and again in the blog posts of Lorcan Dempsey, who at one point in his recent book of essays remarks that libraries of all kinds are going to come to look like the technology corporation Cisco. That is, they will become "flat systems," operating in the "space of flows" with most of their services provided by others.[18] To capture the image, think of shared cataloging and what all libraries will look like when that collaboration becomes operational in most or all of their services.

And then consider how library finances will change to keep up with these vast shifts in work and resource sharing—including staffing.

NOTES

1. *Brainy Quote.* Retrieved on May 13, 2015, fromhttp://www.brainyquote.com/quotes/quotes/i/isaacasimo100104.html#AmPab6h75pk1iBfI.99.
2. Stachokas, George. *After the Book: Information Services for the 21st Century.* Amsterdam, Boston, and London: Chandos, 2014, pp. 1–2.
3. Ibid.
4. Walther, Larry M. *Principles of Accounting.* 2015 Ed. Ch. 21. Planning for Success, [Section on] Budget Periods and Adjustments. Retrieved on August 2, 2015, from http://www.principlesofaccounting.com/.
5. Becker, Samatha, Michael D. Crandall, Karen E. Fisher, Rebecca Blakewood, Bo Kinney, and Cadi Russell-Sauve. *Opportunity for All: How the American Public Benefits from Internet Access at U.S. Libraries. The U.S. IMPACT Study. A Research Initiative Examining the Impact of Free Access to Computers and the Internet in Public Libraries.* Washington, DC: Institute for Museum and Library Services, 2010, p. 8.
6. III, Innovative. *The Open Library Experience.* Retrieved on August 12, 2015, from https://www.iii.com/products/resources.
7. Godby, Carol Jean, Shenghui Wang, and Jeffrey K. Mixter. *Library Linked Data in the Cloud: OCLC's Experiments with New Models of Resource Description.* Dublin, OH: OCLC, Webinar video, May 2015.
8. Buffalo and Erie County Public Library. *Monthly Operating Financial Report.* Retrieved on August 12, 2015, from http://www.buffalolib.org/content/budget-information/monthly-operating-financial-report.
9. Foundation Center. Grant Space. "Knowledge Base: How Long Should Nonprofit Organizations retain Business-Related Records?" Retrieved on April 9, 2014, from http://grantspace.org/tools/knowledge-base/Nonprofit-Management/Accountability/record-retention.
10. U.S. Government, Internal Revenue Services. *Compliance Guide for Tax-Exempt Organizations (Other than 501(c)(3) Public Charities and Private Foundations).* Washington, DC: IRS, 2015 Ed. Retrieved on August 2, 2015, from http://www.irs.gov/pub/irs-pdf/p4221nc.pdf.
11. Martins, Christine S., Esq. and Sophia J. Martins, Esq. "The Impact of the USA PATRIOT Act on Records Management." *The Information Management Journal.* May/June 2005, pp. 52–58. Retrieved on August 2. 2015, from http://www.arma.org/bookstore/files/Martins.pdf.

12. Kugel, Robert. *Applying In-Memory Analytics to Finance Can Boost Business Agility. Tech Target. Search Financial Application.* Retrieved on February 16, 2015, from http://www.bitpipe.com/data/demandEngage.action?resId=1350330387_267. p. 2.

13. Ibid, p. 3.

14. *Agile Adoption Rate Survey Results: March 2007.* Retrieved on April 12, 2015, from http://www.ambysoft.com/surveys/agileMarch2007.html; Williams, Laurie. "A Survey of Agile Development Methodologies." Retrieved on April 12, 2015, from http://agile.csc.ncsu.edu/SEMaterials/AgileMethods.pdf.

15. William B. Rouse. "Agile Information Systems for Agile Decision Making." In Desouza, Kevin C., ed. *Agile Information Systems. Conceptualization, Construction and Management.* Burlington, MA: Elsevier, 2007, p. 25.

16. Ariel Gilbert-Knight, Senior Content Manager, TechSoup Global. *What TechSoup Offers Libraries.* Posted January 16, 2012. Retrieved on February 12, 2015, from http://www.techsoup.org/support/articles-and-how-tos/what-techsoup-offers-libraries.

17. Laura S. Quinn, Executive Director, Idealware; Elizabeth Pope, Director of Research and Operations, Idealware. *A Few Good Accounting Packages.* Posted March 14, 2014. Retrieved on January 12, 2015, from http://www.idealware.org/articles/fgt_accounting.php.

18. Dempsey, Lorcan. *The Network Reshapes the Library.* Chicago: ALA, 2014, pp. 60–62.

CHAPTER 6

Legal Context: Basic Rules
You Need to Know

Ignorance of the law is no excuse.

—John Sheldon, 1689[1]

Laws govern how libraries obtain funds and how they use and report on their use of those funds. Libraries also have accounting practices that staff needs to understand and follow. And of course, all these policies and procedures vary from library to library. Overarching all operations, however, is federal tax law that applies to every library that uses public funds or raises funds privately.

Newly appointed library employees and many library staff who are assigned budget responsibilities need to know basic finance law and recognize its significance. Together, the few terms described here define myriad dimensions of the library's legal context.

FEDERAL INCOME TAX STATUS

The Internal Revenue Code grants tax exempt status to nonprofit organizations in more than 20 categories under Section 501 (c). To aid them in fundraising, libraries usually want to establish a library foundation that has the highest tax-exempt status. A library foundation usually can provide the highest level tax credit for gifts to the library, the kind of deduction that donors expect from a not-for-profit institution. Note that your school, public, or academic library may have its IRS category determined by the status of the host institution. So, when you work with finance, you may find that the documentation for some practices is located in the offices of the school district, university, or other host institution rather than in your library.

IRS 501 (C)(3) INTERNAL REVENUE SERVICE CLASSIFICATION

Most libraries either have or are eligible to have status as an IRS Section 501 (c)(3), which "is the public benefit category, and permitted purposes for organizations in this category include: charitable, educational, and literary." Under this category, libraries may engage in education and promotion of literacy and literature, including administrative and training costs.

Libraries that are categorized as 501 (c)(3)s can create and operate other "captive" not-for-profit organizations for legitimate purposes like fundraising foundations, friends groups, and building corporations. And libraries that have other status in the IRS categories, for example, as government agencies, may also create captive 501 (c)(3) philanthropies. Moreover, for-profit corporations can set up and operate not-for-profit libraries. (See the next section of this chapter.) Corporate special libraries, for example, often are operated by for-profit corporations as nonprofit agencies within full legalities of federal legislation.

Once you have completed your research on any aspect of 501 (c)(3), including looking through relevant documents on the American Library Association website and various IRS websites, contact a legal counsel to discuss and eventually ascertain the nuances of your particular situation.[2]

IRS 509 CLASSIFICATION

A few libraries, usually older ones, are classified as charitable government agencies under the IRS 509 code. That category is an older designation for public libraries that operated almost entirely with "government funds." To reiterate, 509s have differing rates of tax benefits for donors, and most public libraries so designated have found legal means to achieve a charitable designation of a 501 (c)(3) institutions.

If you find any evidence that your library is still relying on its status as a 509 private charity, check with a qualified tax attorney for advice on what to do next. We advise not to attempt to do this reclassification without legal advice; it took one large library several years to obtain a 501 (c)(3) status. A little research demonstrated that the library needed more expert help to communicate the issues of the institution's current status and how the new status would allow the library to present a much clearer financial picture to prospective donors.

FORM 990A

Form 990 is an annual reporting return requirement that certain federally tax-exempt organizations must file with the IRS. It provides information on the filing organization's mission, programs, and finances." Depending on the nature of their charter and/or operational authority, all academic, public, and school libraries have to file an IRS 990A statement each fiscal year to keep their not-for-profit tax status secure. Special libraries may be viewed as part of their corporation's for-profit structure, in which case they would not file a 990A.[3]

GOVERNMENTAL ACCOUNTING STANDARDS BOARD

These Governmental Accounting Standards Board (GASB) requirements are issued to clarify accounting standards required of all public agencies, including libraries with budgets of more than $25,000. This requirement means that all but the smallest libraries need to comply with these standards. For libraries that are part of a larger agency such as a school district, city, or county governmental district or a university, it is important that library managers keep GASB standards in mind even as they conform to the accounting practices of the parent agency. For small- and medium-sized libraries, that don't have access to a professional accountant who is knowledgeable in government accounting, check with your state library agency for training and advice. Also, there may be an accounting professional in your city or county government who can help you comply with GASB standards. Your local United Way or other nonprofit agencies may also offer training or access to knowledgeable accountants at little or no cost.

"The Governmental Accounting Standards Board (GASB) Statements are issued by GASB to set generally accepted accounting principles (GAAP) for state and local governments in the United States of America. These statements are the most authoritative source for governmental GAAP. Other business entities follow statements issued by the Financial Accounting Standards Board (FASB)."[4]

FINANCIAL ACCOUNTING STANDARDS BOARD

Financial Accounting Standards Board (FASB) pronouncements consist of rules and guidelines for preparing, presenting, and reporting financial statements according to (GAAP) in the United States of America.

Together, FASB and GASB define how private and public corporations maintain and present financial records. These standards are tougher than any of the cataloging rules with which librarians are more familiar. (The toughness comes because the rules are quite specific and are often in specialized accounting language.) FASB and GASB rules are where knowledgeable accountants lay down the law about how all kinds of libraries account for, authorize, and disburse money, and the only way to change those laws are through appeals to the FASB and GASB boards or through court cases.

The binding nature of FASB and GASB rules can be seen in this brief decision about what constitutes government. The short document is quoted in its entirety.

THE FASB/GASB DEFINITION OF GOVERNMENT.[5] Public corporations and bodies corporate and politic are governmental organizations. Other organizations are governmental organizations if they have one or more of the characteristics listed below:

a.   Popular election of officers or appointment (or approval) of a controlling majority of the members of the organization's governing body by officials of one or more state or local governments.

b. The potential for unilateral dissolution by a government with the net assets reverting to a government.

c. The power to enact and enforce a tax levy. Furthermore, organizations are presumed to be governmental if they have the ability to issue directly (rather than through a state or municipal authority) debt that pays interest exempt from federal taxation. However, organizations possessing only that ability (to issue tax-exempt debt) and none of the other governmental characteristics may rebut the presumption that they are governmental if their determination is supported by compelling, relevant evidence.

To summarize, most libraries are government agencies, and they have to behave like the pieces of government which they are. This FASB and GASB combination bestows enormous authority and advantage on governments; it also establishes definite limits about what libraries and other government entities may do. The big thing that these standards do is to lay out rules of practice. If librarians stay within these rules, fine. If you do not, officers and the whole institution are exposed to legal peril and, frequently, to bad public opinion as well.

(The) Sarbanes–Oxley Act of 2002 (*Pub.L. 107–204*, 116 *Stat. 745*.) . . . set new or enhanced standards for all U.S. public company boards, management and public accounting firms.

The bill, which contains eleven sections, was enacted as a reaction to a number of major corporate and accounting scandals, including Enron, and Worldcom. The sections of the bill cover responsibilities of a public corporation's board of directors, adds criminal penalties for certain misconduct, and requires the *Securities and Exchange Commission* to create regulations to define how public corporations are to comply with the law.[6]

The basic book on Sarbanes-Oxley for years has been by Greene, Silverman, and Becker.[7] Referencing this book in a Google search will elicit other overviews and current updates, but this volume is probably still the easiest for non-accountants to read and understand.

ACCOUNTABILITY

Government Performance and Results Act (US Congress 1993). The growing importance of spending impact and benefits was seen in this Federal legislation. The requirement is that if any federal money was involved in a program, there had to be some estimation of that expenditure's impact or benefits. In our studies of cost–benefit analysis and outcome-based planning, the authors of this book have pushed hard to bring the significance of such measurement to the attention of professional librarians. In a few words, librarians ought to build assessment and evaluation into their regular budgeting as a matter of good practice. This stipulation becomes an outright requirement if federal grant money is involved.

The Government Performance and Results Act (GPRA) (P.L. 103–62) is a United States law enacted in 1993. It is one of a series of laws designed to improve government performance management. The GPRA requires agencies that accept federal funds, including LSTA funds from the Institute for Museums and Library Services (IMLS)] to engage in performance management tasks such as setting goals, measuring results, and reporting their progress. In order to comply with the GPRA, agencies produce five-year strategic plans, set annual performance goals, and provide evidence of institutional results against goals. To state the matter specifically, if you get federal grants, including LSTA money, you have to create a plan, with goals and outcomes.

Many state and local governments require similar planning as do charitable foundations and private companies. And even if you don't use federal funds, you ought to engage in this planning/outcome process as part of modern institutional management. The benefits of articulating plans and outcomes is that your institution will have a much easier time making a case that you act with planning and best purpose, and that you are willingly accountable to those who provide you funding and those whom you serve.

On January 4, 2011, President Obama signed H.R. 2142, the GPRA Modernization Act of 2010 (GPRAMA), into law as P.L. 111–352. Section 10 requires agencies to publish their strategic and performance plans and reports in machine-readable formats.[8]

To conclude, no matter how large or small your library or the type of library into which it is defined, your financial issues are shaped by externalities like tax law and accounting and audit requirements. Few books on library finance make much of this legal context. We include it here because, as the quote for this chapter states, "Ignorance of the law is no excuse" when you are helping to govern a complex service institution like a library.

NOTES

1. *Duhaime's Law Dictionary.* Retrieved on May 13, 2015, from duhaime.org/Legal Dictionary/I/IgnoranceoftheLaw.aspx.
2. *American Library Association Tax Exempt Status.* Retrieved on February 14, 2015, from http://www.ala.org/educationcareers/employment/resources/alataxexemptstat. ALA should be correct in its own research on this subject, since it is a $50 million annual budget, not-for-profit chartered under the 501 (c)(3) IRS classification.
3. Guidestar. *FAQs: Form 990.* Retrieved on February 13, 2015, from http://www.guide star.org/rxg/help/faqs/form-990/index.aspx?sitelink=1–501&505&linktitle=Form%20 990%20FAQs&gclid=CObzvuzZ4MMCFciBfgodZxsAxg#faq1942.
4. Wikipedia. *List of GASB Statements.* Retrieved on February 14, 2015, from http:// en.wikipedia.org/wiki/List_of_GASB_Statements.
5. This is the agreement of the FASB and GASB on this subject, in its entirety, as reprinted on page 16 of the July 1996 issue of the AICPA's *Journal of Accountancy.* Retrieved on February 14, 2015, from http://www.cg.sc.gov/guidanceandformsforstateagencies/ Documents/GAAP/AgenciesSubmitStatements/FASB_GASB_Def_Government.pdf'.
6. Wikipedia. *Sarbannes-Oxley Act.* Retrieved on February 15, 2015, from http:// en.wikipedia.org/wiki/Sarbanes%E2%80%93Oxley_Act. There is a huge bibliography on Sarbannes-Oxley, with many articles and postings available for free on the Net.
7. Greene, Edward F., Leslie N. Silverman, and David M. Becker. *The Sarbanes-Oxley Act: Analysis and Practice.* New York: Aspen, 2003. Inputting this reference on Google will elicit current updates and other overviews, but this volume is probably still the easiest to read and understand.
8. Wikipedia. *Government Performance and Results Act.* Retrieved on February 15, 2015, from http://en.wikipedia.org/wiki/Government_Performance_and_Results_Act. A practical narrative on the subject of evaluation in which the GPRA is involved is Dresang, Eliza T., Melissa Gross, and Leslie Edmonds Holt. *Dynamic Youth Services through Outcome Based Planning and Evaluation.* Chicago: ALA, 2006. The importance of the legislation highlighted in this paragraph begins on page 8.

CHAPTER 7

Professional Advice

An investment in knowledge pays the best interest.

—Benjamin Franklin[1]

Library professionals often have to handle activities for which they received no formal training and in which they have no previous on-the-job experience. The "up side" of this situation is the opportunity to learn about many new knowledge areas. The "down side" is making poor decisions simply because the decision maker does not know enough about the subject.

Smart librarians have enough sense to get help with finances from knowledgeable, trained professionals, either inside the library, school, university, or corporation or by hiring outside the library profession.

If you don't understand how to use financial forms, for example, ask someone in the business office who can show you; attend training in financial management that is offered in your institution, at local colleges, or professional meetings; and start conversations and get-togethers with non-library professionals from other institutions.

Modern libraries need access to finance professionals to operate successfully in the financial field. The authors of this book have followed their own advice here. We have at various times hired or talked with financial consultants with special knowledge (bonding, fundraising, and marketing), brought CPAs and other financial specialists on full-time staff (regularize budget, tighten budget controls, install new accounting systems), and talked at length with bankers, lawyers (especially tax lawyers), and real estate professionals to get more information with which to frame financial decisions.

Finance is a broad area which has many legitimate areas of expertise represented in other professions. Librarians need to know about the existence of these professionals and when to call on them for advice.

ACCOUNTANT

Look for a certified public accountant rather than a bookkeeper. That person ought to be able to help you set up legal, ethical, and workable accounting systems, as well as decide which of your activities are and are not taxable, particularly in the area of employment.

LEGAL COUNSEL

An imperative financial management advisor. Some libraries negotiate an annual retainer for legal services, then have the counsel's firm bill the institution for work by the hour at a set not-for-profit rate.

AUDITOR

If you need to set up an institutional audit or you just need to keep up on audit rules, a good auditing firm can provide both policy consulting and an institutional audit for your annual financial report.

INSURANCE AGENT

Someone who can make sense of directors and officers insurance, public liability insurance, and the ins and outs of health insurance for staff and vehicle insurance on the library's automotive fleet. The right insurance agent can save the library money and get the necessary insurance as legal requirements change.

FUNDRAISING/COMMUNICATIONS CONSULTANT

A consultant who knows the politics and information flows of the local scene in which the library operates and who will help you learn how to communicate within your community or institution, with elected and civic officials and your elective and user constituency. Fundraising consultants aid library staff, library foundations, or friends groups and library governing bodies with planning and executing money-raising activities.

INVESTMENTS/INCOME MANAGEMENT

Some libraries or library foundations operate under laws that prohibit any but the most conservative investments (e.g., fully collateralized). Your library, however, may be able to rent building space to generate income in the same way that museums often do, for example. Some libraries may have endowments or offer annuities to donors that will need to be managed by licensed brokers.

REAL ESTATE AGENT

A high visibility member of a reputable real estate firm who will advise you on marketing, buying, and selling property, especially if your institution is doing lots of remodeling, including expansion of parking or construction of new facilities

CONSTRUCTION

Hire a space planner, architect, and a construction manager (CM). Of the three, a CM is probably the most critical because a good CM will make construction issues much easier to handle while controlling the costs. We know of a few instances in which librarians have grown into a CM job, but generally you want a building expert (usually a certified architect or engineer) who will act independently to recommend items concerning quality, costs, and project timing. A CM also is a great ally in bidding for the services of engineers and architects, and in how heavily your or other staff members need to negotiate when project change orders need clarification because they involve increased expense for the library or library system. Also, CMs often have valuable knowledge and contacts to help libraries fill minority contracting and construction and building union requirements.

Some library professionals might see this coterie of consultants as a waste of money. Our response is that library staff members should spend as much time as possible doing their core jobs in the most efficient and effective way possible. Financial learning curves are steep, and mistakes often are highly visible to both staff and citizens. After a time, you will know when to call on a consultant specialist as the institution faces a decision. Until then, consultants are a cheaper expense than making decisions that some elected official or civic leader can say was "dumb" even a few years down the line.

ESTABLISH AN APPROPRIATE BANKING RELATIONSHIP

On many occasions, pressures of various kind are put on library financial decision makers to "spread around the funds" into multiple banks. That kind of pressure often comes from banks that do not have any library funds on deposit, and they want some. The difficulty with these requests is that some banks (along with some auditing firms and some legal firms) are better prepared to handle a library's banking needs than others. Here are some differences in how banks treat libraries, based on lots of years of experiences:

- What qualities do you look for in the individual or team that serves as the financial adviser to the library. How long and how easy is it to communicate with the person(s) you need to talk with at a bank?
- Convenience in handling signature cards. We have found lots of variability in handling this relatively simple but legally required item.

- Do you need to or want to open additional accounts at separate banks to keep library deposits below the FDIC insurance limits or for some other reason of convenience or specialized service.
- Handling investments; rate of interest on investments; speed at which library investments are moved from one account to another; bottom line in interest earned along with convenience.
- Handling loans; loan rates, especially short-term credit loans and construction loans.
- Amount of fees that the bank charges for handling payroll withdrawals and payment of library bills. Pennies and nickels do add up to savings and accumulation of interest for libraries, and library leadership needs to be smart about banking issues.

Intuit suggests five things to do to find an appropriate bank for any small business, the category into which almost all libraries fall. These are:[2]

- Know what you want from your bank. What kinds of services to you expect to use most, least? Can you pay? How do you want to pay? And, associated questions.
- Compare small and large banks. For some reason, do you want your bank to know the market in which your library and the bank operates? Have the banks being considered developed a good record in community service and philanthropic relationships?
- Nothing is free. And that is always true when it comes to modern banks. One way or another, every banking service has a price. You may have to compare oranges and avocados but there always is a difference.
- Look into the bank's reputation. For example, does the bank being considered do SBA loans in the community? Is the bank well capitalized? How is any one bank regarded by other not-for-profits that use it?

Establish an ongoing relationship with the bank that gets your business. Forecasting service needs, suggesting investment vehicles, and so forth are relationship features you might want to check out with your new banker friends.

All professional librarians start out as beginners in library finance. That's because the values and the twists and turns of financial decision making and use of money for specific purposes has lots of reverberations that can mess up important library work and cause significant peril for institutional decision makers.

"Who Needs a Librarian When You Have Google? Who Needs a Doctor When You Have Web MD?" This quote from an often used librarian "marketing" poster is seen frequently on the Net. Somehow, this poster message is regarded as a grand and popular defense of library professionalism.[3]

The authors of this volume regard the statement as a masquerade, an attempt to stop significant discussion about an important professional question. Medical and Osteopathic physicians carry their own sets of hard professional questions around with them. Plus, it is difficult to find any aspect of library search that will elicit such explicit subject findings as those that even amateur researchers can find on Medline.

This chapter suggests that professionalism is based on the knowledge and how it is used by persons in different professions. The very nature of their business (i.e., answering other people's questions) is a humbling part of any information professional's self-evaluation portfolio. No library professional will answer every question well. Neither will any architect, insurance broker, lawyer, or banker. We all need help, especially with financial issues, and to get that help, we need to know the financial help that various professional experts bring to our discussion when we ask them a question.

The heart of every profession is not about what you know but what you are willing to admit what you don't know in your professional life. The professionals included in this chapter are those which both authors have used in our various library administrative jobs and consulting. We look to other professionals to provide us with information we need to do our essential jobs in our libraries, many of which have requirements that go well beyond our knowledge, especially in a world of rampant change—and one that involves a good deal of expenditure.

Brenda Roberts, the Bibliotheque of Ottawa Public Library in Ontario (Canada), in a thoughtful essay, "We Build Communities Through Knowledge," in a wonderfully thoughtful book, *Defending Professionalism* (2012), edited by Bill Crowley, writes these words:[4]

> The advent of eBooks underscores the necessity that librarians redefine and then strongly reassert our professional mission to the public. If public libraries are to retain their relevance, our mission must pivot on building communities through knowledge. Professional librarianship is key to that goal and implies a pragmatic approach, one that combines mastery of information in all its forms with the hands-on commitment of a community organizer.

Roberts's words are what this chapter is about. Change requires all librarians to develop new skills by entering and learning significant aspects in new kinds of knowledge communities. To develop those skills, library professionals must master new kinds of knowledge with many different kinds of teachers. Calling on the various kinds of experts for help in doing a library job is a testament to a librarian's willingness to learn knowledge that she does not know. In short, as change occurs, librarians have to acquire new knowledge to better serve their various constituencies. This simple truth, not posters comparing the search behavior of librarians to the treatment behavior of doctors, is the essence of library professionalism.

NOTES

1. Bakke, David. "The Top 17 Investing Quotes of All time." *Investopedia*. May 16, 2011. Retrieved on August 3, 2015, from http://www.investopedia.com/financial-edge/0511/the-top-17-investing-quotes-of-all-time.aspx#ixzz3hndFpCcv.
2. Polevol, Lee. "5 Tips for Choosing the Right Bank for Your Business." *Intuit Quick Books*. December 2, 2014. Retrieved on August 30, 2015, from http://quickbooks.intuit.com/r/banking/5-tips-for-choosing-the-right-bank-for-your-business.
3. Jones, Gwyneth. *The Daring Librarian*. *Blog post*. Retrieved on August 3, 2015, from http://www.thedaringlibrarian.com/2013/04/who-needs-librarian-when-you-have-google.html.
4. Roberts, Brenda. "We Build Communities Through Knowledge: Demonstrating the Value of the Professional Public Librarian." In Crowley, Bill, editor. *Defending Professionalism: A Resource for Librarians, Information specialists, Knowledge Managers, and Archivists*. Santa Barbara, CA: Libraries Unlimited, 2012, pp. 45–46.

SECTION III

Strategic Financial Planning

CHAPTER 8

Annual Report as a Starting Point

I believe—we all pay taxes. I'm happy to pay it, but I hate to have it abused, money wasted, no accountability. That's going to bother you.

—Lou Holtz[1]

WHERE TO BEGIN FINANCIAL PLANNING?

Any library's annual report is the cornerstone of public accountability for funds spent. It is a snapshot of how the library has used its funds and a public pronouncement of what has been accomplished for those served. And it can be used as the basis for what to do next financially.

Years ago, a member of this book's writing team was talking with a soon-to-retire director of a large Midwestern public library system. We complimented him on his wonderful annual reports, with appropriate financial and user statistics, sensitively chosen photographs, and the many short stories on activities through the year just ended. Only a little innocently did we ask him, "And, what do you call those library directors who don't publish up-to-date annual reports." "Idiots!" he said, as he smiled knowingly. "Idiots who don't understand that libraries are about developing and holding long-term relationships, not nickel-and-dime marketing of a few programs." The best annual report demonstrates financial accountability tied to community benefits and builds trust relationships with constituents and funders alike.

ELEMENTS OF THE GOOD ANNUAL REPORT

Wikipedia counts these elements as typical within an organizational annual report.[2]

- **Overview**. A statement to constituents about where the library spent its money and what the constituents received for it. That includes general organizational information, including various kinds of usage statistics, often displayed in simple and highly visual charts and graphs accompanied by photos and other graphics.
- **General Organizational Information**. Highlights of the organizational year, likely to appeal to broadly defined real and potential audiences and supporters, for example, we cut mobile library service. How do we now serve those citizens in schools, daycare facilities, and so forth where we no longer stop. We introduced Electronic City Hall. Now, all of you can get access to local ordinances on the Internet at your library's website.
- **Board Chair/Statement/Director's Report**. These documents set an official institutional tone for annual reports. If there have been controversial events through the year, these overview, introductory documents may provide an institutional perspective on such developments.
- **Operating and Financial Review**. The review ties major operational problems and/or achievements into finances. For example, a newly developed leaky roof may have strained the budget to the point of needing to cut staff or collections. Or a library has received a major art collection from a private donor during the year, raising insurance costs and forcing the rehab of space to obtain appropriate collection storage spaces. The collection, however, is unique to the community and may be of considerable financial value in its own right.
- **Accounting Policies**. "The specific policies and procedures used by a company to prepare its financial statements. These include any methods, measurement systems and procedures for presenting disclosures. Accounting policies differ from accounting principles in that the principles are the rules and the policies are a company's way of adhering to the rules."[3]
- **Balance Sheet**. According to the *Encyclopedia Britannica*, a balance sheet is the "financial statement that describes the resources under a company's control on a specified date and indicates where they have come from. It consists of three major sections: assets (valuable rights owned by the company), liabilities (funds provided by outside lenders and other creditors), and the owners' equity. On the balance sheet, total assets must always equal total liabilities plus total owners' equity."[4]
- **Income and Expense**. Like all businesses, librarians organize their budgets and financial reports by categories and subcategories. There are two principal monetary categories in budgets, monthly financial statements, and annual reports: income and expense. In most cases, the largest income category is sales, but there also may be income from investments and other sources as well. Sales are further broken down into cash and credit, a very important distinction if the business depends upon cash sales to pay its expense. Expense categories often include such things as rent, insurance, utilities, supplies, and salaries. Once the categories are designated, management allocates a dollar amount to each one.
- **Library Income, Allocated or Earned**. Library income often is from a single source, as a budget allocation from a university, college city, country or state, or a financial

office which has collected taxes authorized for the library, thereby sourcing a major revenue stream. Special libraries often receive their money from an organizational entity like a medical school, a legal firm, or a corporate budget.

- **Cash or Credit Sales**. In the private sector annual reports, sales often are further broken down into cash and credit, a very important distinction if the business depends upon cash sales to pay its expense. Expense categories often include such things as rent, insurance, utilities, supplies, and wages.

- **Earned Income**. Some libraries may have income from investments, as with an endowment that either is directly controlled by the library or by the library foundation or friends group. There also may be income from the sale of books, other store merchandise like computer disks, tablets, and writing instruments, or from food and drink in a library restaurant. All such income usually is spoken of as earned income as opposed to income from public or private sources such as taxes. The latter type of income is sometimes designated as allocated because it often has a legislative action involved in its existence.

- **Income and Expense Categories**. In the private sector, the largest income category is sales, but there also may be income from investments and other sources as well. Expense categories often include such things as rent, insurance, utilities, supplies, and wages. Once the categories are designated, management allocates a dollar amount to each one.

- **Cash Flow Statement**. Exactly what its title indicates, but usually does not appear in library annual reports because of the minimal nature of income sources that fuel the library.[5]

- **Non-Audited Information**. Texas A&M University handles this definition in one brief description, which reads: "The documents in the Financial Disclosure section are provided for informational purposes only and must not be considered to be an offer to sell or the solicitation of any offer to buy any securities of the A&M System in any jurisdiction, which offer or solicitation may only be made by an official statement or other offering document."[6]

- **Profit and Loss Account.** The profit and loss statement is a wonderful tool to ascertain the amount of variance you will find among organizational entities issuing annual reports and other regular financial documents. The enormous variance in this tool's report arrangements can be seen at a search site which appears in a Google search for "Annual Report Profit and Loss Statement."[7]

- **Notes to the Financial Statements**. Notes to financial statements contain all kinds of disparate information. In understanding financial statements, think of notes as explanatory footnotes. For example, a private historical society library may have a stock of original paintings that have a value in the millions of dollars. For all kinds of good operational and legal reasons, this kind of asset should not be hidden. If you think this category is farfetched, consider that a library finance office safe might contain patents or rare papers that may have a very high appraisal, bearer bonds, insurance policies, and cash receipts from multiple branch locations. Consider as well that Buffalo-Erie County Public Library holds a manuscript for Mark Twain's *Adventures of Huck Finn*, the story of which is told both briefly and clearly in a Net note published by BECPL.[8]

- **Auditors Report**. This report sometimes is not included in the annual report, but is issued separately to the library's governing and/or its administrative officials. The principal feature of this report is one that offers a judgment as to whether the audit is issued on a "qualified" or "unqualified" basis. An "unqualified" statement is high praise for the library's financial officials, a statement that internal money flows/controls work correctly. A "qualified" judgment suggests that there are problems in the way money flows through the organization. The "qualified" decision often has suggestions for remedies to be installed.

The Internet contains many examples of annual reports from various kinds of libraries. In them, you will see the huge variance in the amount of financial information that the organizations make available in this public document. Here are a few examples demonstrating differences:

Harvard University Library. A wonderful annual report, but hardly a word about finances.[9]

University of California at Berkeley. This annual report has two purposes: first, to highlight the year's outstanding library developments and appointments and, second, to thank major donors to the various affiliated libraries by name. So, it is both about money and building relationships, but without dealing with most of the typical financial topics that one usually would find in an annual report.[10]

Tulsa City-County Library. A complete annual report, one that ties special programs, service statistics, and the year's finances reports altogether.[11]

Some individual school libraries and school district libraries do annual reports. As Library Girl says in a blog posting: "Annual reports were never required in my district or by my principal, but after seeing the work of other librarians whose districts did require these types of reflections, I knew I wanted to make completing one for my library a part of my year end routine."[12] She goes on to give a variety of sample annual reports and an excellent summary of what they contain. Most do not contain budget information, but as planning documents they can be most helpful.

NOTES

1. *Brainy Quote*. Retrieved on June 6, 2015, fromhttp://www.brainyquote.com/quotes/quotes/l/louholtz629659.html#m7MsOHtVDSu9kDti.99.

2. *Annual Report*. Retrieved on October 23, 2014, from http://en.wikipedia.org/wiki/Annual_report.

3. This definition is retrieved on October 22, 2014, from http://www.investopedia.com/terms/a/accounting-policies.asp.

4. Retrieved on October 23, 2014, from http://www.britannica.com/EBchecked/topic/49778/balance-sheet.

5. For more information, see http://en.wikipedia.org/wiki/Cash_flow_statement. Retrieved on October 22, 2014.

6. See http://www.tamus.edu/apps/soba-afr/disclaimer.aspx?report=SOBAFY2013UNAUDLTR. Retrieved on October 23, 2014.

7. Retrieved on October 22, 2014, from https://www.google.com/search?q=annual+report+profit+and+loss+statement&rlz=1C1QJDB_enUS595US596&espv=2&tbm=isch&tbo=u&source=univ&sa=X&ei=IPrwU-OsLYnuoATg14CQAw&ved=0CDsQsAQ&biw=1014&bih=622.

8. Retrieved on October 28, 2014, from http://www.buffalolib.org/content/grosvenor/mark-twain-room/huck-finn-manuscript.

9. Retrieved on October 28, 2014, from http://library.harvard.edu/annual-report-fy-2013.

10. See http://www.lib.berkeley.edu/give/fiatlux/fiatlux29.pdf for the 2012–13 annual report from which this brief description is drawn. Retrieved on October 28, 2014.

11. Retrieved on October 28, 2014, from http://www.tulsalibrary.org/sites/default/files/pagefiles/TCCL_ar_11.pdf.

12. Library Girl Blog. Retrieved on June 7, 2015, from http://www.librarygirl.net/2013/05/school-library-annual-reports.html.

CHAPTER 9

Purpose Documents as a Starting Point for Financial Planning

If you don't know where you are going,
you'll end up someplace else.

—Yogi Berra[1]

Along with starting your annual financial planning by examining your annual report, you also can start to consider your financial plan by reviewing your institutional purpose documents. You might want to pay special attention to these documents, if your library is just starting to bring finances into its annual strategic planning update or if your leadership group wants to improve the quality of your fiscal planning. Library purpose documents are summarized briefly below.

VISION STATEMENT

The vision statement articulates the hopes for the organization. It is a framework for marking out major targets in the strategic plan. The vision statement reminds you of the whole structure you are trying to build and articulates where you want your organization to go.

The primary audience for the vision statement is internal, that is, those already associated with the organization. That, of course, includes staff, governance, and fund raisers.

Here are some questions that will help you think about your vision statement—and the whole budget planning process:[2]

1. **Where Are We Now?** The first step is to capture the library's current situation. What is happening in the library's operating context? Successful libraries cannot operate as if they are isolated from their physical or demographic environment. Sizing up awareness of the institution's advantages is the first step in planning awareness.
2. **Where Do We Want To Be?** What do you want the library to be known for? What should typify your organization in the eyes of your customers and business associates? What do you want your employees to say about you? This series of questions helps you develop your vision of a desired future.
3. **Why Is This Important to Us?** At times, organizations prepare vision statements more as a fad or something which they need to do, since almost everyone else is doing it. Making a vision statement without understanding why it is important to organization staff or constituents is meaningless. If you are going to move your vision beyond a cheerleader's game-rallying cry, you need a specific strategy to work toward it.
4. **What Are the Obstacles In the Way?** Knowing what we want is one thing, knowing how to get there quite another. It is useful to identify in a proactive manner the possible obstacles that you foresee in the way to achieving your vision. These obstacles may be geographic, may be related to people or to financial resources or even environmental factors that could adversely impact our actions.
5. **What Actions Can We Take to Overcome Them?** All planning actions are important, but laying out an action scenario is crucial. Who will do what and when? What changes are clearly within your control and can be initiated early? What will require time and effort to initiate in the longer term? These actions are the most important part of the execution. Without them, the vision remains a dream.
6. **What Are Our Priorities?** It is tempting to try to change everything at once. Prudence dictates that you work on the basis of defined priorities. Without priorities, you will squander valuable resources, time, and effort in working on relatively less important actions.
7. **When Will We Know We Are on Track?** Knowing how we are doing is an important element in implementing any change process. You need to monitor results against stated actions and track your progress toward achieving that vision.

Those who are familiar with formal planning techniques will realize that the suggestions here fit easily into a SWOT analysis (i.e., an assessment of Strengths, Weaknesses, Opportunities, and Threats). The movement forward can be charted with another formal planning tool, Critical Path Analysis, and measurement of whether the effort is on track is part of Return on Investment or other Impact Analyses or Cost–Benefit Analysis. There is a growing literature to be consulted on each of these methodologies, including such methods isolated for libraries. Our later chapter on assessment, benefits, and impact should be useful to those who have little knowledge in these areas.

We mention these strategies to let you know that there is more that can be learned about organizational planning, including about financial planning. Also, if you want a planning tool that is simpler even than what we have presented here, there are guidelines in a Vision Statement Formulation Package on the net that might be fun to use in some library planning session.[3] If you want more institutional planning training, you can start with other Google searches on the net. For our purposes in this book on library finances, however, we say simply, "Think about the money." To what ends will you spend it? How will you spend it to achieve those ends?

MISSION STATEMENTS AND TAGLINES

The summation of purpose documents in modern institutional promotion is the summary tagline which increasingly appears with the logo on all marketing documents. An exercise like that outlined in the preceding section of this chapter was the basic first step in producing taglines and mission statements for many different institutions. Here are some examples:

American Red Cross. Always there. Touching more lives, in New Ways, under the Same Trusted Symbol.

Emory University. Emory: A destination university, internationally recognized as inquiry driven, ethically engaged and diverse community, whose members work for positive transformation in the world through courageous leadership in teaching, research, scholarship, health care and social action.

The South Orange Public Library will be the integral physical and virtual gateway by which our broad and diverse community may access information, congregate to freely exchange ideas, celebrate literacy and cultural growth in a leisurely yet lively atmosphere. The South Orange Public Library will provide individualized services delivered in a professional manner while being fully responsive to individual needs.[4]

IFLA identifies several vision statements from libraries around the world. For example, The National Library Board of Singapore will be "An inspiring beacon of lifelong learning, bringing knowledge alive, sparking imagination and creating possibility for a vibrant and creative Singapore."[5]

Libraries have mission statements to state their fundamental purpose to those who use their institutional services—that is, customers and clients. Library budgets should be mission driven. That is, the budget should reflect the priorities and goals stated in the mission statement just as the library's services and programs should be designed to further the library's mission. A good example comes from Dedham Massachusetts School Library which offers this mission statement:[6]

The mission of the Dedham Public Schools, in partnership with the community, is to promote excellence in learning, self-discipline, and motivation.

From the document the school published on the net, it is clear that some thoughtfulness and modeling from other school libraries went into the development of this concise mission statement. Fundamentally, the mission statement should answer the question, "Why do we exist?"

Mission statements need to be focused, then widely disseminated. Our favorite one, still, is the mission statement devised by the board of directors of the St. Louis Public Library which continues in use more than two decades later.[7]

The St. Louis Public Library will provide learning resources and information services that support and improve individual, family and community life.

The SLPL board then appended value statements which have been used to guide planning discussions since they were approved. The value statements read:

To support this mission, the library will organize and prudently manage its resources to:

- Ensure that the library's resources are available to all.
- Promote use of the library.
- Assist children and adults with life-long learning.
- Promote literacy for all ages.
- Assist individuals in finding jobs and educational opportunities.
- Assist businesses with their development and growth.
- Provide current information.
- Provide recreational reading resources, media materials, and programs.
- Promote public use of modern information technology.

The library's intent was and still is to improve individuals, families, and the whole community. The value statements extended the improvement theme—putting special emphasis on helping kids, businesses, job hunters, community leaders, and illiterates. Just as with many other large public libraries, SLPL set out to become the city's principal voluntary educational institution and to assist in every way possible to use public money to fuel the city's economic and cultural development.

It is a big deal when a library articulates a reform rather than a service theme. The reform theme suggests that the library will help the community change in measurable ways, for the better. It is an even bigger deal when libraries self-consciously spend their funds on services that carry out the reform objectives articulated in their mission.

In a recent article, futurist Carl Grant, now at the University of Oklahoma, provides a nice transition to end this chapter with his comments about the mission statement that David Lankes recommends to the readers of his *Library Encyclopedia*. Lankes's mission statement is as dramatic as it is simple: It states:

The mission of librarians is to improve society through facilitating knowledge creation in their communities.

Grant utilizes this mission statement because it puts libraries in the business of improving their communities through knowledge creation.[8]

Adding to that discussion is the work of Brandon Gaille, who collected numerous taglines from the nation's 121,000 different libraries in 2013.[9] Gaille points out that slogans and taglines have the purpose of marketing in synoptic forms. His list includes: the ever-popular Check It Out, Know Better, Keys to the Past—Gateway to the Future, Explore Today—Discover Tomorrow, and Your Guide to Answers.

When you think about institutional planning, consider Yogi Berra's clear statement about the importance of developing and financially resourcing a clear purpose: "If you don't know where you are going, you'll end up someplace else." Using a library's core documents to interpret the intention of spending in an annual budget is likely to take the institution to the place where its planners want it to be.

NOTES

1. Goodreads.com Retrieved on June 6, 2015, from http://www.goodreads.com/quotes/tag/planning.
2. The questions are reproduced from a blogger, Prem Rao. "7 Steps in Formulating Your Vision." In *People at Work & Play*. Posted October 8, 2015. Retrieved on January 18, 2015, from https://bprao.wordpress.com/2008/10/08/7-steps-to-formulating-your-vision/.
3. *Vision Statement Formulation Package*. Retrieved on January 19, 2015, from http://vision-statement-formulation-package.soft112.com/download.html.
4. South Orange Public Library. Retrieved on June 7, 2015, from http://www1.youseemore.com/southorange/contentpages.asp?loc=10.
5. The National Library Board of Singapore. Retrieved on June 7, 2015, from http://www.ifla.org/files/assets/government-libraries/publications/MissionStatements2010–07–28.pdf.
6. Dedham Public Schools Mission Statement. Retrieved on June 7, 2015, from http://www.dedham.k12.ma.us/pages/Dedham_Public_Schools.
7. St. Louis Public Library Mission Statement. Adopted by the St. Louis Public Library Board of Directors. Adopted January 31, 1994. Retrieved on January 19, 2015, from http://www.slpl.lib.mo.us/kidzone/using/kdmiss.htm.
8. Grant, Carl. "It's Time to Define a New Brand for Libraries. Let's Make Sure It Leaves People Soaring, Not Snoring." *Public Library Quarterly*, 34:2 (2015), pp. 99–106.
9. Brandon Gaille. *List of 37 Catchy Slogans and Taglines*. Posted September 8, 2013. Retrieved on January 19, 2015, from http://brandongaille.com/list-37-catchy-library-slogans-and-taglines/. A somewhat different purpose—that of marketing an image in very synoptic form.

SECTION IV

Budget Basics

CHAPTER 10

Budget Planning

It's clearly a budget. It's got a lot of numbers in it.

—George W. Bush[1]

Like other budget novices, new hires in organizations like libraries often view budgets as numbers and see managing the budget as a mathematical task. More accurately, as Jacob Lew, former director of the Federal Office of Management and Budget, says, "The budget is not just a collection of numbers, but an expression of our values and aspirations."[2] To adapt a line for libraries from the 1976 movie, *All the President's Men*, which popularized the cliché, if you want to see what any library values, "follow the money."[3]

In all public service institutions, including libraries, the budget has two functions. First, it begins as a spending plan, limited by amounts which are available within a certain time period. Notice how general that definition is. The definition does not say, "to spend the cash on hand" or "to budget this year's revenue." That's because a budget is the organization's creation. It articulates how the institution will use some of its available assets to carry out a set of prioritized work tasks.

Second, once the budget is adopted by an official governing board or the host institution, the budget becomes either a legally binding document or a binding policy document. In either case, the library staff is expected to work within and carry out the financial mandates articulated in the budget's terms.

In libraries, the terms are these: The budget states the amount that is to be spent. And most library budgets are for one year, named the fiscal year, no matter when the 12-month period begins or ends. Annual library budgets are more complex than most personal or family budgets, because they serve multiple purposes and cover a variety of expenditures.

To meet their legal or policy-mandated fiscal requirements, library leaders have to spend funds as delineated in their budgets as closely as possible.

A decade ago, Judith Dossett, in writing about the finances of special libraries, summarized the three administrative purposes of a budget. They are:

- Planning: The allocation of resources in a timely way.
- Coordination: Resource how individuals and library units will work together.
- Control: Avoid running out of money; irresponsible behavior.[4]

Supreme Commander of the Allied Forces in World War II and later U.S. President Dwight Eisenhower articulated the importance of planning before starting any military campaign. He noted, "In preparing for battle, I have always found that plans are useless, but planning is indispensible."[5]

As Eisenhower found for war, budget planning in libraries also is indispensible. That's because budget planning is the fiscal process where the professionals who operate the library lay out how the organization will use its resources, including both money and time, to move the library to its new service future. Table 10.1 articulates a view for how this process occurs in one library system.

The Pierce County Library System (PCLS) outside Tacoma, Washington, is independent from the county and funded by a separate taxing district. It is careful and thoughtful in its budget creation and produces financial documents that it uses and that it provides publicly, so that government officials, civic leaders, and taxpayers can see how it uses its money to do important work for the community.

The material from PCLS in this chapter is available on the Internet, and it is part of a lengthy analytical article that appeared in *Public Library Quarterly* in early 2014.[6] We use the documents from Pierce County because the Government Finance Officers Association in 2012 gave Pierce County the Distinguished Budget Presentation Award. And in 2013, it won the same award for a second time.

Table 10.1   Pierce County Library System Budget Preparation Calendar

July	Strategic priorities created	Budget calendar created	Revenues estimated	Budget instructions to managers
August	Managers develop budget proposals	Board review budget process		
September	Managers present budget proposals	Budget team develops estimated budget	Board study session on budget	Board review of estimated budget
October	Director's approval for draft balanced budget outline	Preliminary certification of revenues	Budget team develops draft balanced budget	Board review of draft budget
November	Budget team develops budget document	Public hearing and first reading of budget		
December	Final certification of revenues	Budget team revises budget	Public hearing/board passes budget	Final budget and pamphlet published

Source: Based on Pierce County Library System 2011 Annual Report at https://www.piercecountylibrary.org/files/library/2011-annual-report.pdf

Table 10.1 is Pierce County Library's budget process in the form of an annual calendar. Note how the library is essentially working on three budgets a once: As PCLS spends down from its current FY budget, its administrative officials close out the previous year's budget, including preparation and cooperation in the audit of the previous year's accounts. With the official closing of the previous year's books and completion of the audit, PCLS publishes an annual report.

Meanwhile, the careful control of money is displayed as the staff adjusts budget spending midyear, depending on the most recent new information on revenues and spending gathered in the spring. In the second half of the year, library staff plan and create the next year's budget to submit to the library board for approval.

The clarity of this process displayed in the calendar is a nice model for other libraries no matter what their size. The implicit confident attitude displayed in this document, the budget, and the other financial documents it makes public is "Please look at this financial information. We do many good things with the money we are given, and our spending produces remarkable positive results."

PCLS budget preparation is a good model, because libraries are idiosyncratic on how the budget gets constructed. In general, most library administrators and many library staff participate in developing the library's annual budget. It is time-consuming work that eats up available time spent on service assignments, and depending on the organization's budgeting style, it may involve a large number of staff. Those realities are true whether the budget is increasing or decreasing.

In libraries where the revenues are growing, the libraries' budget may be based on the previous budget with slight increases in most budget lines, but even in good times staff have to be savvy to get the budget they need. In times of economic downturn, staff has to figure out how to work with less.

In many libraries, managers are asked to submit a budget request for administrative approval and inclusion in the library's budget. This information may include several budget lines such as collection, programs, staff, staff travel or training, and electronic upgrades. In larger libraries, specialists may only need to submit a collections budget with staff and other budget lines included in the administrative budget. In some school districts, building-level staff may have informal discussions of budget needs, but it is the district-level administrator who does the budget request.

Whatever the case, staff should know what budget work and the specificity of budget compliance expected of them, so they can carry out policy mandates and meet the deadlines the library has in its budget process. It is important to know what is expected or to ask questions to clarify what is expected. It is important to understand the basic accounting practices and terms to be effective in playing the expected role in budget management.

TYPES OF BUDGETS

If your job is in a just-established library, where financial operating policies have not yet been set, you and your professional peers would have lots of significant policy decisions to make immediately. One of these would be what type of budget your library was going to use. You would make that decision early in your budget planning process, because the type of budget in which you operate will require some data that other budget types do not require.

The point of this section is to inform you about basic types of budgets. Knowing the type of budget that your library uses may help you understand more quickly how your particular institutional budget works or the aspects of your program that it emphasizes. Dossett says she has found all these six types of budgets presented here in special libraries.[7] Our search has found each of these types in other libraries, as well. Sometimes, budgets receive different names than the ones we present here. To understand what is really happening in the budget, follow the processes we lay out here and in the next chapter.

Here are six basic budget types:

- **Lump Sum Budget**: Duke University Office of Research Support defines this term as identifying a "very general, non-specific approach to budgeting which leaves a great deal of discretion to the owner [manager]" of a budget. One figure includes all possible expenditures.[8] For example, a school library might receive a collection budget of $1,000. The building librarian would use the district's collection development procedures to purchase as many books as possible for $1,000. She would not have to spend 25 percent on paperbacks, 50 percent on reference materials, and 25 percent on Spanish language books, as the spending requirements of the budget is not divided in any way.
- **Formula Budget**: A mathematical budgeting technique, in which the cost of a particular category is figured by formula as "X full-time-equivalent employees at Y average salary produce a budget estimate of Z amount for the coming year." Forecasting errors are a critical feature of formula budgeting.[9] For example, 10 physics journal subscriptions at $500 each will produce a $5,000 budget. Adelphi University has used the technique in materials budgeting.
- **Line-Item Budgets:** These are the most frequently used type of budgets in special libraries, according to Dossett, and in most other types of libraries as well. Line-item budgets "facilitate low levels of detail for both planning and cost control."[10] "The line item budget is organized around categories or lines of expenditures, and shows how much is spent on the various products and services that the library acquires." If more detail is needed, it is carried in subaccounts which feed into the lines in this budget.[11] Many libraries present line-item budgets in a way to help staff directors see how funds are spent for major priorities of library expenditure. Two examples follow.
- **Program Budget**: "The program budget, designed to assist with planning, is organized around service programs (such as children's services, young adult services, reference services) and helps the library board and director see how much is spent on these individual areas. A program budget is usually presented in a line-item style, so that the individual categories of expenditures for each program are also recognizable."[12]
- **Performance/Function Budget**: These budgets highlight work tasks to be performed rather than programs. Usually, these library tasks include cataloging and other technical services. Some librarians anticipating Return on Investment (ROI) studies break service functions into performance budgets.[13]
- **Zero-Based Budgets:** These are clean-slate budgets. Here, the budget makers start with mission and updated goals, disregard previous budgets, and in effect ask, "What will it take to achieve X or Y?"[14] Most library budgets are based on the previous year's budget. For example, the budget is increased by 2 percent, so if the administration wants to start with equality as a priority, a certain percent will be added to all of last year's budget items. By contrast, zero-based budgets start with every budget line at zero. This beginning allows the library staff to reexamine priorities, as the budget does not reflect prior budgets.

Various experts and organizations will put different versions of budget types into a basic list. If you want to see some of this variety, just Google "budget types" or "library budget types" into your net access computer and see the various lists of terms that pop out. We have listed the budget types above because they seem to appear most of the time in library financial outputs.

We close this chapter with a quote from Meredith Schwatz's 2013 article in *Library Journal*. She began her summary of the library budget scene with these words: "Though there aren't a lot of whoops and cheers to be heard, a cautious optimism seems to describe the 2012 library budget landscape, according to *LJ*'s annual survey. Some 60 percent of libraries increased their funding, while 36 percent decreased it. Only four percent stayed the same."[15]

This quotation seems an appropriate place to end this chapter on library financial planning within easily recognized budget types. Financial planning is mapping the adaptive route to institutional change. And that activity always is accomplished within an institutional context: by type of library, by whether or not the annual revenue is going up or down, and the style of management which the institution's leadership uses as it prioritizes its annual budget planning.

The Pierce County Budget Document cited earlier is a good place to begin that study. It is clear that those who operated the institution were not about to slack off on institutional adaptation just because the budget cupboard was bare of new money and shy on old resources, as well. In the end, in every type of library, great budget planning is born from solid financial leadership.[16]

NOTES

1. *Brainy Quote.* Retrieved on July 8, 2015, from http://www.brainyquote.com/quotes/quotes/g/georgewbu382358.html#BkJ4jIwWHUkQRv5i.99.
2. *Brainy Quote.* Retrieved on July 8, 2015, from http://www.brainyquote.com/quotes/quotes/j/jacoblew442942.html#KTHTiA2tOgysKvSy.99.
3. For attribution to this source, see "Follow the Money" in *Wikipedia*. Retrieved on August 5, 2015, from https://en.wikipedia.org/wiki/Follow_the_money.
4. Dossett, Judith. "Budgets and Management in Special Libraries." CLIS 724. Special Libraries and Information Science. Dr. Robert Williams. April 28, 2004. In Williams, Dr. Robert C. *Special Libraries Management Handbook.* University of South Carolina, College of Library and Information Science, 1993–2004, 2007. Retrieved on June 19, 2015, from http://faculty.libsci.sc.edu/bob/class/clis724/SpecialLibrariesHandbook/INDEX.htm.
5. *Brainy Quote.* Dwight D. Eisenhower Quotes. Retrieved on January 16, 2015, from http://www.brainyquote.com/quotes/quotes/d/dwightdei164720.html.
6. See Parikh, Neel, Clifford Jo, Georgia Lomax, and Sally Porter Smith. "Making the Case for Budget Reductions: Pierce County Library's FY2013 Budget." *Public Library Quarterly*, 33:1 (2014), p. 25.
7. Dossett, loc. cit.
8. Duke University, Office of Research Support. *Lump Sum Budgets.* Retrieved on June 20, 2015, from https://ors.duke.edu/orsmanual/lump-sum-budgets.
9. Hanushank, Eric. "Formula Budgeting: The Economics and Analytics of Fiscal Policy Under Rules." *Journal of Policy Analysis and Management,* 6:1 (Autumn 1986),

pp. 3–19. Retrieved on June 20, 2015, from http://hanushek.stanford.edu/sites/default/files/publications/Hanushek%201986%20JPAM%206(1).pdf. Or see Smith, Debbi A. "Percentage-Based Allocation of an Academic Library Materials Budget." Delivered at Nelinet Annual Collection Services Conference, April 15, 2009. Retrieved on June 20, 2015, from http://www.slideshare.net/kramsey/percentage-based-allocation-of-an-academic-library-materials-budget.

10. Dossett, loc. cit.
11. Wisconsin State Library, Public Library Development. *Developing the Library Budget.* Retrieved on June 20, 2015, from https://www.google.com/webhp?sourceid=chrome-instant&rlz=1C1QJDB_enUS595US596&ion=1&espv=2&ie=UTF-8#q=library%20line%20item%20budget.
12. Ibid.
13. See, for example, National Archives and Records Administration. *2012 Performance Budget. Congressional Justification.* Retrieved on June 20, 2015, from http://www.archives.gov/about/plans-reports/performance-budget/2011/2012-performance-budget.pdf.
14. Sargent, C.W. "Zero-Based Budgeting and the Library." *Bulletin of the Medical Library Association,* 66:1 (1978), pp. 31–35. Retrieved on July 20, 2015, from http://www.ncbi.nlm.nih.gov/pmc/articles/PMC225295/?page=1.
15. Schwartz, Meredith. "The Budget Balancing Act: LJ's Budget Survey Shows Modest Improvement, and Signs of More to Come." *Library Journal.* January 9, 2013. Retrieved on August 5, 2015, from http://lj.libraryjournal.com/2013/01/funding/the-budget-balancing-act-library-budgets-show-modest-improvement-and-signs-of-more-to-come/#.
16. Parikh, Neel, Clifford Jo, Georgia Lomax, and Sally Porter Smith, pp. 33ff.

CHAPTER 11

Basic Library Budget Language

Every one has experienced how learning an appropriate name for what was dim and vague cleared up and crystallized the whole matter.

—John Dewey, *How We Think*[1]

WHAT'S DIFFERENT ABOUT LIBRARY BUDGETS

It's unlikely that a library budget is going to look much like the ones that families use when they plan their purchases. The latter mostly think in terms of cash accounts, such as, "Our family has the cash or can get the cash to make a purchase now or we can use our future income to pay off any installment loans we take out to buy something we need right now."

Rather than cash accounts, libraries use **Fund Accounting**. *Wikipedia* defines fund accounting as *"an accounting system emphasizing accountability rather than profitability, used by non-profit organizations and governments.* [Emphasis added.] In this system, a fund is a self-balancing set of accounts, segregated for specific purposes in accordance with laws and regulations or special restrictions and limitations."[2] In practice, what fund accounting means is that all income and expenditures are placed in categories, so there is the general fund, a capital fund, and different kinds of special funds.

For library staff, fund accounting means you ask for funds from the correct account and spend money from fund accounts only for the fund's stated purpose. Usually, you buy books from a book account and book cases from a furniture account. Even if you have "extra" funds in a collection account, it can't be spent for a much needed book case—without a public action transfer that falls within the by-laws or other formal financial policies and procedures determining how library money will be handled.

Accountants usually recommend both fund accounting and double-entry bookkeeping to institutions like libraries, because financial integrity and openness is of such great importance in nonprofit agencies. To reiterate, fund accounting emphasizes accountability, not profit making.

DOUBLE-ENTRY BOOKKEEPING—CHART OF ACCOUNTS

Double-entry bookkeeping is the handmaiden of fund accounting. Double entry means that every transaction involves two accounts. For example, when a company borrows money from its bank, the company's cash account will decrease and its liability account Loans Payable will increase.

For every budget, there is a General Ledger which serves as a chart of accounts (i.e., table of contents) to the budget entries. Robert H. Burger, one the few gurus of library finance, in his introductory course outline on this subject, notes the importance of the chart of accounts in the operational budget when he states that library accounting in "a budget and cost analysis produce resolution only as good as chart of accounts allows them to be."[3]

Along with a chart of accounts, there also is a "journal" or "general journal." *Wikipedia* does a nice job of summarizing activity in the general journal. The entry notes:[4]

> The journal is where *double entry bookkeeping* entries are recorded by *debiting* [subtracting an amount from] one or more accounts and *crediting* [adding the same amount to] . . . one or more accounts with the same total amount. The total amount debited and the total amount credited should always be equal, thereby ensuring the *accounting equation* is maintained [i.e. balanced].

> "In accounting and bookkeeping, a journal is a record of financial transactions in order by date." Historically, the journal was "the book of original entry" that included an explanatory narrative to clarify the nature of the transaction. As with other kinds of budgetary documents, there can be specialized journals for certain functions. . . . A general journal entry includes the date of the transaction, the titles of the accounts debited and credited, the amount of each debit and credit, and an explanation of the transaction also known as a Narration.

BUDGET CATEGORIES

Authorized library budgets usually have a couple of spending categories that contain more funding than the other accounts and, even if relatively smaller, they require more attention than other budget categories.

The first of these is for personnel or staffing; the other is for collections. Both of these are collective categories. Staffing, for example, may include estimated amounts of salary based on union agreements and benefits, including estimates of salary that include vacation and sick leave.

Collections usually include both books and serials and increasingly e-collections, as well. A relatively new library question about e-collections is whether or not the item should be placed in chart of accounts as an information technology expense or a materials collection expense. Information technology, including public and staff computers or electronic devices, operating software and data storage, and often the library's catalog and circulation systems, is a large and growing budget category.

Every library has many other types or categories of expense. What are the main types of expenditures in your library? Check your library's public budget documents. You will probably find staff, collection/materials, technology, construction, systems maintenance, and outreach away from buildings.

Many library budgets classify lots of expense as "operations," which is a general or miscellaneous category. Every type of library has standards—or at least expectations—about what percentage of all expenditures should be used in each category.

Professor Burger is correct in his suggestion that no chart of accounts is very good if it does not allow resolution of income and expenses in a way that helps the budget makers to know that what they want to happen financially is occurring. Burger's suggestion is about how adherence to the budget is used to coordinate and control various types of operations or functions.

BUDGET IS AN AUTHORIZATION DOCUMENT

To remind readers again, the budget is the basic authorization document for institutional expenditure. Like most everything else in library land, spending money is authorized and legitimated by prior paper or electronic records. Typical of expense authorizations that flow from an approved budget, libraries have buying/purchasing guidelines that state the rules about

- spending limits that unit work managers follow to request funds before purchases of more than X amount of money;
- travel expenditures, including who can get library reimbursement, what receipts are needed, and when a travel advance will be given;
- how to get office supplies or new and replacement furniture (like new displayers);
- how to set up financial agreements for outside contractors or performers;
- how and when to order serials, books, and eBooks;
- how to handle cash received as well as purchases made in cash.

Library staff also will have developed competitive bidding terms (i.e., rules) for selecting vendors and how to select materials for the collection. Most libraries bid out contracts for vendors and for service consultants (e.g., architects, engineers, and attorneys) every few years and expect staff to use these vendors for all purchases in their respective categories.

In this way, specific library purchasing is legitimized: It is part of a fiscal planning, budgeting, authorization, ratification process that is marked out in library policy documents and procedures based on federal, state, and local law. The more purchasing is accomplished outside the rules, the more likely it will cause official trouble within the institutional framework of monetary controls.

So, your first financial job is NOT to exceed the operational budget authority that has been granted to you. You can have conversations about budget items, but you should not even give the impression that you have budget authority if you do not. A good library supervisor at any level will not and should not take your financial misstatements casually. Money is not something that you joke about in not-for-profit institutions, including libraries, where accountability is an ongoing watchword.

BUDGET EXAMPLES

Figure 11.1 is the 2011–2013 Comparative Budget for the Pierce County Library System. A thorough in-house presentation on this budget by Pierce County Staff was featured in a 2014 issue of *Public Library Quarterly*.[5]

OPERATING BUDGET	2011 ACTUALS	2012 FINAL (12/10)	2013 BUDGET (12/12)
New Revenues	$29,111,096	$26,694,758	$24,616,725
Use of Fund Balance	0	175,127	807,172
Total Available Funds	29,111,096	26,869,885	25,423,927
Less:			
Operating Costs	26,572,741	26,069,042	24,931,592
Set Asides and Transfers	1,731,183	800,843	492,335
Total Expenditures	28,303,924	26,869,885	25,423,927
Net of Revenues and Expenditures	**$807,172**	**$0**	**$0**
CAPITAL IMPROVEMENT BUDGET			
New Revenues	$196,379	$0	$0
Transfers from General Fund	6,376,043	800,843	492,335
Use of Fund Balance	0	1,194,857	1,139,665
Total Available Funds	6,572,422	1,995,700	1,632,000
Less:			
Capital Project Costs	5,452,432	1,995,700	1,632,000
Net of Revenues and Expenditures	**$3,855,066**	**$0**	**$0**
DEBT SERVICE FUND			
Revenues	$156	$0	$0
Expenditures	0	0	0
Net of Revenues and Expenditures	**$156**	**$0**	**$0**

2013 Combined Fund Balances (Cash Reserves)
General, Capital Improvement, and Debt Service Funds

Begin Balances, Jan 1	$16,212,990	$13,701,636	$12,046,697
Net of All Revenues, Expenditures, Transfers	(2,511,355)	(1,654,939)	(1,946,838)
End Balances, Dec 31	$13,701,635	$10,913,343	$10,099,859

Figure 11.1   2011–2013 Comparative Budget for the Pierce County Library System

Every library budget divides revenues and expenditures into several accounts. The annual budget for Pierce County is comprehensive, in that it includes all revenues and expenses. In other libraries, some of that revenue, like that for capital construction and special projects, totals show up in other budgets separate from the general budget. This document, however, is the overall budget for the system; it contains all of the revenue and expense, including that to be used for special purposes other than operations.

To provide perspective to the persons who examine it, Pierce County's annual budget also contains three years of financial figures: Actual for 2011, Final for 2012 (the "final" designating that it is the last budget document available for that year even though official closure of the budget appears to be pending), and estimates for 2013. Note the language progression in the budget totals for the three years. In the way this budget presentation is printed, it is saying, "This library adapts to change. Our three-year revenue trend is downward—from $29 million to less than $25 million, a cut of $4.5 million or 15%, and we are adjusting to that cut."

The first financial adjustment to undertake an activity for which there is no money in the anticipated annual allocation is to use money from a "fund balance," which yields over $800,000, reducing the planned cut back from 15 percent to 12.7 percent. The second is to add funds from "Set-Asides and Transfers," which makes the amount available for 2013 to be $25.4 million.

CAPITAL IMPROVEMENT BUDGET

Another feature of the Pierce County budgeting report is to present the "Capital Improvement Budget" as part of the Operating Budget. This summary shows that no new revenues are anticipated from grants or gifts in 2013. However, there is General Fund money—including use of the "Fund Balance."

The Capital Improvement Budget for 2013, therefore, shows $1.6 million in anticipated revenue—a little less than the amount in the 2012 budget and a lot less than in the 2011 budget.

DEBT SERVICE FUND

With only an incidental revenue item in 2011, the debt service fund is dormant for the year, with no reportable activity for the 2013 budget.

The 2013 Combined Fund Balances (Cash Reserve) includes the accumulated and anticipated reserves (excess of income over expense in the General, Capital Improvement and Debt Service Funds.

Different libraries calculate their Cash Reserve balances in slightly different ways. The Pierce County Budget demonstrates that the system has a healthy reserve that is invested; but it has been hitting that reserve hard since 2011. That reserve is going to be hit again by anticipated construction projects, taking the reserve down to $10 million.

The Pierce County explanation of this budget item appears in this summary statement:[6]

After implementing $2.2 million in reductions, the Library will use $807,172 of cash reserves to mitigate [negative] service impacts. The budget is presented as balanced by fiscal management policy: source of all revenues and use of fund balances equals expenditures.

The fiscal challenge remains. Sustain services, improve, innovate, and perform to Library Priorities, while living in times of dwindling revenues and increasing costs. The Library expects its leadership and staff to address challenges and remain strong in their focus on public service, [and] their actions and ideas are presented throughout this [budget] document.

Finally, Figure 11.2 is a budget graphic to help staff and customers understand how the library budget is spent.

Figure 11.2 makes clear the library's priorities from the library users' perspective. This graphic also articulates time. Operations (staff, collections, buildings, vehicles, and technology) occupy a total of 91 cents out of each dollar in income. An intriguing choice is to budget the executive office and finance operation as a separate item outside of staff, because that inclusion in staffing would have raised the category of expenditure by a few points. The other item of particular interest is that even in tight times, 2 percent of each $1 in income is being earmarked as "Savings for Infrastructure Projects," that is, building construction or restoration.

Communicating the library's budget to the public is an important part of the budget process and will be discussed in greater detail in later chapters focusing on different types of budgets.

Figure 11.3 shows an example of a small library budget that serves a small private school. It does not include the librarian's regular salary or benefits as these are included in the salary budget for the school. Also not included are any utility (light, heat, computer costs) or custodian costs as they are also covered in the larger school budget. The summer work for the librarian and assistant are included as this time is considered "extra" or over and

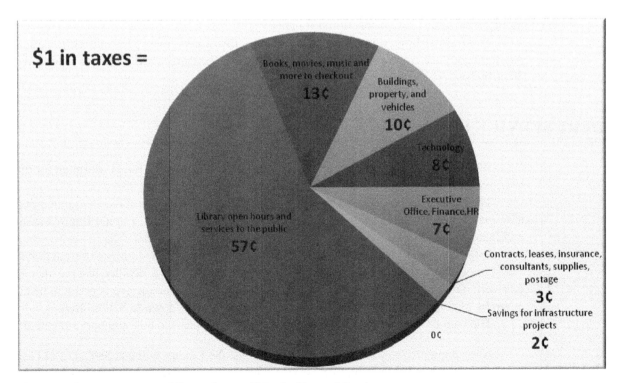

Figure 11.2   Pierce County Library System Value by Type of Service

Library Budget

1. Book Budget	$8,000	
1. DK Eyewitness, Eye Wonder, Eyewitness Readers		$2,000
2. True Books 100 at $8 (paper)		$800
3. Twelve selected countries		$1,000
4. Other countries		$1,000
5. Other nonfiction		$2,000
6. Fiction		$200
7. Reserve/Teacher request		$1,000
2. Supplies	$2,500	
3. Catalog	$8,500	
1. Supplies (labels, label covers, laminate)		$750
2. Librarian August work (12 days)		$2,000
3. Summer assistant 100 hours @ $10		$1,000
4. Fall assistant (425 hours)		$4,250
5. Reserve		$500
Total:	**$19,000**	

Figure 11.3   Sample Small Library Budget

above the regular nine-month salaries for these staff. This budget was approved by the school's governing board, but not funded. The librarian and board members raised the funds from private donations and by holding a "For the Love of Reading" party for parents and friends of the school.

Other small libraries may include many other categories, including staff costs, building maintenance, insurance, computer, and e-costs as well as a more varied materials budget. Budgets can be simple, but should account for all the costs needed to run the library.

FINANCIAL TERMS

Some budget terms are so basic and used so often that anyone who "knows anything" about library finance ought to have these terms in her or his head. We begin with the vocabulary related to timing of the budget year.

Timing of "Budget Year" or "Fiscal Year."

- **Fiscal Year.** The start-up and end dates for the annual budget are set by the organization's by-laws, authorized by law, or enacted by board decision as the board acts under its legislative authority.
  - If a library budget runs from January 1 to December 31 of a single year, the "budget year" or "fiscal year" is identical with the calendar year. Most frequently, the fiscal year dates are set as an accommodation to an income cycle. ("Our library receives its main funding in the month of X. Therefore, our fiscal year starts on the first day of the next month.")

- Governance bodies and parent institutions, however, have all kinds of "good reasons" for setting fiscal years. Some may want to match meeting dates of governance boards or legislatures, because of custom or for some other reason. So, a fiscal or budget year can vary from the calendar year.
- Since watching over expenditures and annual budgeting is a set of activities that usually occurs on a regular cycle, if you are in any way connected with the budget/expenditure process, you need to find out the timing of that fiscal cycle and recognize that some of your professional and personal life will be determined by it.
- **Authorized Budget.** Budgets move from a "proposed" or "tentative" category to "official" or "authorized" when the appropriate persons, as a governance board or particular budget officers, like the chief executive officer, school superintendent, head librarian, and chief financial officer, agree that this budget document is the one that will be in effect in the coming fiscal year.
  - Authorized budgets are official documents, and those who run the library and groups that present various citizen interests expect involved staff members to follow the budget cycle, not make a shambles out of the budget that has been authorized.
- **Budgets Vary in Detail and Flexibility**. Some budgets are very detailed. Others are quite general. Usually, the more detail there is in the specifications for budget expenditures, the less flexibility there will be to shift available dollars from one budget category to another. For example, when a budget proposes a specific amount to be spent on books to be used in library outreach by the extension or bookmobile division, then that requirement may preclude expenditure of that money for another book category, much less for any other type of expenditure.
  - Why that lack of flexibility? Less from a sense of recalcitrance usually than because a change in budget lines can bring conflicts both within an organization and between a library and its parent institution or its governance group. In other words, moving money from one category or another usually requires the action of someone in authority or even of some formal legislative body. So, recognize that one reason there is so much discussion over budgets before they are put in place may be because it is so hard to change them once they are in place.
  - To sum up the issue of flexibility, the amount of play (i.e., change) that is possible in budget lines is limited by the amounts involved and the very real policy and political issues that may be involved in shifting money from one budget line to another.
- **Encumbrances.** An amount due carried forward for payment at a current or future time. An encumbrance is an impediment or burden. Libraries typically use it to move a financial commitment from one FY to another. For example, "Since we didn't get our new ILS system purchased in the last FY, we will take that $850,000 and encumber it to pay for it in the coming FY." Some libraries are prohibited from encumbering their annual budgets; others can encumber under specific rules. When the budget is tight, encumbrances usually fall off because policymakers regard money as less flexible than when times are flush.[7]
- **Funds Budgeted on Speculation**. Some fund amounts may be budgeted on speculation, as, for example, on the basis of earned income from the library store or restaurant or from a special fundraising campaign. The former amount usually is set by the sales from the previous year. The latter amount is, quite simply, a guess based upon any number of factors. In libraries, this speculation is most frequently based on prior experiences within the institutions—or by borrowing reliable figures from other, similar organizations.

- **Critical Path Budgeting**. "Critical Path Budgeting is introduced as an integrating tool for project planning, coordination, and control. Through a synthesis of budgeting and critical path scheduling, it is possible to treat the time and cost variables of a project explicitly."[8] Critical path budgeting lays out what should be done first, second, third, and so on at what cost, to bring the project to completion on its intended start-up date. This kind of budgeting is a cousin to a Gantt Chart, a type of bar chart . . . that illustrates a project schedule . . . , that is, the start and finish dates of the terminal elements and summary elements of a project.[9]
- **Unfunded Mandate.** An unfunded mandate occurs when the national, state, or local government legally requires another government agency or set of individuals to perform certain actions but provides no funding to carry out the action.[10] A good example of an unfunded mandate for libraries is the Americans with Disabilities Act (ADA), which requires libraries to design buildings and provide services in certain defined ways with no funding from the Federal government which passed the ADA legislation. Another unfunded mandate occurs when a legislative body requires particular types of libraries to provide technology education, youth services programs, or outreach efforts without funding authorization or even possibility to accompany the legal requirement.
- **Bid Specifications**. The library's first offer to a vendor indicating "types, quantities, and agreed prices for products or services," that is, terms or bid specifications to which it will usually agree, a seller bids on the option.
- **Purchase Orders**. When a library issues a purchase order, and it is accepted by a vendor, those actions establish the terms of a contract. The same thing occurs when the library is a seller and accepts a purchase order that establishes a contract.[11] In modern libraries, purchasing is accomplished in several different ways.
- **Library Credit Cards**. In modern libraries, using a credit card for a purchase is one way to purchase an item that is needed by the library. For example, a library maintenance person needs a specific kind of elbow joint to make a plumbing repair. The person uses a credit card that maintenance persons carry to make the purchase, often at neighborhood stores selected in advance by the library which may have selected them for contracted discounts.
  - Many staff may carry library credit cards. Typically, these are used for direct billing to the library during in-person or telephone customer purchases. Such credit cards might be used by librarians who deliver programs throughout a state involving overnight stays at hotels and motels and the purchase of meals, fuel, taxi rides, and other incidentals during the required travel. The use of credit cards does not obviate the need for documentation by staff who make purchases, but they do cut down the number of reimbursements (and, therefore, checks) between the institution and the individual staff member.[12]
- **Cash Reimbursement**. The maintenance person can spend cash and get a receipt, and then be reimbursed for the amount of the purchase.
- **Credit Accounts of Suppliers**. Maintenance staff might need to purchase items to repair machinery within a branch of a library system. Van or bookmobile drivers may have the ability to charge fuel and maintenance at certain garages.

The examples in this section demonstrate how the library budget becomes the basis for legitimating certain kinds of financial transactions, whether for purchase process or direct cash expenditure. Remember that accountability is the primary reason for these precautions. Convenience is a granted ideal only within the accountability requirement.

NOTES

1. Goodreads. Retrieved on September 21, 2015, from http://www.goodreads.com/quotes/tag/vocabulary.
2. *Wikipedia,* Fund Accounting. Retrieved, the free encyclopedia. Retrieved on June 18, 2015, from https://en.wikipedia.org/wiki/Fund_accounting.
3. Burger, Robert H. *Financial Management of Libraries and Information Centers. (Currently GSLIS 590FM).* Fall, 2010. In possession of author.
4. *Wikipedia,* General Journal. *The Free Encyclopedia.* Retrieved on June 18, 2015, from https://en.wikipedia.org/wiki/General_journal.
5. Parikh, Neel, Clifford Jo, Georgia Lomax, and Sally Porter Smith. "Making the Case for Budget Reductions: Pierce County Library's FY2013 Budget." *Public Library Quarterly*, 33:1 (2014), pp. 23–75.
6. Parikh et al., pp. 32–33.
7. *Merriam-Webster,* Encumbrance. Retrieved on April 18, 2015, from htp://www.merriam-webster.com/dictionary/encumbrance.
8. Dervitsiotis, Kostas N. *Critical Path Budgeting: A Synthesis of Budgeting and Critical Path Scheduling.* Corvallis: Oregon State University, Scholar's Archive MA in Mechanical and Industrial Engineering, 1965.
9. *Wikipedia,* Gantt Chart. *The Free Encyclopedia.* Retrieved on August 6, 2015, from https://en.wikipedia.org/wiki/Gantt_chart.
10. *WiseGeek*, Unfunded Mandate. Retrieved on April 19, 2015, from http://www.wisegeek.org/what-is-an-unfunded-mandate.htm.
11. Dobler, Donald W, and David N. Burt. *Purchasing and Supply Management, Text and Cases* (Sixth Ed.). Singapore: McGraw-Hill. 1996, p. 70.
12. University of Minnesota. University Policy Library. *Using the University Procurement Card.* 1996. Retrieved on June 15, 2015, from http://policy.umn.edu/finance/procurementcard.

SECTION V

Income

CHAPTER 12

Shifts in Library Service Demands and Income

Court to State: Pay Up! Justices Order
$100K-a-Day Fines over Inadequate Education Spending.[1]

WHAT AMERICANS WANT FROM LIBRARIES

In Chapter 2, we noted some facts about the extent of the financial illiteracy of Americans. That lack of knowledge sometimes is used by elected officials to make policies and to adjust spending that does not always meet their own legal requirements.

That situation was reflected publicly in the August 13, 2015, Washington State Supreme Court Sanction on the state legislature and the governor. In this McCleary Decision, the Court in effect said that the elected officials had broken their own laws in their low level of support for K-12 education, which the Court reminded the Legislature was the "paramount duty" of state financial support. *The Seattle Times* reported,

> At $100,000 per day, the fines would amount to more than $14 million by January, when the Legislature convenes for its next scheduled session. That's a pittance compared with the state's $38 billion 2015–17 operating budget, and a fraction of the billions needed to fully comply with the McCleary decision. . . .

Not everyone looked kindly on the court's order. Rep Matt Manweller, R-Ellensburg, tweeted that the Supreme Court had "gone rogue", suggested the justices be impeached. . . . [and stated that the ruling] "was the sign of a court that is just absolutely detached from any understanding of its own role in government."[2]

We start with this legal decision because of the unlikely possibility that this kind of court decision will help any type of libraries. That's because university, public, and special libraries generally do not have the status of public education in federal, state, or local budgets. And even in states or locales with mandated aid-to-libraries formulae, it is unlikely that a sanction like McLeary would occur.

That legal weakness in funding would not be so important for libraries if they were not expected to fill so many service needs on behalf of their constituents. Libraries historically are expected to expand their services to meet constituent needs whether the economy is rising or declining. In recessionary periods, libraries have added services or found valid ways to escalate the quality of services already in place. During the Great Depression, for example, with so many children on the street and not attending school, libraries expanded the number and quality of youth services; and in the Great Recession of 2007–09, many public libraries reemphasized children's services and vastly increased job training and application services to meet the changing family and job needs of their constituents. Or, as we recounted earlier, they simply promised "to do more with less."

The difficulties with these positions is that many, even most, Americans expect libraries generally to do more and more kinds of services without more funding. This view is upheld time after time in the multiple surveys taken by the Pew Research Foundation. Here are some of the summary findings drawn from one major Pew Research survey.

Begin with changing technology: Computers have changed the communication "landscape, libraries are trying to adjust their services to these new realities while still serving the needs of patrons who rely on more traditional resources." Pew surveys show that Americans ages 16 and older want more of what they regard as basic services for the same amount of money the institutions currently receive. Specifically,

- 80 percent of Americans say **borrowing books** is a "very important" service libraries provide.
- 80 percent say **reference librarians** are a "very important" service of libraries.
- 77 percent say **free access to computers and the internet** is a "very important" service of libraries.

These three services, favored by about 80 percent of those surveyed, represent both the traditional book-oriented library and the computer-centered information library.

Moreover, a notable share of Americans say they would embrace even wider uses of technology at libraries. They would like libraries to install electronic appliances, databases, and materials to support:

- **Online research services allowing patrons to pose questions and get answers from librarians**: 37 percent of Americans ages 16 and older would "very likely" use an "ask a librarian" type of service and another 36 percent say they would be "somewhat likely" to do so.
- **Apps-based access to library materials and programs**: 35 percent of Americans ages 16 and older would "very likely" use that service and another 28 percent say they would be "somewhat likely" to do so.

- **Access to technology "petting zoos" to try out new devices**: 35 percent of Americans ages 16 and older would "very likely" use that service and another 34 percent say they would be "somewhat likely" to do so.
- **GPS navigation apps to help patrons locate material inside library buildings**: 34 percent of Americans ages 16 and older would "very likely" use that service and another 28 percent say they would be "somewhat likely" to do so.
- **"Redbox"-style lending machines or kiosks located throughout the community where people can check out books, movies, or music without having to go to the library itself**: 33 percent of Americans ages 16 and older would "very likely" use that service and another 30 percent say they would be "somewhat likely" to do so.
- **"Amazon"-style customized book/audio/video recommendation schemes that are based on patrons' prior library behavior**: 29 percent of Americans ages 16 and older would "very likely" use that service and another 35 percent say they would be "somewhat likely" to do so.

In the words of practicing librarians, their constituencies want books and computers and online reference and telephone reference and opportunities to meet authors and meeting rooms for all manner of classes and discussions and church services, and so forth.

And the situation gets more complex when surveyed Americans are asked why they personally use the library. Figure 12.1 contains their answers. Look at the small size of each user cell. And then, in Figure 12.2, why patron use of the library declined.

Main reasons patrons cite why their use **increased** 26 percent of recent library users ages 16+ say their use of libraries has gone **up** in the past 5 years. N=351

Enjoy taking their children, grandchildren	26%
Do research and use reference materials	14%
Borrow books more	12%
Student	10%
Use library computers and internet	8%
Have more time to read now, retired	6%
To save money	6%
Good selection and variety	5%
ebooks, audio books, media available	5%
Convenient	5%
Reading more now	5%
Library events and activities	4%
Good library and helpful staff	3%
Quiet, relaxing time, social locale	2%
Use for my job	2%

Source: Pew Research Center Internet & American Life Project Library Services Survey. October 15–November 10, 2012. N for recent users ages 16+ = 1,361. Interviews conducted in English and Spanish and on landline and cell phones.

Figure 12.1   Why Library Use Increased

Main reasons patrons cite why their use **decreased** 22 percent of recent library users ages 16+ say their use of libraries has gone **down** in the past 5 years. N=292

Can get books, do research online and internet is more convenient	40%
Library is not useful because my children have grown, I am retired, I am no longer a student	16%
Too busy, no time	12%
Cannot get to the library, moved, do not know where the library is	9%
Prefer eBooks	6%
Prefer to buy books or get books from friends	5%
Not interested	4%
Health issues	3%
Do not read much these days	3%
Do not like local library or staff	3%
Children are too young	2%

Source: Pew Research Center Internet & American Life Project Library Services Survey. October 15–November 10, 2012. N for recent users ages 16+ = 1,361. Interviews conducted in English and Spanish and on landline and cell phones.

Figure 12.2   Why Library Use Decreased

So, what we have in general is a set of reading and research services that many—even most persons—say they want. And these service desires change as families, jobs, and residences change. Therefore, the library user base tends to be very unstable; it shifts dramatically with economic, job, and social group changes in the potential user constituency.

According to *Library Journal*, we are entering another period in which more libraries are gaining income than losing it. But the funding situation is idiosyncratic. One significant analysis done in the 1950s can be found in the *Public Library Inquiry*, which was intended to "legitimize librarianship, raising it from its marginalized professional status while improving the public image of the institution, thus increasing patronage and federal financial support."[3]

Healthy financial times mean more libraries, more services, and a hugely expanded attention to professionalism. The hope was to get federal funding to mitigate the effect on libraries of the swings of the economy. The Library Services and Construction Act was passed in the 1960s to help with capital building projects.

Even in times of substantial and expanding budgets, libraries sometimes lack the funds to modernize and are again thrown into budget difficulties. For example, with the advent of computerized communications there were new spending needs for all types of libraries. In response, large grants from the Bill and Melinda Gates Foundation for public libraries, and then a positive turn from the Federal Government with passage of E-Rate tax support for school and public libraries made a measurable difference in helping fund the modernization of many libraries. The difficulty with the latter investment was the need to keep up with rampant change in both machinery and software and to fight off the financial cutbacks of legislators and administrators at the state and local level who saw E-Rate income as another good excuse to cut back on support to libraries of all sizes.

These increased spending levels for technology meant that lots of librarians had to look for new sources of funding, especially when traditional sources took either short-term or long-term hits. Those hits came frequently, especially in the public sector, because of the heavy dependency on any downward fluctuation in the national, state, or local economy made good political fodder for some elected official to suggest that, because of the Internet, public funding of libraries could be cut and usually cut savagely.

PUBLIC FUNDING HAS NOT KEPT UP WITH LIBRARY SERVICE POSSIBILITIES

Some politicians and some librarians do not seem to know that solid tax revenue in the public sector lags some months and even years after a recession or an upswing hits the general economy. In the Great Recession of 2007–09, for example, library tax revenue often remained healthy for libraries from one to three years after the recession hit. The impact does occur, however. Public funding for libraries is still being challenged because of funding cuts to state and local government growing out of the Great Recession more than half a decade ago.

Strikingly, finding out the number of libraries that have been hard hit by recessionary turndowns is difficult at best. As library budgets always do in any year, some go up and some go down. A *USA Stateline* column reported the following:[4]

Overall, states slashed funding to public libraries 37.6% from fiscal 2001 to 2010, from $1.28 billion to $799.4 million, [a 2010 Institute for Museums and Library Services (IMLS) survey reported]

Meanwhile, local revenue dedicated to libraries grew 23.5% over the 10 years, from $7.76 billion in 2001 to $9.59 billion in 2010.

States provide only about 7.5% of operating revenue for public libraries; local governments shoulder 85%. Gifts, fines, fees and grants contribute about 7% and the federal government just 0.5%, according to the institute.

The shape of the cuts for other types of libraries is just as anecdotal and piecemeal. We are told that, for example, libraries on college and university campuses get less than they did before the recession.[5]

School library funding is even grimmer. Many school libraries have been closed in recent decades. Many, even most, school library professionals were told to move on because their jobs were being classified out of existence. One article notes, "While there are no national figures detailing the total number of public schools affected by library staff cuts and closures, according to the American Association of School Librarians, data for individual cities beyond Los Angeles suggest an alarming trend." This article then pointed to Philadelphia where out of 214 school libraries only 16 had a school librarian.[6]

In the United States, with its continuing emphasis on the value of education in family and individual upward mobility, who in the library community could have imagined that, in the information-rich decades of the 21st century, the time would come when some elected officials and civic leaders would argue with conviction that libraries and librarians had no value worth preserving with public funds? Yet, since this mood is pervasive among many different groups, libraries have to be especially cognizant about positioning their institutions to shake off such attacks before they occur—and to always be prepared to answer back when they occur.

The lesson of this chapter is clear: Massive technological change has been matched by huge uncertainties in library funding. No librarian should pretend that the current times are not financially perplexing for libraries nor that it is unnecessary for library professionals to pay any attention to how their institutions are financed.

That is why library income has its own section in this book. There are many ways to get money and different libraries make use of all of them. To know about library money, you have to know about library income.

NOTES

1. *The Seattle Times.* August 14, 2015, announcing its decision on K–12, public school funding by the State of Washington in the McCleary Decision, on August 13, 2015, p. A1.
2. Ibid., p. 6.
3. *Public Library Inquiry.* Retrieved on February 26, 2014, from http://libraryhistory.pbworks.com/w/page/16964698/Public%20Library%20Inquiry.
4. Mercer, Marsha. "Libraries See Light After Years of Cuts." *USA Today Stateline.* Retrieved on February 23, 2015, from http://www.usatoday.com/story/news/nation/2014/06/04/stateline-libraries-funding-public-books/9950647/.
5. Mitchell, Michael, Vincent Palacios, and Michael Leachman. *States Are Still Funding Higher Education Below Pre-Recession Levels.* Washington, DC: Center for Budget and Policy Priorities, May 1, 2014, pp. 27. Retrieved on February 20, 2015, from http://www.cbpp.org/files/5–1–14sfp.pdf.
6. Shou, Solvej. *How Cuts and Closures of Elementary School Libraries Are Hurting Our Kids. From Los Angeles to New York City, Budget Cuts Are Affecting Public School Libraries.* Retrieved on February 28, 2014, from http://www.takepart.com/article/2014/02/28/read-public-school-libraries-suffer-staff-cuts-and-closures.

CHAPTER 13

Primary Sources of Income

I hate paying taxes. But I love the civilization they give me.
—Oliver Wendell Holmes Sr.[1]

Almost all libraries have a major or a single source of funding on which that organization depends. That generalization is especially true since most U.S. libraries are public sector tax-supported institutions: That includes almost all municipal, school, state college, and university libraries, plus government libraries like those in federal and state government, plus libraries that serve historical societies and museums. That does not mean that all of these get their revenues from the same principal sources. Though not tax supported, private libraries also rely on a single source of income.

Libraries fall into one of five legal situations. Briefly, these are:

- **Libraries as Independent Taxing Districts**.

Libraries with the clearest source of revenues are those that are quasi-independent agencies, that is, they function as independent taxing districts, drawing their principal revenue from a tax levy passed by voters. St. Louis, for example, abounds with independent taxing districts supporting libraries: Both St. Louis (City) Public Library and St. Louis County Public Library operate as independent taxing districts. The library at the University of Missouri at St. Louis and that at the Southern Illinois University at Edwardsville draw most of their income from the state. In the same city, corporate special libraries abound. Ameran (Energy), Anheuser-Bush (Brewing), HOK (Architects), Purina (Pet Care), and Tyco (Home Safety) are special libraries operating within private sector companies.

Each of these libraries has independent relationships with its funding constituents; and all are self-conscious about developing and maintaining their funding relationships. Marketing for all such libraries is a continuing exercise in relationship building and fiscal cultivation.

In the 2007–2009 Great Recession, some libraries that functioned as departments of larger independent governments said that the cuts on the library budget by the larger government entity had become too great, and they sought independent status. Seattle Public Library, for example, successfully went to the city's voters to establish its own taxing district with a levy separate from the whole city budget.[2]

As many libraries found out in the Great Recession, anytime an institution receives lots of money from a local, state, or the federal government, they must recognize that such funding can be cut off. Governor Jay Nixon of Missouri, a self-proclaimed friend of libraries, in the spring of 2015, took away virtually all of the $6 million of the state grant for public libraries in order to balance his $26 billion state budget.[3]

- **Libraries as Departments**.

Many libraries operate as departments of a larger governmental unit. These include some city libraries, many university libraries, virtually all school libraries, and many museum libraries. These libraries receive their revenue from larger host agencies such as a university, a federal, state, city, or county government. St. Louis again is a good example. Metropolitan St. Louis has a Zoo-Museum Taxing District, which provides the major funding for the Missouri Botanical Garden, the St. Louis Zoo, and the St. Louis Art Museum, among other not-for-profit institutions. The research libraries of these institutions are funded in the main by public revenues allocated by the agencies' various governing boards, which allocate operating revenue to their institutional libraries.

Examples of departmental libraries include the Library of Congress, which is the nation's major public research library, or the Wyoming State Library, which serves both the Wyoming legislature and Wyoming's public libraries. Many universities have departmental libraries within the building housing a disciplinary department such as an education library in the School of Education.

- **Libraries as Independent Philanthropies**.

Libraries are also operated independently as 501 (c)(3) libraries. These are funded by foundations, individuals, and users with gifts, grants, and fees. The St. Louis Law Library, for example, is funded by the memberships of legal firms in the St. Louis Law Library Association, which has operated continuously since 1839. The Huntington Library, Art Collections and Botanical Garden in San Marino, California, is another excellent example. In such an institution, finances and fundraising is never out of the attention of those who manage the institution, especially when the investment economy declines, bringing a major downturn in spendable income from endowment.[4]

- **Libraries That Serve For-Profit Organizations**.

Many corporations or businesses maintain libraries and/or research departments. The budgets for these libraries come from the parent corporation. For example, the aeronautics firm Boeing maintains a Mathematical/Statistical Library with corporate funds. Or it may be the practice to bill clients when the library is used on their behalf as in law firms.

- **Libraries Run by Volunteers**.

Some libraries essentially run with no source of income. The collections are donated and staffing is done by volunteers. Some volunteer libraries have a small budget of money raised from donations or grants to cover processing materials, space rental, and insurance. Often, volunteers start a library with the view that they will eventually have a permanent source of funds and have paid staff. Many public and school libraries were started by civic-minded groups with an expectation that the library will be funded by cities or schools. Volunteers often start and operate private school libraries.

An example of volunteer libraries is the Little Free Library movement. Little Free Library is a nonprofit organization that supports the worldwide movement to offer free books housed in small containers to members of the local community. The organization is based in Hudson, Wisconsin. Little Free Libraries are also referred to as community book exchanges, neighborhood book exchanges, book trading posts, pop-up libraries, and micro libraries.[5]

Another example is the brainchild of Seattle civic leader David Brewster who, as this book goes to press, is preparing to open Folio, the Seattle Athenaeum of the Seattle YMCA. The practical idea, according to Brewster, is to form a reading room which will be "a place to be alone, but not alone." If it succeeds, it will become a downtown membership library charging $125 annually per member.[6]

To sum up, almost all libraries in the United States rely heavily on a single source of funding, whether those monies are from the public or private sector, and whether they come from independent tax districts or a larger parent organization. No matter where you work as a library professional, you need to recognize the significance of this primary or single-source funding relationship.

The implication of this single-source funding issue is that the financial destinies of almost all libraries have little flexibility and almost no financial safety net. University and school libraries are in the hands of institutional administrators or elected or appointed boards of trustees. So, too, are public libraries that are departments of city governments and special libraries, which operate for some agency or some for-profit organization. Even libraries which are independent taxing districts have governing boards that can shift budget items in a major way, usually with a simple majority vote.

To sum up this synoptic categorization, libraries are always dependent on the financial support of others. Library professionals may choose to not think of themselves as fundraisers, but they must consider the reality that every one of them is dependent for their institutional employment on their library's relationships with constituents. The best library professionals always have this fact in their minds as they work with the members of their various communities.

NOTES

1. Goodreads. Retrieved on June 15, 2015, from http://www.goodreads.com/quotes/tag/taxes?page=2.
2. See Seattle City Library. *Levy Annual Report, 2013*. Retrieved on February 28, 2015, from http://www.spl.org/Documents/about/LFA2/levy-annual-report/2013Levy-report-bookmark.pdf.

3. Herndon, Barbara. "Governor's office tells librarians to 'shhh'." *Missouri Times*. March 18, 2015. Retrieved on March 21, 2015, from http://themissouritimes.com/17153/governors-office-tells-librarians-to-shhh/.

4. See the extensive discussion of Huntington Finances. Retrieved on February 24, 2015, from http://huntington.org/uploadedFiles/Files/PDFs/ar07finances.pdf.

5. Wikipedia. Retrieved on June 16, 2015, from https://en.wikipedia.org/wiki/Little_Free_Library.

6. Gwinn, Mary Ann. "Quiet, Please: A membership Library That Is All About . . . Reading." *Seattle Times*. May 24, 2015, p. H5.

CHAPTER 14

Ways to Increase Funding

A large income is the best recipe for happiness I ever heard of.

—Jane Austen[1]

We use a quote from Jane Austen to open this chapter, because more library money does not guarantee happiness at your work but more income certainly is better to obtain operational happiness than less in the institutional budgeting process.

Even if libraries don't change the services offered or have increased demand, operating costs increase. Staff salaries increase, material and electronic prices go up, and building maintenance costs more. In addition, many libraries do grow; they offer more services and a larger more diversified collection, they meet increased demand, they build new facilities, and employ more staff. Librarians need to find ways to increase funding to keep healthy. Depending on the source of library income, there are several ways to increase funding.

BUDGET ADJUSTMENTS

For many libraries and most library staff, the most likely way to increase funds is to be effective in requesting greater funding through the annual library budget process. Most academic, school, and special libraries operate as departments of a larger organization, and are not in a position to increase tax revenues or even apply for grants unless given permission. Many public libraries are departments of a city, county, or other governmental division and must compete for budget dollars with other city agencies.

Chapters 10 and 11 discuss budget fundamentals. General knowledge of budgeting is helpful, but the first step to a successful budget request is to understand the who, what, why, and when of the budget process where you work. Who do you ask for more money? What is this person going to need to know from you? What is the budget calendar? And why will your library's budget officer(s) entertain the prospect of a serious proposal from you or the work group you represent? In short, know the rules, both formal and informal, for budgeting in your library before seeking to improve upon your allocation.

Rarely is it appropriate, for example, for the newest teen librarian in a multibranch library to ask the library director for funds without approval of the unit supervisor or the head of branches. The supervisor of a college library should know what format is used for budget requests and when input on budget creation is welcome before making an effective request.

The other key to successful budget requests is the justification that accompanies the request. If there is an urgent need to upgrade computers in the high school library, make clear why there is a need, what is the best way (cheaper? Most effective?) to meet the need, and what are the benefits to the library and library users that will result from spending more money. If costs have gone up, demonstrate this escalation with actual cost figures. If a new program opportunity has presented itself, explain how the library and its constituents can best solve the problem or improve service. Do your research, present facts and figures that support your request, and be brief.

If you are successful in getting more money, report how the budget is being spent and what actual benefits (and problems) resulted from the increased spending. If you are unsuccessful, be sure you understand why so you can do better next time. Successful budget requests are both those that conform to the "rules" and capture the imagination of the budget officers. Library staff who are able to do both are more likely to increase their unit funding through the budget process.

GAINING OR PROTECTING THE LIBRARY'S TAX-EXEMPT STATUS

Another feature of library finance is a way to increase donations and decrease costs. That feature concerns a library's tax-exempt status.

Most libraries are qualified to be tax exempt: Either they operate under the IRS 501 (c)(3) status, or exist as a bona fide government agency which holds one or another IRS Section 501 tax-exempt status. As stated in Chapter 6, being tax exempt has numerous benefits, including not paying sales tax on library purchases and in allowing donors to get a tax deduction for their gifts to the library.

Once your library has tax-exempt status, it is important to understand the rules for keeping it. The IRS provides not-for-profits with both summary and detailed information about how to lose a 501 (c)(3) status.[2]

The major easy ways to **lose** nonprofit status are summarized below:

- **Private benefit/inurnment**. All funding gained under the 501 (c)(3) status must be used for an exempt purpose carried out in the public interest. Inurnment specifically means that no single individual, including high-ranking library officials or board members, can gain monetarily in a personal way from library activities set up for their institutional benefit. Specifically, prohibited inurnment includes "the payment of dividends, the payment of unreasonable compensation to insiders, and the transfer of property to insiders for less than fair market value."

- **Lobbying**. Only certain kinds of lobbying are permitted. For example, a library director may travel on library time to testify before a legislative committee, but usually no other salaried or hourly staff member can lobby while being paid by the library organization. So controversial is lobbying that the IRS has set up an "expenditure test" to see if an organization is doing too much lobbying. The rules for this test are spelled out by the 501h section of the IRS code. To use this test, an organization must file another IRS form in advance of any lobbying.
- **Political campaign activity**. Library officials may not campaign for or against any local, state, or national official. Organizations like libraries can encourage voter registration and voter turnout, but not in such a way as to favor certain candidates and not others.
- **Unrelated business income (UBI)**. Organizations like not-for-profit libraries must be careful about the amount of income they generate from activities that are unrelated to the exempt function of the organization.[3] "Some of the most common UBI generating activities include: the sale of advertising space in weekly bulletins, magazines, journals or on the organization's website; the sale of merchandise and publications when those items being sold do not have a substantial relationship to the exempt purpose of the organization; provision of management or other similar services to other organizations; and, even some types of fundraising activities."
- **Annual reporting obligation**. Based upon the size of their gross receipts, libraries have to file one or another form of the 990 income statement described earlier in this book. Not filing would lose the library's 501 (c)(3) status.
- **Operation in accord with stated exempt purpose(s)**. For example, if you stop checking out books, which has been your principal activity since your library opened, and move on to pursue some other educational purpose, to keep your tax-exempt status, you need to notify the IRS in advance of the giant shift. And if, for example, you go out of the education business and go into the paid contract researcher business, your nonprofit status certainly can be challenged by the IRS.

INCREASE REVENUE BY PASSING A REFERENDUM

Most tax systems allow the library board to tax up to a particular rate, meaning that the library can tax at a lower rate, but not a higher rate without a constituent vote. In most locations, public libraries that are independent taxing districts have to ask the voters to increase the taxing rate and thus the amount of taxes that can be collected on its behalf. Some municipal public libraries that are city departments may be able to set a separate library tax rate and still remain a city department. State and local laws govern the rules for increasing library tax rates.

The overarching challenge of developing a successful referendum campaign is to build trust and establish a compelling need. Meeting that challenge requires a campaign that clearly identifies three key things for staff and constituents alike: (1) the amount of money needed, (2) how long the tax will last, and (3) a justification that resonates with the community.[4]

Here are major campaign elements that have helped many different libraries win tax referenda.[5]

- **Seek legal advice**. Make sure you and the library board understand the legal rules for running a tax campaign, the timetable for filings, ballot language, and campaign finance.
- **Hire a consultant**. Hire a consultant who has a winning record in passing referenda. Such consultants are available nationally and locally. There are, for example, not-for-profit organizations like EveryLibrary[6] and for-profit fundraising firms like Skystone Partners that provide referenda support.[7]
- **Formulate a marketing strategy** that entails a demographic assessment of your voters and whether or not you are going to set your referendum for an off-year election or for a presidential election year. You may decide a lower or higher turnout will help the library issue more, but you need to know that, not guess about it.
- **Set the amount of money to request and detail how it will be spent and what benefits will be gained by the community served with the increase**.

LEGISLATIVE ACTION/GOVERNMENT GRANTS

Some state legislatures give funds directly to specific libraries, in addition to funds given to universities or other government agencies. For many years, the library at the University of Illinois Urbana-Champaign received its budget from the university and an allocation directly from the state budget. In return, the library greatly facilitated interlibrary loan of its materials to public and academic libraries within the state. To get such legislative support takes political clout and effective lobbying, but can greatly enhance collection budgets.

On the federal level, the Institute of Museum and Library Services (IMLS) funds libraries both directly through a competitive grant process to individual libraries and through federal funds that go to state library agencies for them to distribute to libraries. Some state legislatures fund operational grants to local libraries that are administered by the state library agency. Each year, over 2,500 Grants to states projects support the purposes and priorities outlined in the Library Services and Technology Act (LSTA). State library agencies may use the funds to support statewide initiatives and services, and they may also distribute the funds through competitive awards to, or cooperative agreements with, public, academic, research, school, or special libraries or consortia (for-profit and federal libraries are not eligible). For more information on this program, visit your state library website or the IMLS website.[8]

The U.S. Department of Education has some funding programs to support school libraries. Some state education agencies make grants to individual school districts.[9]

Another federal program that benefits libraries is the E-Rate program. E-Rate is the commonly used name for the Schools and Libraries Program of the Universal Service Fund, which is administered by the Universal Service Administrative Company (USAC) under the direction of the Federal Communications Commission (FCC). The E-Rate program provides funds for telecommunications and Internet access for libraries that serve low-income communities. E-Rate reduces communications costs through grants to individual libraries.

FOUNDATION GRANTS

Along with IMLS grants and other federal and state grants, libraries can receive grants from private foundations. These grants are targeted funds and usually cannot be used to pay ongoing library costs, and often the library is expected to provide matching funds and/or pay staff and overhead costs that are required by implementation of the grants. When applying for grants, choose projects that are central to the library's mission so that the project can be continued after the grant funding ends.

Once you have an idea for a grant and a clear description of what you want to do, it is important to get permission to pursue the grant. Most libraries have protocols for how grants are applied for, so the first step in grant writing is to be sure to know how to write a grant for your institution, including who should be involved and how to get approval from the library administration and/or library board or advisory committee. Even if this approval is not required, these groups can offer good advice about how to handle various grant approaches.

The next step is to find potential granting agencies. The Foundation Center, a clearing house for foundations, has a useful website (http://foundationcenter.org) which provides information on individual foundations, reports on grants awarded, and information on how to write a successful grant. *The Chronicle of Philanthropy* (http://philanthropy.com), though not library specific, also has up-to-date information on fundraising and grant opportunities

Some grants requests are very time consuming and elaborate, while smaller grant requests may only require a letter to request funding. Most large libraries have a person who writes grants, while in smaller libraries grant writing may be managed by the director. If you are unfamiliar with the grant writing process, perhaps a member of the governing officials for your library may be able to help you. School librarians can usually get help from someone at the district office.

In any case, it is important to read the grant description carefully, gather facts that support your request, and to meet grant application deadlines. Grant writing is a valuable skill, but it usually takes training to keep fundraising skills up to date.

Grant writing also can be important in solicitations to local charities, philanthropies, and to individuals. Our best advice for going after these kinds of grants is to start with a telephone call, e-mail or Facebook, or other electronic inquiry to find out about grant opportunities. A meeting may be appropriate as a follow-up on this kind of activity. Or you may learn enough in electronic communication to lay out ideas or even a full proposal. Grant writing is hardly ever a bad option because it helps shape strategic funding visions for your library. It is wrong to think that all libraries are looking only for leaders who are strong in fundraising, but it is unusual for any modern library not to have fundraising capacity from someone on staff or in a regular consultant position.

NOTES

1. *Brainy Quotes.* Retrieved on July 7, 2015, from http://www.brainyquote.com/quotes/quotes/j/janeausten148332.html#c6WQ8cKudGat2jBK.99.
2. NonProfit Risk Management Center. *How to Lose Your 501 (c)(3) Tax Exempt Status Without Really Trying.* Retrieved on February 28, 2015, from https://www.nonprofitrisk.org/library/articles/How_to_Lose_Your_Tax_Exempt_Status.shtml.]

3. *How to Lose Your 501 (c)(3) Tax Exempt Status.* Ibid.

4. Rosa, Kathy. "Referenda Roundup. An Overview of How States Performed on 2013 Ballots." *American Libraries.* December 16, 2013. Retrieved on August 20, 2015, from http://americanlibrariesmagazine.org/2013/12/16/referenda-roundup/.

5. St. Louis Public Library won two tax referenda between 1994 and 1997, tripling the institution's income from $6 million to almost $20 million annually in a very conservative financial city which had not increased the library's revenue base for over 20 years previously.

6. Retrieved on August 21, 2015, from http://everylibrary.org/5-tips-successful-infor mationly-campaign/.

7. Retrieved on August 21, 2015, from http://www.skystonepartners.com/.

8. The IMLS website. Retrieved on August 21, 2015, from http://www.imls.gov/programs/ default.aspx.

9. *Improving Literacy through School Libraries.* Retrieved on August 20, 2015, from www2.ed.gov/programs/lsl/index.html.

CHAPTER 15

Fundraising

Fundraising is an extreme sport!

—Marc A. Pitman[1]

If your library is unable to increase its income through budget or tax increases, then you still probably will need to shop for other sources of income. There are lots to choose from.

The library's regular budget supports most of the library's collections, services, and programs, but it rarely supports all the library could or should do. Libraries like other institutions have become more dependent on outside funding to meet even basic services. "If libraries are to sustain current levels of excellence, and if they are to grow to meet the needs of a technologically sophisticated age, they will have to discover new networks of funding."[2]

The major responsibility for fundraising for the library rests with the executive director, the library's or university's development officer, or the library foundation, but individual staff will need to be involved by articulating needs, writing proposals, and meeting with donors.

Libraries also ask for very specific support. A school library might ask parents to honor their children's birthdays by donating funds to purchase a book for the collection. Or a university library may accept donations to purchase materials to honor a retiring professor, or how about a mailing and counter piece asking for help to hire more storytellers for little kids? Or more books for adults? Or more eBooks for teens?

Remember that the basic tenet of fundraising is its basis in a relationship with potential donors which already has been built up. Within that context, the development of specialty donor groups makes a lot of sense for libraries.

WHY PEOPLE GIVE

Several decades ago, a couple of prominent library representatives summarized philanthropic giving in their seminars for various librarians. Hartsook and Walters noted that the motives for giving were:[3]

- Demonstrated spiritual love of humankind gained from spiritual teachings.
- Philanthropic concern for humankind through gifts of time or resources or both.
- Personal gratitude for life or services rendered.
- Perpetuation of personal ideals, values, and goals.
- Joining in success to assure organizational goals.
- Fear, prevention of want, assurance of service.

They summarized the meaning of this list with this sentence: "The decision to give or not to give to any particular organization is based on non-tax considerations first, given the options to give to several thousand other philanthropies." Tax considerations followed all of these.

FUNDRAISING TIPS

For those new to fundraising or for those who are taking on more responsibility for fundraising, it can be a bewildering field. Can I just go ask for funds for my program? Can I hold a bake sale when the PTA meets? How do I attract and impress important donors? The guidelines that follow will help you get organized.

- **Know the Rules**.
  Any large institution will have rules about how staff can be involved in fundraising. These polices are in place to prevent donors from getting multiple requests for funds from the library in the same year and to make sure the library is able to meet the requirements for spending and reporting of each donations. If the library, university, or school has a foundation, there may be even more rules about who can ask for donations. It is important that donations are logged and spent as directed by the donor and accounting procedures are followed.
  In small libraries, it is important to know simple rules. For example, how should cash donations be recorded, how should checks be made out, how do you keep track of donations, and who is authorized to spend donated funds?

- **Be Strategic**.
  Karen Brodsky tells how the Sonoma State University Library in Rohnert Park (California) raised funds for a new art gallery, but one without a budget hard line. She writes,[4]

  There is no line item for the gallery in the library budget, so expenses come directly out of the library operating budget or from fundraising. . . . The exhibit dictates where we look for funding. Departments on campus, donors in the community, external grants, and even the student clubs have all helped cover costs. . . . The gallery is only one of many library services, and we don't ever want to compete with ourselves for donations. Because of this, we act very strategically when asking for support.

- **Use Sophisticated and Varied Approaches**.

    All library users are not alike, and you should not assume that all of them will want to give your library money for any single reason. The following situation adds support for this assertion.

AN EXAMPLE OF A DONOR REQUEST

In mid-January 2014, the authors of this volume received yet another mailing asking for still one more donation from *Consumer Reports* (CR), which is, like many libraries, an agency funded by its user members. This was not your typical "Just Give Still More" fundraising appeal. Rather, the letter opened with a fake handwritten note which read, "Glen Holt. Thank you for standing with us during these difficult times." The appeal was to give to a special category of funding.[5] In CR's case, the appeal was for funding to support "Product Testing." The heart of the appeal went this way:

> In the fiscal year ahead, we are committed to investing more than $25,000,000 into Product Testing. Because of the difficult economy, some people have suggested we cut back on this critical work. However, we are faced with a stark reality: Our work has never been needed more! Due to the tough economic conditions, we're seeing evidence that some manufacturers are beginning to "cut corners," in ways that will undermine product quality, and may even jeopardize product safety.

The CR request then was made for a donation smaller than the one which we had given previously; in fact, a range of five different donations, each smaller than the original gift. In other words, the interpersonal relationship strategy was "Thanks, you understand us and what we do, we need more funding for what you understand is basic to our services for you, please give again to this specific, earmarked purpose." We found it hard to resist this personalized (i.e., categorized) appeal and sent another small donation.

- **Communicate Effectively**.

    Library staff need to build a relationship with both the institution's constituents and donors (who probably are different from user constituents) to be credible. This might mean regularly reporting the benefits or positive impact that the funding for libraries brings to constituents, plus the placement of the facts of these papers in the library's social media, on its website, and in speaking before citizens groups and meetings of elected officials. Donors want to know how they have made a difference.

    Successful fundraisers communicate regularly with constituents, especially those who are the principal influentials who have a positive voice with their constituents. The principal problem that librarians make in constituent communications is they say something once or twice, then go on to something else. The key to success in constituency support is sustained communication, over and over and over again. The words can vary, even the nature of the appeal may shift, but sustaining the communications relationship ought to be built into every approach.

    Regular communication means in-person communication, specifically a staff or board member who takes part in the community meeting, even to the point of holding office in the community organization. That representative needs to be a regular contributor to the agenda. The topic always is the same: What the Library is Doing: For

You, For Your Children, For Your Students, For Your Property Values, For a Bright Future for the Library. Hand out your newest brochures and counter pieces. Like every good "store" where these folks shop, including those online, you want the value of your "store" to grow in how it fills its users' interests and needs.

- **Say Thank You.**
  Whether the gift is big or small, say thank you. In fact, say it several times. Give a written acknowledgment of the gift, thank individual donors personally if possible, and develop ways to recognize donors publicly. Have a list of donors in your newsletter, create a donor wall, or sell naming rights be it for bricks, furniture, computers, or whole buildings. Give donors the option to be anonymous and find creative ways to thank people for gifts to your library.
  The reason that so many different organizations raise funds the same way is that these methods work. The organization's message, of course, is personalized and, in the case of some libraries, downright unique. But the approaches by mail, by radio spot ads, by TV ads, by electronic communications on social media greatly resemble each other. As any fundraising seminar will emphasize, copying the success of others in fundraising campaigns is a virtue, not a vice.

NOTES

1. Goodreads. Retrieved on August 7, 2015, from http://www.goodreads.com/quotes/tag/charity?page=3.
2. Steele, Victoria, and Stephen D. Elder. 2000. *Becoming a Fundraiser: Principles and Practice of Library Development*. Chicago: American Library Association.
3. Hartsook, Robert, and Suzanne Walters. *Resource Development for Libraries*. Wichita, KS, and Denver, CO: By the authors, 1992, p. 9. Typescript. Copy in authors' possession.
4. Smallwood, Carol. *Librarians as Community Partners: An Outreach Handbook*. Chicago: American Library Association, 2010, p. 81.
5. *Consumer Reports* to Glen Holt, January 2, 2014.

CHAPTER 16

Other Sources of Donations

When we give cheerfully and accept gratefully, everyone is blessed.
—Maya Angelou[1]

PARTNERSHIPS WITH OTHER AGENCIES

Sometimes, pooling funds or staff resources is a way to fund a project of benefit to more than one library or community agency. These include different kinds of libraries and libraries of the same kind in other geographic settings. Sound partnerships also can include age-specific volunteer organizations such as AARP, skill- and knowledge-based professional organizations of attorneys and accountants, benevolent organizations like Elks and Masons, and nonprofit organizations and churches as well. The advantage of successful partnerships is that all the participants get benefits from pooling expertise, audiences, and funds that they cannot get working alone.

The problem here is that many of these organizations want to talk with the decision makers of the university, school, or public library because they think that funding for the libraries is greater than their own. Often, they are looking less for true partnership than a large single donation or an ongoing donation of services like regular outreach stops, operation of a branch in a community, or regular program that contributes to the quality of their operations without additional cost.

PLANNED GIVING

Planned giving refers to gifts made either over time or upon the death of the donor. Many libraries are miles behind in developing and advertising their planned giving programs. If your library is one of these, the institutional leadership needs to organize and implement the program.

Donations and other kinds of current gifts are provided by donors in the here and now. Planned giving is a promise of a future gift. By definition, it is any major gift of value whether promised in the "lifetime or at death as part of a donor's overall financial and/or estate planning."[2]

> Planned giving, sometimes referred to as gift planning, may be defined as a method of supporting non-profits and charities that enables philanthropic individuals or donors to make larger gifts than they could make from their income. While some planned gifts provide a life-long income to the donor, others use estate and tax planning techniques to provide for charity and other heirs in ways that maximize the gift and/ or minimize its impact on the donor's estate.

Planned giving usually takes one of three forms:

First, outright gifts that use appreciated assets as a substitute for cash. An example might be paintings from a family art collection with substantial appraised value, but with no stipulation as to whether the library has to hold or can sell these assets.

Second, gifts that return income or other financial benefits to the donor in return for the contribution. In this case, the planned gift might be a gift of stocks, which the library holds and pays an annual income to the donor from some of the dividends of the stocks that the library now holds.

Third, gifts payable upon the donor's death. An example would be a substantial donation derived as a portion of the donor's estate; for example, the value of a specific insurance policy.

Why do persons make planned gifts to libraries? As the previous list suggests, planned gifts allow the donor to receive benefits from assets before death with a settling up at death as the estate is calculated and various bequests are handed out in response to mandates set by the gift giver. The general reason for planned gifts is twofold: A sense that the balance of the estate is no longer needed and/or the use of a planned gift to minimize the tax consequences of an estate. In other words, a planned gift may inure to the donor or heirs by the way it is handled in terms of projected income or tax benefits.

The successful growth of planned giving for any library is to find ways to call its benefits to the attention of those who have the capability to give bequests which are of positive consequence to the institution, providing some form of high value without a huge amount of annual costs to maintain the gift. The American Library Association (ALA) has at least three electronic documents to help libraries deal with planned giving. One of these is *Marketing Your Planned Giving Program*.[3] A second is *Implementing a Basic Planned Giving Program*.[4] The third is *Planned Giving: Encouraging People to Leave a Legacy*.[5]

ALA offers an older book on planned giving as well: Amy Sherman Smith and Matthew D. Lehrer, *Legacies for Libraries: A Practical Guide to Planned Giving* (2000) is still a good overview of the planned giving process in spite of its advanced age.[6] Or, if you need a general book rather than a computer screen on planned giving, you might want to order a copy of the 2015 edition of *The Ultimate Quick Reference Planned Giving Pocket Guide*.[7]

Individual libraries also share their planned giving websites with other institutions along with potential donors. Just plug in the search term "Library Planned Giving" into Google or other search engine and watch the hits pop up.

To reiterate an important final point for this section, if you're going to have a planned giving program, you must have a systematic method in place to get the information about this program to likely donors. That takes more than a couple of mass mailings. You probably will need a planned giving website tailored to your library, regular mentions in your monthly electronic and published materials, counter pieces, posters, and so on. The list is as diverse as a library's communications program with its constituents.

One of the closing comments of the ALA outline notes, "Remember—your prospects need to work with their attorney, financial planner, accountant or other professional advisor before finalizing their gift." The same warning needs to be given to library professionals who want to start a planned giving program.

ENDOWMENTS

An endowment is a donation of money or property to a nonprofit organization for the ongoing support of that organization. Usually, the endowment is structured so that the principal amount is kept intact while the investment income is available for use, or part of the principal is released each year, which allows for the donation to have an impact over a longer period than if it were spent all at once. An endowment may come with stipulations regarding its usage.[8] Endowments can be part of estate planning and may be set up by one individual or family or by many donors.

Endowment development can be for a building, building wing, program support, collection, or staff. A university may create an endowed professorship to support a subject specialist in collection development or a school library may have an endowment for expanding the nonfiction collection or the collection as a whole. Libraries of any kind may develop an endowment to support building a new facility.

Like planned giving, however, endowment development may take a lot of effort to create and funding may be slow to arrive. The additional problem with endowments, of course, is that unless a library is hugely endowed, income from that source usually grows more slowly than the needs of the institution. There may be income as well from investments, as with an endowment that either is directly controlled by the library or by the library foundation or friends group.

Setting up an effective fundraising, planned giving, or endowment income program for most library professionals is not unlike buying a used car. There is one reason to undertake the fundraising exercise: to increase income; and there are myriad reasons why such fundraising programs often have difficulty built into them. For example, the library and museum field is populated with numerous individuals who want some not-for-profit institution to pay for their education as they learn various aspects of fundraising.

In an earlier chapter, we emphasized the importance of looking at the good ideas of institutions in other communities for models of successful fundraising. On the other hand, we note that major fundraising is sufficiently different from community to community that it sometimes is difficult to replicate successes from one city to another or one constituency to another. Keep this point in mind when you and your associates consider hiring fundraising counsel to help you with a major donor campaign or when you are ready to hire a fundraising professional to add to library staff.

NOTES

1. Goodreads. Retrieved on June 19, 2015, from http://www.goodreads.com/quotes/tag/charity.
2. *Planned Giving 101*. Retrieved on March 26, 2015, from http://www.plannedgiving.com/what-is-planned-giving.
3. ALA. *Marketing Your Planned Giving Program*. Retrieved on March 26, 2014, from http://www.ala.org/advocacy/advleg/frontlinefundraising/marketingprogram.
4. ALA. *Implementing a Basic Planned Giving Program*. Retrieved on March 26, 2014, from http://www.ala.org/advocacy/advleg/frontlinefundraising/basicplannedgivingprogram.
5. ALA. *Planned Giving: Encouraging People to Leave a Legacy*. Retrieved on April 12, 2014, from http://www.ala.org/advocacy/advleg/frontlinefundraising/legacy_.
6. Smith, Amy Sherman, and Matthew D. Lehrer. *Legacies for Libraries: A Practical Guide to Planned Giving*. Chicago: ALA, 2000.
7. *The Ultimate Quick Reference Planned Giving Pocket Guide*. Planned Giving.com, 2015 Ed. Retrieved on May 26, 2015, from http://www.plannedgiving.com/downloads-tools/downloads-in-house-tools/planned-giving-pocket-guide.
8. *Wikipedia*. Retrieved on August 1, 2015, from https://en.wikipedia.org/wiki/Financial_endowment.

CHAPTER 17

Earned Income

Some people regard private enterprise as a predatory tiger to be shot.
Others look on it as a cow they can milk. Not enough people see it
as a healthy horse, pulling a sturdy wagon.

—Winston Churchill[1]

Almost all libraries earn income in the form of overdue charges, lost materials fees as well as from copy machine charges, room rentals, and by selling computer flash drives and other office supplies. While most libraries could not exist on this income alone, these earned income funds do contribute to the financial well-being of the library.

Earning income does not make most libraries into for-profit organizations, as the major source of funds probably will remain public funding and fundraising. So, the answer to the question "How do libraries make money?" is:[2]

Libraries don't make money. That was not why they were established. They provide a service—public libraries provide it free of charge. They are supported by local counties and special governmental tax districts, and organizations . . . [and individuals paying] a property tax. They are part of the free educational services like our schools, which don't make money, either.

After this broad disclaimer, however, the writer of this online posting granted that there were a number of exceptions, and that libraries indeed did make money. The posting noted:

Some libraries offset their costs by fundraising from private nonprofit organizations like "Friends Of. . . . . . . Library." Contributors, such as individuals and corporations,

109

new computer companies, help with internet access and use of free computers for students and members of the public. A few might charge a small fee, but it does not offset the costs of providing the computers. Some charge a small amount for a rental for loans of DVD's or CD's, but, again, it doesn't pay the entire cost of the service.

CHARGING FOR LIBRARY SERVICE

In discussions a couple of decades ago, someone always would rise to point out that library services were irreplaceable, and that therefore a library could charge for services if no other funding could be found. After all, Americans believed that all persons should have access to information, and all kinds of libraries were at the heart of this proposal. Libraries were essential in keeping the bounty of information available. The rapid movement of so many librarians to install public access computers was a response to a changing information market.[3]

Then, of course, things changed. Information came to be regarded as a commodity, and the Internet redefined place in the accumulation and dissemination of information. Many thought libraries could then charge fees to use computers or to have library staff do research for a fee. Then, new kinds of businesses appeared redefining how people could find and compile reading and information on their own. Examples of such businesses were Amazon.com, Apple.com, and Netflix.com operating as part of Google or Yahoo. The net effect of these new developments was the creation of an extensive research organization next to a bookstore adjacent to a library.

At Amazon Prime or Netflix, a reader/researcher could check out unlimited electronic books or videos or music for a set monthly fee. They could turn to Google Scholar to get answers to advanced questions about various subjects, or to WebMD for medical advice, or MyAttorney for legal help, and Edward Jones and a dozen otherbrokers for retirement help and Ancestry.com for genealogy leaves (family history leads). There were so many sources of bestseller information that it was hard to pick one or two as standouts. If you could find it and knew how to bring what you wanted to your screen, the Internet truly did bring something for any computer user no matter where that person was located or the nature of the individual's interest.

Because of these changes in the market place, most United States public libraries did not end up charging computer use fees or to make use of reference services. Rather, most of them adjusted their missions to provide information and computers to their users without fees, and with reference and search help as an essential free library service.

EARNED INCOME—EXAMPLES

As principal source-budgets tightened, libraries became more expert in earning income. In 2013, Librarian Otis Alexander in *Public Library Quarterly* remarked, "The financial policy issue is how far public libraries should go to get the money they need to fund their mandated civic mission. At the crux of the issue is the question: Should libraries charge some of their users for services to make library services available to others?"[4]

Here are ways that libraries earn income:

- **Book Sales**. Part of nearly every library's earned income regimen comes from big places like Seattle Public's annual book sales and from small libraries, to smaller institutions like the smaller Texas libraries like those in Largo and Conroe which operate ongoing book sales to serve their users. There are overview guides to such sales, simple and free in some cases. The Booksale Manager on the net is one such guide.[5]
- **Food Services**. The University of Santa Cruz Global Village Café operates inside the lobby of the McHenry Library, including acceptance of phone orders.[6] The Whispers Café at Olin Library at Washington University in St. Louis adds to the celebratory mood of the facility. Fifteen patron-use computers create the ambience of an Internet Café.[7] Many larger libraries have successful food services but few run them. Usually they are operated by franchise companies (e.g., Starbucks) or university food services. Libraries rarely get a part of the profits, but do get a rental or service fee for the use of library space.
- **Print Market**. For a couple of decades, various St. Louis libraries hosted Print Market, which brought collectors to that library site to purchase art prints for their collections. Print Market raised about $6,000 for each library as well as additional income for the organizers.
- **Flea Market**. Built on the principle that "one man's trash is another man's treasure," the Upper Dublin (Pennsylvania) Public Library operates a flea market.
- **Fees for Services**. New York Public Library developed a fee schedule for ILL for independent researchers.[8] Many, if not most, libraries charge for either ILL or courier service to deliver materials from one library to the other, while Cornell University Library (does not charge for ILL, but has charges for delivery of the documents).

Otis Alexander's (2013) published survey dreportrss several other different examples of public library earned income to end sentence. These included:

- Computer usage without a library card is $5.00 for a half hour at the Belmar Public Library, Belmar, New Jersey.[9]
- The charge for non-residents (out-of-state) is $45 at the Prescott Public Library, Prescott, Arizona.[10]
- The Library charges $0.15 per page for Black and White Prints/Copies and $0.50 per page for Color Prints/Copies at the Contra Costa County Library in California. Cash or Print/Copy cards can be used to make Copies or Print. To purchase a Print/Copy card use the card dispensing machine. The cost of the card is $1.00 and it comes preloaded with $0.50 in Print/Copies.[11]
- Exam Proctoring. Charges a $35 per test fee for proctoring services at the Prince William Public Library, Prince William, Virginia.[12]
- Gift shop items—priced individually are marketed by the Friends of the Gary Public Library Gift Shop, Gary Public Library, Gary, Indiana.[13]
- Parking Fees. Parking is available for a fee in the Library underground lot at Spokane Public Library, Spokane, Washington.[14]
- Room Rental Charges. Fees of $10 to $50, depending on the size of the room and the time of the rental, are the prices of room rentals at Vespasian Warner Public Library District, Clinton, Illinois.[15]

EARNED INCOME ISSUES

- **Taxes and Bookkeeping**. It is important to get advice from an auditor or lawyer before entering into earned income projects. As mentioned in Chapter 10, most publicly supported libraries have a tax exempt status, and thus do not have to collect sales tax on items sold by the library or on fees or damaged materials charges; but regulations are set at the state and local level as well as the federal government, so it is good to check.

  If the library is renting real estate, running a coffee shop, or any other business operation that does not directly relate to its service mission, it may be necessary to run these operations separately and pay appropriate taxes and fees. As with other library fund accounts, business accounts should follow standard accounting procedures and be audited regularly.

- **Planning**. With earned income, it is best to take a "don't count your chickens until they hatch" attitude. Over time, earned income is predictable. Most librarians know how much they will collect in overdue fines or other fees. At the other end of the earned income spectrum, it might be more difficult to predict how much money a book sale will take in or will be made in the library store.

But things happen. The library board may decide on an overdue amnesty program or a Starbucks may open up across from the library and income drops. Or the school district may decide that any profits from library bakes sales have to go to the district office for distribution. Many libraries apply earned income funds to the next year's budget, so it is known how much there is to spend before allocating it.

In good times and in bad, earned income is a standard part of the library budget. As public agencies become more entrepreneurial, librarians will likely find new ways to earn income to supplement the regular budget. Earned income allows libraries to keep up with rising costs as well as start new projects and services.

NOTES

1. *Brainy Quote.* Retrieved on July 12, 2015, from http://www.brainyquote.com/quotes/quotes/w/winstonchu165926.html#8UfS2ebufX5rR3Hk.99.
2. *How Do Libraries Make Money?* Retrieved on March 17, 2015, from https://answers.yahoo.com/question/index?qid=20080218233642AAAiWfr.
3. Kinney, Bo. *Access to Computers and the Internet in Public Libraries: Growth, Influences, and Impact. Report to the U.S. Impact Study Project Team.* Seattle: University of Washington Information School, June 12, 2009.
4. Alexander, Otis D. "Free Public Libraries Charging for Survival." *Public Library Quarterly*, 32:2 (2013): pp. 138–149.
5. *Find Book Sales with Book Sale Manager.* Retrieved on March 17, 2015, from http://www.booksalemanager.com/.
6. Retrieved on May 17, 2015, from http://housing.ucsc.edu/dining/global-village.html.
7. Retrieved on May 17, 2015, from http://library.wustl.edu/about/olinlibrary.html.
8. Retrieved on March 19, 2015, from http://www.nypl.org/help/research-services/interlibrary-loan.
9. Retrieved on March 19, 2015, from http://belmarlibrary.homestead.com/.

10. Retrieved on March 19, 2015, from http://www.prescottlibrary.info/.
11. Retrieved on March 19, 2015, from http:/www, http://ccclib.org/.
12. Retrieved on March 19, 2015, from www.pwcgov.org/library.
13. Retrieved on March 19, 2015, from http://www.garypubliclibrary.org.
14. Retrieved on March 19, 2015, from www.sbplibrary.org.
15. Retrieved on March 19, 2015, from http://www.vwarner.org/.

SECTION VI

Spending and Expenses

CHAPTER 18

Dispelling Financial Mythologies

The great enemy of truth is very often not the lie—deliberate, contrived and dishonest—but the myth—persistent, persuasive and unrealistic. . . . We enjoy the comfort of opinion without the discomfort of thought.

—John F. Kennedy[1]

COMMONPLACE FINANCIAL MYTHOLOGIES

Like all institutions that serve the public, libraries exist in a world of public opinion, which consists not only of opinions, observations, and facts, but also rumor, half-truth, and made-up notions. If someone reads on a social media posting that a library in another state or another nation has a particular kind of financial problem, this "fact" may be the basis of a question about your library from a user, a journalist for a commercial publication, or someone who writes a blog. Therefore, one financial job for a staff member is to know about spending and expenditure mythologies that plague libraries, and know what to say if that issue occurs in any venue in or outside the library.

For example, when the authors were engaged in a tax campaign to increase the library's annual revenue, the library director received a phone call saying that a staff member was handing out a poster in his neighborhood telling all his neighbors to vote against the tax increase because the library had "a huge amount of funds in a secret savings account which the library was not telling anyone about."

In fact, the library did have a substantial cash reserve, which was a matter of public record, and the reason we had it was to have a way to keep our staff paid for several months if we had to make an adjustment to some money emergency. We also built the cash reserve as we were creating architectural and engineering drawings for several new and rehabilitated branches.

Once the staff member found out the facts about the reserve fund, he stopped handing out the circulars. The attention from administration during the campaign plus financial assistance to pursue library studies made him a much more engaged employee, who went on to become a mid-level administrator in the library system.

Following up on that story, we begin this section on "Spending and Expenses" by providing readers with a dozen financial mythologies which have been accumulated and posted on one library-focused blog. What follows is a list of typical financial myths about libraries that staff hears from users, nonusers, and even other staff.[2] This particular list is centered on public libraries, but similar mythologies involve other types such as school and university libraries. Here is the list of accusations with correct but quite general responses to the charges made by users, the unserved, and cocktail party constituents.

My library has plenty of money—it just opened a new computer lab. Response: Many public libraries receive local, state, and federal grants to pay for everything from renovations to specific programs. These dollars cannot be used for anything but what's specified in the grant.

Why would my library need money? We passed a levy only a few years ago. Response: Operating levies and referendums [sic] usually aren't indefinite and often expire within 5–10 years. Your library may be renewing the current levy or asking for additional funding based on future need or to offset cuts in state or federal funding.

Libraries have too many employees—can't they save money by letting some of them go? Response: There is a lot that goes on at a library besides what patrons see—such as planning, purchasing, cataloging, training, marketing, maintenance, and community partnership activities. Also, keep in mind that many of the helpful people you see stacking books or assisting with classes are volunteers.

A new library building means that the library has loads of money in its budget. Response: Most libraries have a capital budget, for maintenance or expansion projects, and an operating budget, for staff salaries and other operating expenses. Also, the money used to build the new library was probably a combination of a separate levy, donations, and grants.

Now that libraries have e-readers and other Internet-based technology, they can downsize to save money. Response: New technology available through your local library costs money and can create ongoing charges and the need for more technology-savvy staff. Also, access to this technology often increases library traffic, making it even more important to evolve the library building and staff skills.

Public library funding is the state's responsibility. Response: While state money does help support local libraries, these dollars can be inconsistent and prone to cuts, and for most libraries, a very small portion of the overall budget. Local dollars make up the majority of budgets for almost all American public libraries.

The busier the library, the more money it receives. Response: Unfortunately, library funding is not based officially on use or demand. Most libraries work on annual budgets based mainly on city or county allocations, or a form of local property tax allocations.

The federal government funds U.S. public libraries. Response: Actually, the majority of library budgets come from local sources; state and federal dollars usually make up the smallest portion (almost always less than 5 percent of the total income).

I'm already funding the library by paying my late fees and purchasing items at book sales. Response: Late fees and book sale dollars provide a very modest contribution to libraries and support replacement of materials lost or items not returned. Fees and fines are not sufficient to support operating or program activities.

Every public library in the United States is funded in the same way. Response: Even though all public libraries are funded by some combination of local, state, and federal dollars, the mix is unique. To learn more about how your library is funded, contact your local library's administrative offices.

Libraries use private donations for extras. Response: Some do, but many libraries across the United States report that they are also starting to use non-tax revenue, such as donations, to help pay for critical budget items such as staff salaries and collections.

If I do not vote in support of a library operating levy or referendum, other funding from the state or federal government will make up the difference for my library. Response: When a library or library system loses a local operating levy or referendum, it can mean cuts in programs, staffing, and collections, or closing its doors. In the majority of cases, there is no mechanism for state or federal funding to supplement local support.

Several libraries have used this "countering the myths" technique in their communication with users. Kent (Michigan) District Library, for example, has a connection from its website to the electronic website we have just quoted.[3]

OTHER EXAMPLES OF FINANCIAL MYTHBUSTING

Dayton (Ohio) Metro Library takes a more humorous tack, posting *8 great library myths busted* still primarily about finances, but using the theme to broaden communication with possible constituents. Here is the Dayton Mythbuster posting:[4]

Welcome to the page where your old-fashioned notions about libraries are debunked! If you think libraries are dreary, boring, staid places full of musty books and librarians who shush you, we're here to bust your mistaken perceptions. Today's Dayton Metro Library is nothing—*nothing*—like that.

"If you don't have a fresh perspective on what your Library has to offer, you're missing some great opportunities," said Rachel Gut, Deputy Director for the Dayton Metro Library. "The Library is always evolving, adapting to social change and reinventing itself to meet the needs and expectations of our community," she said. . . . The major financial myth follows:

Libraries are funded by overdue fines.

Truth: Overdue Fines Are Less Than 1% of Our Revenue

Because local property values and Ohio's general revenues have fluctuated dramatically in recent years, the Library's operating budget is currently lower than in 2005. Our costs to operate have increased significantly in the last 10 years, while funding has not kept pace with demand. The State's Public Library Fund supports about half of our operating budget, which is generated through Ohio's general revenues and distributed locally among Montgomery County's four public library systems (Dayton Metro, Wright Library in Oakwood, Centerville-Washington Township and Germantown). Most of the rest of our operating budget is generated through the property tax levy in our service area, and the balance comes from contracted services, fees and fines, grants and donations. (The Facilities for a Smarter Future plan is being funded by a five year bond issue, passed by local voters in 2012, and cannot be used for operations.) Overdue fines are less than 1% of our revenue!

School libraries,[5] special libraries (like medical libraries),[6] and academic libraries[7] all have used this mythbusting format to convey messages about their institutional services to potential and current users and the public generally. The Medical Library Association presentation, a high-quality PowerPoint program of 41 slides concludes with these points[8]:

In-house libraries managed by qualified librarians provide the most cost effective, efficient means to manage and locate quality medical information.

A balance between print and electronic resources augmented by interlibrary loan services will best serve the needs of health care professionals.

Librarians are part of the health care team. Finding the right information for the healthcare professional is Mission Critical. The end result is improved patient care.

THE BOTTOM LINE

What follows are some random financial myths from the PubLib website:

- That publishers are required to give books to us—we don't have to buy them. That we are REQUIRED to put on the shelf certain books that the "government" tells us to. That we are REQUIRED to put on the shelf any book anyone wants us to . . .
- When my fellow teachers ask how the contract affects me (uh, I have a K-12 teaching cert so the same as you) and was SHOCKED that I had a student teacher. Librarians are TEACHERS not SUPPORT STAFF.
- This reminds me of the only time when our budget did not pass and that it was suggested that we staff the reference desk with volunteers because people basically ask the same 3 or 4 questions!
- People think the publishers GIVE us all those books. "You mean, you have to BUY the books?" Well, yeah, we do; with the fine money that is surely our only source of income (don't people look at their property tax bills?)
- I am surprised by how many people ask, "How much does it cost to get a library card?" We have a fair number of immigrants in our community, and they are often surprised to learn that public libraries are free.[9]

To sum up, the mythbusting format often leads to the core of a meaningful impression delivered to a general audience from outside the library profession. Mythbusting does not solve all the misapprehensions about library expenses and operations, but it can be a good place to begin training staff in helping to explain what the budget pays for and where the budget money comes from.

For years, when one of the authors of this volume was the director of a large public library, he had a speech in his computer labeled "My Rotary Speech." That speech never ran more than half an hour and mostly 20 minutes, always to an audience of business or church persons. That speech used specific electronic and reference questions as the grist for points about what a library staff did.

Here are some of the finance-related points from "My Rotary Speech":

A. The library owns and maintains 17 buildings. We are spending on average $5,000,000 annually on facilities. Mostly we are spending money in the neighborhoods—but also downtown. Critical public investments. Hope we will induce private investments.

B. A major SLPL visitor destination. SL Cardinals served 2.5 million persons at the Stadium through the whole baseball season. SLPL had 1.75 million visitors and .75 million outreach contacts—or 2.5 million through the same calendar year.

C. One third of our use is by persons under age 18. Very much a child-focused institution and nationally recognized for our youth work.

D. We program and take materials to 225 daycare centers and 100 senior centers monthly. We visited every St. Louis school classroom at least once and most twice through the last school year. We reached out to people wherever they were.

E. We are in the culture business. We had 6 major author lectures last year. They included David Halberstram, Toni Morrison and Gail Sheehy. We had dozens of lesser known and local authors. Most of costs of these speakers were paid for by the Friends of the St. Louis Public Library. You should join.

F. Staff—Labor force is very well educated—We speak 11 or 12 languages.

G. Staff—Provide important first-job entry point, including first (on the job training) for cleaners, clerks, shelvers, and volunteers. Send a lot of people to the private sector—and are proud of the fact that our staff often leave our employ to get higher paid jobs.

H. Staff—Problem: finding staff who are well enough educated to do the work. 40% of all those who apply for shelving can't pass the shelving test which is arranging 40 cards by alpha and decimals. So we provide educational incentives to staff including tuition grants to get better educated and get degrees.

I. Staff—We tend to grow a lot of our own—with tuition remission program and finding scholarships for our staff.

J. Point 4: We are in the answer business. Answer hundreds of thousands of reference questions a year:
    Most frequently asked questions at SLPL.
    1) Spelling of Mostaccioli. Information on all the saints. Business reference and health reference questions. Legal next.
    2) Serve the pathetic, fearful, hopeful—who go to the library to ask an anonymous question. How do you know if you have AIDS? Is my doctor telling me the truth that I am dying from cancer. Ratings of insurance companies? How to get a patent? How to get a copyright? Lots of small business questions, especially about how to get funding to start one: How to get rid of a bad

neighbor? How to get rid of your neighbor's bad dog without murdering the dog or your neighbor?

   3) Reference sequence: Ask a relative, friend, minister or priest, consult yellow pages, go to the library.

   4) Most interesting recent questions: At what temperature does wood burn? For a patent search. What is the origin of the Swivel Chair? For another patent search.

   5) Most frequently asked questions about current St. Louis: Such questions have led to a brochure publication, *St. Louis by the numbers*, which has all kinds of questions about demographic and wealth-holding in the city.

K. Question I am most frequently asked: What is the most frequently stolen library item?
   A Testing materials and job search manuals,
   B Books on the Bible, theology, philosophy and religion.
   C Recipe books
   D Boy scout manual.

L. We do a great job for the people of St. Louis. Know that because of Cost Benefit Analysis. Two methods yielding a benefit to the community of $4–$10 for each dollar invested. In other words, we do our business with a positive impact in the community.

Each library has its own financial facts and its own story to tell, and each community has its own culture of disbelief and misinformation. It is important that library staff all know the financial "facts" for their institution, so that they can help dispel any financial myths about the library on campus, in the classroom, or in the community.

NOTES

1. Goodreads. Retrieved on August 11, 2015, from http://www.goodreads.com/quotes/tag/myth.
2. Kent (MI) District Library. "Debunk the Myths." Retrieved on June 21, 2015, from http://www.kdl.org/about/go/funding_myths.
3. Ibid.
4. Dayton (OH) Metro Library District. *8 Great Library Myths Busted.* Retrieved on June 21, 2015, from http://www.dayton.com/news/news/local/8-great-library-mths-busted/nkpzS/.
5. Kuhlthau, Carol Collie. *Guided Inquiry: School Libraries in the 21st Century School of Communication and Information.* Rutgers: The State University of New Jersey, School Libraries Worldwide, January 2010, Volume 16, Number 1, 17–28. 17 *School Libraries Worldwide.* School Libraries Worldwide, January 2010, Volume 16, Number 1, 17–28. Retrieved on July 8, 2015, from https://comminfo.rutgers.edu/~kuhlthau/docs/GI-School-Librarians-in-the-21-Century.pdf.
6. Medical Library Association. *Myths and Truths about Library Services.* Retrieved on July 8, 2015, from http://search.myway.com/search/GGmain.jhtml?searchfor=myths+about+medical+library+services&st=tab&ptb=95424992-CBD3-429A-93F0-7C530482DD4E&n=781b3b07&ind=2015050503&ct=SS&pg=GGmain&tpr=tabsbsug&p2=%5EY6%5Exdm267%5ETTAB02%5Eus&si=CI2KoKfSq8UCFdKIfgodaKwA2A.

7. Mason, Moya K. *Myths Associated with Undergraduate Use of Academic Libraries. 2015*. Retrieved on July 8, 2015, from http://www.moyak.com/papers/academic-library-anxiety.html.

8. Medical Library Association, loc. cit.

9. PubLib. Retrieved on August 14, 2015, from https://bestofpublib.wordpress.com/2011/02/25/library-and-librarian-myths-and-legends/.

CHAPTER 19

Purchasing: Your Part in Spending Library Funds

If you are buying a cow, make sure that the price of the tail is included.

—Tamil Proverb[1]

Almost all library staff handle money and many purchase materials or services on behalf of the library. At first, purchasing seems like a slam dunk; who doesn't like shopping? But, as well as making sure you get the most for library dollars spent, you must do it by following the rules for purchasing at your library.

As this chapter demonstrates, when you are in any agency that operates on a budget, and that includes all libraries, whether they serve a university, school, community, or as a special library for some particular type of organization, you need to recognize that all librarians need to know two languages. The first is the language of their specialty. The University of Illinois has compiled an excellent glossary of library terms, including "truncation," "stopword," and the now-obsolete "gopher."[2] The second is the accounting language that outlines and categories how funds are to be handled within the library organization.[3] (See The Glossary of Financial Terms following Chapter 25.)

Even if you don't have any say in the development of the organization's annual budget, your salary and the program in which you work set out the possibilities and limits of what you can and should do in order to follow the financial rules of your work. That always includes helping keep the organization budget "balanced," that is, spending no more than a specifically authorized amount.

PURCHASING CONTROLS

Most library financial problems involve the use of staff wages and hours or the spending of library funds to purchase goods and services. Library purchasing policies are easy to find on the Net. A very clear library purchasing policy is the one for Aurora (Illinois) Public Library.[4] Or see Northwestern University institutional Purchasing Policy within which the library has to work.[5]

When you deal with purchases, you will encounter terms that may be new to you.

- **Compliance Terms**. Reimbursements frequently have compliance terms, which might include the amount of detail about the expense and the place and date of the expense required by your organization or the institution or company. Compliance also is a term used in purchasing and contracting. Products and services delivered to the purchaser must be in compliance with the terms of the contract before payment can be issued.
- **Petty Cash**. All kinds of libraries fall down in the handling of petty cash. The term marks out a small amount of funds so little that using a credit card or writing a check seems too much trouble. Typically, in a library, the petty cash fund takes two forms: the amount of cash kept at the desk to accept fine payments and to make change for fines, small sales in the library store, and so forth; or the amount of cash kept on hand in the finance office to pay to employees who make small purchases while working. Most small businesses keep up to $100 in petty cash, which is sufficient to attract dishonest employees who see the fund as potential expense money. "Oversight of petty cash is important because of the potential for abuse. Examples of petty cash controls include frequent (usually daily) oversight by a staff member, monthly audits by someone who does not work regularly in the unit and a way to record income and disbursements even though they are small."
- **Petty Cash Controls**. In many libraries, petty cash is a particular trouble spot, mostly because the controls are inadequate and theft from these loose funds is too tempting. Petty cash expenditures usually are highly visible, however, making theft from this money relatively easy to detect. Emphasize the need for honesty in this trove, and make sure that daily cash balance and deposit policies are followed rigorously. Always follow up if there is a discrepancy.
- **Terms** are specifications for legitimating expenditures. See Compliance Terms above, but the word. "Terms" appears frequently on short notations about how to pay a bill (e.g., "Net 30 days") or some other piece of information that an accounting department or finance office is required to use on a financial document.
- **Reimbursement**. Or, reimbursement request, reimbursement claim, or request for payment. Some libraries have forms; others simply ask for a statement with accompanying original receipts. Most frequently, this document has to be offered by the person seeking reimbursement for expenses incurred on travel, program preparation, and so on. If you are engaged in a job in which you record mileage and are reimbursed for your expenses in your vehicle—or when you make a fuel purchase in a library vehicle—you will come to understand reimbursement policy very quickly.
- **Contract**. "A contract is an agreement in which the library and a vendor (or the library may be the vendor) agree on the performance or carrying out of a lawful task such as creating software code or erecting a building." A contract creates legal obligations, which means a contract can be said to be a "mutuality of obligation." The elements of a contract are "offer" and "acceptance" by "competent persons" having legal capacity,

who exchange "consideration" to create "mutuality of obligation."[6] Here are important terms in the contract process.

- **Contract Formation**
  - **Offer and Acceptance**
  - **Firm offer and Tentative Offer.** The tentative offer is made during negotiations; the firm offer usually comes at the end of negotiations.
- **Defenses against Formation.** This term is a legal term, involving defenses against fraudulent behavior on the part of buyers and sellers. The terms that follow this term are clarifications of important kinds of illegal behavior in the purchasing process.
  - **Lack of Capacity.** It is potential fraud if either party in a contract does not have the capacity to carry out contract promises.
  - **Duress and Undue Influence**
  - **Illusory Promise and Statute of Frauds.** An illusory promise is one that appears to guarantee performance, but when examined is an illusion. Again, a potential fraud.[7]
- **Contract Interpretation.** Talk with a knowledgeable attorney representing the library.
  - **Excuses for Nonperformance**
  - **Mistake or Misrepresentation.** Either can cost your institution. Mistakes are often found in construction specifications of the owner—in this case, the library. Make sure the items you want included in the contract are worthy of that inclusion and won't cost a fortune, besides.
  - **Frustration of Purpose.** This is a defense against enforcement of the contract. It amounts to a case in which both parties in the contract were aware of a problem that invalidated the contract, but they signed it anyway.
  - **Impossibility of Completion.** When circumstances have changed, as when a disaster knocks down a neighborhood and there is no need for a new library.
- **Third-Party Rights and Benefits**
  - **Minority, Disabled, Women.** Set Aside for Percent of Work on the Job. These are "set asides" for participation in the contract by minority firms or employees, or disabled, or women. A library frequently finds that its set asides as stated by its governing boards are not being met by contractors or the construction manager. Usually, the library sees that problem when the contractor says that non-set aside group members are available, or if they are, they come at a much higher price than regular union workers.
  - **Unions Right to Participation.** May be specified in either monetary terms and/ or number of workers in a particular piece of a contract.
- **Breach of Contract**
  - **Change Order.** All changes in a building's erection have to be accepted with change orders proposed by the builder and signed by the owner. The change orders are a shift in the scope of work to be accomplished by a builder, usually at an increase in price or in greater time. Hence, change orders always involve higher expenditure or longer time periods in the construction process, which usually mean higher costs as well.[8]
  - **Exclusion Clause** is the contractor's statement of the fourth Amendment, in that the fruits of illegal searches of the building site cannot be used to accuse a contractor or an owner of wrongdoing.[9]
  - **Deviation.** A term that indicates that some item in a contract is not carried out appropriately. A change without a change order would be a deviation.

- **Check Request**. A standard way to pay "accounts payable" is also called a purchase requisition form. This form and most other business forms used in libraries are available at Biztree.com. Related documents are included, as well.[10]
- **Invoice and Packing Slip**. An invoice can be used as a noun or a verb; it is an itemized bill for goods sold or services provided containing individual prices, the total charge, and the terms of payment due.[11] Often confused with an invoice, a packing slip is a shipping list (an alternate name) inside a shipping pouch or the package itself. This list covers only in this package, which in libraries often is not the whole order.[12]
- **Bid Specifications**. No single document causes librarians as much trouble as bid specifications, because specifications often are stated in specialized terms by engineers, space planners, binderies, or technology specialists. Bid specifications or bid requirements are written, minimum acceptable specifications, qualifications, conditions, terms, and so on, set out by the principal (customer) in the invitation-to-bid (ITB) document. Under appropriate legal terms, the invitation, with its specifications, may be sent to one, a few, or many (including self-defined) as eligible to bid.[13]
- **Checks and Balances**. "The various procedures set in place to reduce mistakes or improper behavior. Checks and balances usually ensure that no one person or department has absolute control over decisions, and clearly defines the assigned duties. The existence of checks and balances within an organization prevents any one person or department from having too much power, and forces cooperation in completing tasks."[14]
- **Audit**. An official inspection of an individual's or organization's accounts, typically by an independent body. In libraries, the audit typically is conducted by certified public accountants who are NOT the regular accounting personnel for the institution. The best finding for an auditor's report is that it is "unqualified." If an audit is highly qualified, a legally responsible agency conducts an "Investigative or Fraud Audit" of public sector libraries.[15]

INSURANCE LIABILITY, DIRECTORS, AND OFFICERS INSURANCE

Insurance is not something that most new library directors or board members think about. Hosting a gala fundraiser, especially when lots of the work is done by the staff, is glamorous. Deciding the terms of an insurance RFP is about as exciting as checking out the differences in the lug nuts on the wheels of a 20-year-old bookmobile.

Insurance coverage is best when it anticipates accurately. How long should the warranty be on the new computers? What kind of insurance should be written for a 15-year-old air conditioning unit? When is a user or board member or a dissatisfied citizen going to sue your appointed or elected officials? What if the charge is made that your gala manager walked away with a lot of the funds raised by the event? Is the insurance company one that will pay off on a library claim?

At an even more pedestrian level, what happens when a woman decides to sue the library because she fell on the ice in the parking lot or her child was groped by a registered sex offender in a library restroom, or your delivery van runs into a transit bus. (your van driver tells you that there were only 12 people riding on the bus when he hit it) But 23 persons register with a local contingency attorney who publicizes that he is organizing the class action suit against your library because of the accident;

How best to handle insurance issues? One way is to hire a knowledgeable insurance broker as a policy consultant. Such a broker is not affiliated with just one company, and she/he helps you prepare the contractual specifications to seek out appropriate vendors from which your administration or board can choose.

Among all types of insurance, one of the least understood is Directors and Officers (D&O) liability insurance. D&O pays directors and/or officers "indemnification" (i.e., reimbursement) for losses or advancement of defense costs in the event "an insured suffers such a loss as a result of a legal action brought for alleged wrongful acts in their capacity as directors and officers", including defense costs over both criminal and regulatory charges. Such coverage can extend to defense costs arising out of criminal and regulatory investigations/trials as well; in fact, often civil and criminal actions are brought against directors/officers simultaneously.[16]

PRACTICAL APPLICATION OF SPENDING POLICIES

Even if you are the newest of the new kids on the library block, the first financial matters that are likely to come your way will involve your role in purchasing items and services the library needs—and making sure that the library payment system works to reimburse your staff and you for your expenses—and to pay vendors with whom you work.

Another form of financial mythbusting for library staff is to articulate personal behavior guidelines for becoming effective in spending the library's money. Kate Capps, an ALSC member from Olathe (Kansas) Public Library authored a blog posting on "Budget Tips for the New [Library] Manager."[17] Along with reference issues, Capps claims that children's services management and budgeting issues are among the most significant financial allocation issues facing libraries trying to sort out a bright future for libraries in the 21st century.[18] Capps writes, with our own additions to her comments bracketed:

So you've landed your dream job–congratulations! It won't be long before you discover that there will be dozens of projects and materials vying for your funds. Here's a handy tip sheet that may help you get started:

1. Set your priorities–and make sure to consider the administration's priorities for the department as well. (Are you going to be a team player or march to your own drummer when it comes to carrying out the institutional budget?)
2. You should have separate budgets for collection development and programming. (We're going to cover collection development in another chapter, but Capps has advice on that as well as what we have selected for publication here.)
3. Depending on your organization's structure, supplies, equipment, and continuing education/travel may or may not be included in your budget. Ask whether you have a copying and printing budget.
4. Once you know what your budget encompasses, you can start planning. (Which means consulting with the staff you supervise and other knowledgeable managers to devise a budget document that you will attempt to have integrated into the institutional budget in preparation.)
   a. What kinds of programs does your department offer or do you want to offer? Do you have materials (such as flannel boards, a CD player, etc.) for use in those programs?

      b.   What do you need for your summer reading program? Does your state participate in the Collaborative Summer Library Program? If so, you can purchase professional full-color materials that will please your patrons and save you time and money.

5.   Keep track of everything you order/spend. A spreadsheet is easily created and can be as basic or detailed as desired. I suggest that you include the following:

      a.   Date ordered
      b.   Purchase order number
      c.   Supplier name
      d.   Estimated amount (of purchase)
      e.   Actual total cost
      f.   Notes (this can include type of item ordered, number of items ordered, etc.)

The above information will enable you to track purchases and reference delivery/nondelivery. (You may save yourself time and trouble by a quick meeting with the staff member who will receive the purchasing information you are compiling. If you have that, you can simply fill in the draft form as you go and have it ready to send forward when you have processed all the information you need to provide.)

SUMMING UP YOUR RESPONSIBILITIES: HELP LEGITIMATE LIBRARY EXPENDITURES

Find out how expenses are legitimated in your organization. Once they are approved, purchases can be made—and/or bills can be paid. Here are some important steps.

- **Does the item purchased match the contract terms.** If it does, the receipt and the paper surrounding it validates the contract terms. That is true for collections, equipment and services. The content of that document ought to include:
  a.   Library wants to buy this amount at this price with delivery by this date.
- **Do the terms follow the description in the library's purchase order policy?**
  a.   Do the terms fit the library's purchasing procedures and legal regulations?
  b.   Is the purchase authorized by the correct person or official representative?
  c.   How can you know (or can you check) to find out if the funds are available to pay for this purchase?
- **Encumbrances and Payments**. An amount due carried forward for payment at a current or future time. An encumbrance is an impediment or burden. Librarians typically use it to move a financial commitment from one FY to another. For example, "We will encumber $8,000 from the FY2015 unused salary budget to YA electronic book purchasing in FY2016." If this action is accepted, the $8,000 jumps from one FY to another FY, but with a specific purpose. Some libraries are prohibited from encumbering their annual budgets, others can encumber under specific rules. When the budget is tight, encumbrances usually fall off because policymakers regard money as less flexible than when times are flush.[19]
- How does the **electronic purchasing** and payment system work in your library?

Librarians sometimes believe that whether they manage to purchase the cow with (or without) the tail doesn't much matter as long as the purchase was approved by a supervisor.

Navigating institutional rules for purchasing may seem tedious or overly complex, but the alternative is that money gets spent and nobody quite knows how or for what or if a good price was paid. Accountability, both for individuals and institutions, demands that purchasing rules be followed.

NOTES

1. Dumb.com. Retrieved on August 14, 2015, from http://www.dumb.com/quotes/buying-quotes/.

2. University of Illinois at Urbana-Champaign, University Library. *Glossary of Library Terms.* Retrieved on June 21, 2015, from http://www.library.illinois.edu/learn/intro/glossary.html#Z.

3. Glossaries of financial terms are far more plentiful than those for library terms. One general financial glossary is Reuters. *Financial Glossary.* Thompson-Reuters, 2015. Retrieved on June 21, 2015, from http://glossary.reuters.com/index.php?title=Main_Page.

4. Aurora Public Library, Aurora, Illinois. *Purchasing Policy.* Retrieved on February 12, 2015, from http://www.aurorapubliclibrary.org/about-the-library/policies/purchasing-policy/.

5. Northwestern University. *Purchasing and Payment Policy and Procedures.* December 1, 2008. Retrieved on June 15, 2015, from http://www.northwestern.edu/uservices/purchasing/policy.pdf.

6. Wikipedia. *Contract.* Retrieved on April 18, 2015, from https://en.wikipedia.org/wiki/Contract.

7. *Free Dictionary of Farlex. Illusory Promise.* Retrieved on June 15, 2015, from http://legal-dictionary.thefreedictionary.com/Illusory+Promise.

8. *Wikipedia. Change Order.* Retrieved on June 15, 2015, from https://www.google.com/webhp?sourceid=chrome-instant&rlz=1C1QJDB_enUS595US596&ion=1&espv=2&ie=UTF-8#q=change%20order.

9. Cornell University Law School. *Exclusionary Rule.* Legal Information Institute. Retrieved on July 15, 2015, from https://www.law.cornell.edu/wex/exclusionary_rule.

10. Biztree.com. *Check Request Form.* Retrieved on April 19, 2015, from http://www.biztree.com/doc/check-request-form-D670.

11. Dictionary.com. *Invoice.* Retrieved on April 19, 2015, from http://dictionary.reference.com/ browse/invoice.

12. Wikipedia. *Packing slip.* Retrieved on April 19, 2015, from http://en.wikipedia.org/wiki/Shipping_list.

13. Businessdictionary.com. *Bid Requirements.* Retrieved on April 19, 2015, from http://www.businessdictionary.com/definition/bid-requirements.html#ixzz3XnufDv7a.

14. Investopedia. *Checks and Balances.* Retrieved on April 19, 2015, from http://www.investopedia.com/terms/c/checks-and-balances.asp.

15. Julie Davoren. "The Difference between a Qualified and Unqualified Audit Report." smallbusiness.chron.com. Retrieved on April 19, 2015, from http://smallbusiness.chron.com/difference-between-qualified-unqualified-audit-report-66670.html.

16. Su Epstein, *Disaster of the Month: D&O Insurance.* Retrieved on November 5, 2014, from http://arsl.info/2014/06/disaster-of-the-month-do-insurance/; "Directors and

Officers Liability Insurance," Wikipedia. Retrieved on November 6, 2014, from http://en.wikipedia.org/wiki/Directors_and_officers_liability_insurance.

17. Capps, Kate. "Budget Tips for the New [Library] Manager." ALSC Blog. Posted on May 21, 2013. Retrieved on June 6, 2015, from http://www.alsc.ala.org/blog/2013/05/budget-tips-for-the-new-manager/.

18. Holt, Glen E., and Leslie Edmonds Holt. "Library Card Campaigns and Sustaining Service: How Do Public Libraries Best Serve Poor Children?" *Public Library Quarterly*. 34–3. September 2015, pp. 270–278.

19. *Merriam-Webster*. Encumbrance, Retrieved on April 18, 2015, from htp://www.merriam-webster.com/dictionary/encumbrance.

CHAPTER 20

Staff Costs

During fiscal year 2012, academic libraries spent about $3.4 billion on salaries and wages, representing 49 percent of total library expenditures.

Total operating expenditures for public libraries were $10.7 billion in FY 2012, and of this amount, 67.6 percent was expended for paid staff.[1]

—ALA Fact Sheet, No. 4.

ALL LIBRARIES ARE STAFF INTENSIVE

Library staff members make libraries work, but they also are the most significant cost in almost all libraries. Library organizations, including those in the foreseeable future, are labor intensive because they are personal service (including electronic service) intensive.

Great libraries and outstanding library services require substantial budgets, no matter what the level of government or whether the library service is delivered in a community, on a college campus, or within a corporation, or a school.[2] Even in academic libraries with heavy annual investments in serials, in only a few places and usually in relatively few years do staff costs exceed 50 percent, while even when paper-based and electronic materials together do not come up to 40 percent. School libraries do not report salaries as part of the whole school library budget; but in 2012 the median school librarian salary was $55,000 with a median collection budget of $5,000.[3]

The elements of staff costs include salaries, hourly wages, benefits (including family leave, family counseling, vacation, sick leave, and insurance—both medical and life), training, contract staffing (accomplished both on and off site), work study benefits, internships, terms of union contracts, separation payouts, and salary administration. The latter includes the costs of calculating benefits for employed workers, the tabulation of used benefits, costs of time sheets and other internal controls, and the preparation and issuance of payroll checks, with work accomplished both inside and outside of physical library buildings.[4]

LIBRARY STAFFING IS CHANGING DRAMATICALLY AND WILL REQUIRE MORE SOPHISTICATED ACCOUNTING TO CONTROL COSTS

Like jobs in other information intensive industries (finance, insurance, and real estate), there was a merging of library responsibilities and an increasing number of jobs that encouraged applications from LIS degree holders outside libraries. This shift in library job titles provides a gross indication of important changes. Recent new titles included knowledge management, social media management, digital asset/digital content management, including such positions in archives, museums and public libraries, and project management, plus data analysis in both the academic world and in private industry. Some staff surveyed in work and salary analyses describe their principal responsibility as "rovers;" others categorize themselves as "user service specialists" and "e-service librarians." Public libraries have "community connections librarians." Also apparent was an upward blip for teachers of library educational specialties for users. These include digital content development and tutoring.[5] Since 2009, several large public libraries have hired social workers to deal with both staff and patron issues in cities as diverse as San Francisco (California); Washington, DC; Edmonton, (Alberta, Canada); and Dallas, (Texas).[6]

WAGES AND BENEFITS

Many librarians claim they work as librarians because they love the business, whether it is interpersonal helping contacts, its focus on the work of knowledge organization, or the ability to assist particular user groups, like the elderly or children. Still, most library staff members are not in a personal position financially that they can work without salary.

Whether they work because they love library research or services, or because it's the best job they can find just then, staff wants the employer's compensation program to work reliably and fairly. Payroll issues, after all, involve real and symbolic issues around compensation for a staff member's most valuable asset: his or her time. No issue will cause more quicker, greater, seething resentment in a library than a payroll system that some staff members brand as unfair, illogical, or one that seems to be cheating them personally within the rules under which they work.

TYPES OF COMPENSATION

The payroll system is often made more complex because a library is operating two different compensation systems within the organization. The first of these systems is rewards to salaried workers, who in pay parlance work for so much per year. Some of these, even most of them, may have written contracts with some variances in how the system works for them.

The second system rewards hourly workers, who are paid on the basis of the number of hours they work at an hourly rate. Obscured by these two systems of paying library staff is the use of "comp time," which involves giving certain staff paid time off as if they were working regular hours when they are not present in compensation rather than paying them at overtime salary rates.[7] "In the United States, such comp time arrangements are currently legal in the public sector but not in the private sector." So, public sector libraries, like academic, public, or school may, use compensatory time, but a corporate library may be prohibited from doing so.

Library compensation issues are made more complex because staff members often have their own informal, arithmetic methods for determining their compensation, which inevitably do not agree with the organization's payroll system's methods for determining how much a staff member is owed. Therefore, persons who handle payroll in house have to be good explainers, who know all the ins and outs of the library's payroll policies and procedures and who have the ability and the authority to correct inevitable errors in records that establish the amount of money that employees were paid or are to be paid.

To sum up, payroll is complex both from a human and recordkeeping standpoint, and if payroll is not accomplished in a regular, timely manner, penalties for breaking laws or disregarding written policies can be expensive. New librarians who are casual about payroll records they handle and approve inevitably find difficulty in dealing with the financial demands of supervision.

The best advice for a director of a library of any size, but especially those which have more than a few employees, is to have access to a human resources (HR) officer who knows the law about such issues, a finance officer who understands the recordkeeping about payroll, and the ability to construct a request for proposal from professional payroll services like Automatic Data Processing (ADP) or Paychex. The latter company advertises the range of its services as "a provider of payroll, human resource[s] . . . and benefits, outsourcing solutions for small- to medium-sized businesses." On May 31, 2014, Paychex had over 100 offices and served 580,000 payroll clients.[8] ADP is perhaps a little more publicly opaque, having been tarred with some of the banking scandal fallout from the mid-2000s. ADP also has been evolving as a corporation within the last few years.[9]

If you are managing a small library, seek the help of someone from your city agency. If you are a school librarian, the school district will have someone in charge of HR.

Using such systems, specialists in HR and/or Finance accept payroll reports from work units, stating how much salary a staff member has earned. This kind of recordkeeping needs to be accomplished on a software system that is updated annually, as wage and tax laws are changed at the national, state, and local level.

ITEMS IN LIBRARY PAYROLL RECORDS

Here is a list of various items that regularly find their way on to library payroll records.[10]

W-2 Wage and Tax Statement
    Qualified Retirement Plans
    Social Security & Medicare Tax

Health Savings Accounts
Dependent Care Benefits
Group Term Life Insurance (Often involving both Employer and Staff Payments)
Tax-Free Commuting Benefits (Travel and Parking)

Beyond the W-2 Guidelines, there are additional entries as follows:

Other Forms of Compensation
Bonuses
Cafeteria Plans
Accident and Health Benefits
Health Insurance
Flexible Spending Arrangements
Health Savings Accounts (HSAs)
Dependent Care Benefits
Disability Insurance/Income
Life Insurance
Deferred Compensation
Simplified Employee Pension Plans (SEPs)
SIMPLE Retirement Accounts
Employee Business Expenses
Auto Allowances
Personal Use of a Company Car
Qualified Transportation Benefits
Educational Assistance
Job-Related Education
Working Condition Benefits
Employer Provided Cell Phones
Sick Pay
Uniform Allowances
Achievement Awards
Gifts
Moving Expenses
Membership Fees
Multi-State Employment Tax Issues
State Withholding
State Unemployment
Local Employment Tax Issues (For example, a local city earning's tax)

1099 INFORMATION RETURN REQUIREMENTS

We have entered a complete payroll information list without further references. Most libraries will not use all the entries. Many will use only a few of them. The list does suggest the range of special information topics that can find their way into the payroll equation of not-for-profits or for-profit libraries.

THE IMPORTANCE OF PAYROLL RECORDS

The complexities of payroll is attested to by the fact that Pennsylvania has issued a public library accounting manual which is open only to people with appropriate passwords.[11] The note on entry states, "The Pennsylvania Public Library Accounting Manual is available in electronic format only. It is available as a password-protected Word document on WebJunction."[12] Security is the obvious concern; obviously that is more important than easy information gathering by library employees and representatives of non-Pennsylvania State library systems.

PAYROLL AUDIT OF A PUBLIC LIBRARY

The significance of payroll in library finances is made clear by an unscheduled audit made by the New York State Comptroller of the Baldwin (New York) Public Library reported in January 2014.[13] The audit's purpose was "to assess the adequacy of the internal controls put in place by officials to safeguard Library assets." The audit began by an assessment of internal financial controls. In that review, the auditors "determined. . . . that risk existed in the payroll area and in information technology controls." They also determined that the Baldwin Public Library IT staff had sufficient risk to limit the Comptroller's communication on this subject to private communications with Baldwin Library administrative officials. Financial issues like this one often are treated as executive communications and are protected from public scrutiny out of fear of harming those who might be negatively affected by the publication of the information. The choice of public versus private communication sometimes is used as a legitimate communication methodology in audit reporting. This seal can be broken only for legitimate cause by the successful appeal for a court order.

The New York State Comptroller's office conveyed the essence of the public audit finding in one paragraph. It reads:

> We found that the Library's Business Manager ensured that individuals reported and paid on the payrolls were bona fide employees and, as such, were paid at their approved salaries and wages and received only the benefits to which they were entitled. However, we determined that there was inadequate supervision and oversight of the payroll process.

The essence of the problem, the auditors found, was that many payroll functions were handled without the checking of a second person. For example:

> The Business Manager records all salaries and wages, along with employee resignations and retirements and their effective dates in the Board minutes. The Business Manager also enters all new employee information into the payroll system and inactivates payments to employees who resign or retire, without anyone reviewing her work. In addition, the Department heads do not review and approve the timesheets and leave requests. Without these reviews, the Library cannot ensure the accuracy and validity of the information provided.

These and other work procedures had similar problems. All involved the need for more "segregation of duties in the payroll process."

The Baldwin Library complied with the audit improvement recommendation, hiring a part time staff member to oversee and handle independently some of the procedures which had been handled previously in a cluster of duties executed by the business manager. In addition, the Board was told "to continue to monitor the payroll process to ensure duties are properly segregated or mitigating controls are in place." This very simple audit illustration is a good example of how an audit works, and the potential for any audit to become a public relations communication advantage or a trouble spot in the life of the organization.

LIBRARY LABOR UNIONS

While payroll is a ubiquitous topic for all libraries, labor unions are not to be found in every library. Operating under its tag line "We Make America Happen," The American Federation of State, County & Municipal Employees (AFSME), which is generally considered the largest library union, claims (a total of) 25,000 workers nationwide (not all of whom are library staff members). In general, library unions are strong in strong union communities like Boston, New York, District of Columbia, Chicago, and Los Angeles; but AFSME chapters, according to a union publication, can be found in "public, school, college and university libraries" across the United States.

The right to organize a public organization union, of course, is one issue that pops up in libraries. To recount typical union events reported in the library press in 2015, local AFSME chapters reportedly joined in a fight against privatization of local public libraries in Bakersfield (California); documented "underfunding and understaffing at Queens, NY, Public Library; advocated for public service worker (including library staff) pensions in Indiana; and opposed a $140,000 office renovation by the president of the library in Queens at a time when he was eliminating 130 library jobs for budget reasons."[14]

AFSME workers also were involved in winning wage and benefits increases at Erie County Public Library. Workers in the Civil Service Employees Association at Onondaga County, New York Public Library won a contract with increased wages and improved health insurance contributions. So did Oakland (California) Library Workers as part of a labor agreement for 3,100 city workers who held membership in Service Employees Union International (SIUE).[15]

Unions, of course, are a financial issue in many libraries. Their history can be tracked back to before the beginning of the 20th century, when industrialization brought issues of efficient work and pay scales into discussions with library workers in many different locations. U.S. factories and large libraries that were run like factories needed much human labor. Workers, including children, were abused, and workers organized for higher salaries and better working conditions. Advocates who track workers' wages say that the salaries of union labor are 8–12 percent higher than non-union workers. There are too many variables in the local salary equations, however, to take this differential a totally accurate estimate in the 21st century.

Thus, labor unions span the whole range in libraries—from no organizations in some locations to quite significant worker organizations in others. Where the unions have organized effectively, they have considerable power that must be taken into consideration as part of the library financial equations that involve wages, hours, and benefits in the institutions where they exist.

One example should suffice. In 2007, the leadership of King County (Washington) Library System announced a plan to put the system's 43 libraries in the hands of multiple "cluster managers," each of whom would oversee several branches and move staff about to make "operations more efficient and flexible." Washington Council of County and City Employees (WCCCE)/AFSME Local 1857 protested, saying they did not have a voice in the restructuring. "Under a three-year contract . . . by 550 WCCCE-represented librarians and assistants" (the administration had to ease back on its requirements to put more current workers into the category). Instead, "workers previously assigned to a single library won't be required to work at other libraries in the cluster."[16]

In financial terms, the union members who had been in the system longer and presumably were paid more than new workers would not have to move about; they would work in only one assigned place. The net effect of that decision was to raise the hourly and daily operating costs of the branches where they worked and lock their skill sets into place, as well.

We are not suggesting that library unions are bad. We are suggesting that where library unions are respected for their own representational strength, the decision-making process is different than where no formal labor unions exist.

SCHOOL LIBRARIANS AND MEDIA SPECIALISTS: SPECIAL FINANCIAL PROBLEMS

School librarians are often left out of budget descriptions because so much of what they do financially is subsumed into teachers' salary budgets or whole school system budgets. School library and book budgets are usually based on one of the following wants/needs:

- Format
- Services
- Circulation
- Curriculum

When money is tight, these categories and their subcategories tighten and often are set up to compete with each other for available funds. Then, school librarians, like librarians in lean times everywhere, have to make hard decisions about funding. Special projects, however, remain a part of the construct, as this quote from a school librarian course outline indicates:[17]

School fund accounts are often categorized by information format: books, periodicals, nonprint, computer software, computer equipment, etc. Budgets based upon services are categorized/grouped under headings such as curriculum resources, recreational reading, general reference, management costs, special projects, etc.

These budget divisions often place varied outcomes in competition with each other for available monies. Some school librarians and administrators maintain that budgets for their library collections should be based upon "evidence of use." Hence, circulation data would be gathered to find distribution shifts and budget allocations would shift accordingly. Those areas showing more use or demand would receive an expanding budget portion.

Some finance offices and development offices are highly attuned to project budgets, including estimates of "benefits" in the form of estimated salaries from volunteer time and food donations from local restaurants and stores. If your finance group is not so attuned, then tune them up. Fundraising of all kinds, including for special projects, needs a large dose of plain old-fashioned entrepreneurship.

That advice may seem simplistic and even irrational to those school librarians who have lost their jobs because policymakers have lost their faith in the ability of schools—much less school libraries—to have any positive impact on children. Quoting one of their own complaints helps demonstrate the often perilous financial situation they face. A school librarian writes:[18]

> Publicly financed libraries in schools, cities, and universities are basically supported through some combination of sales tax, property tax, and state income tax. Welcome to the triple whammy of declining retail sales, diminishing real estate values, and rising unemployment. You can't get blood out of a rock. I know this sounds defeatist and pessimistic and it's not politically correct, but it is what it is. Wishing will not make it so.

BUDGET TOOLS FOR CONTROLLING STAFF COSTS

If there are no budget increases, what budget tools are available to deal with rising staff costs? The policy alternatives seem decidedly limited:

- **Cut hours and staff when budgets decrease**.
- **Full-time versus part-time staff costs**. Used to institute more flexible hours and, in most cases, to eliminate some benefits costs as well.
- **Change staff mix of professional, paraprofessional, clerical, and other employees**. "Deskilling is the process by which *skilled labor* within an industry or economy is eliminated by the introduction of technologies operated by semiskilled or unskilled workers. This results in cost savings are due to lower investment in *human capital*,[19] and reduces barriers to entry, weakening the bargaining power of workers to negotiate improved positions. It is criticized for decreasing quality, demeaning labor (rendering work mechanical, rather than thoughtful and making workers automatons rather than artisans), and undermining community." Librarianship is one of several professions that is being deskilled, according to critics of the process.[20] Deskilling is a relatively old Library and Information Science (LIS) issue. It was treated as a growing problem in a professional LIS reference book in 1968, as improved post–World War II technology was making its way into the library.[21]
- **Training current staff for new work**. This point leads naturally to one of the most famous quotes from Microsoft founder Bill Gates, who in an oft-cited statement noted, "We've got to put a lot of money into changing behavior."[22]

TRAINING COSTS

Training budgets in most libraries are too small for what we expect them to do. Until the last decade, comparable budgets in the Finance, Insurance, Real Estate (FIRE) sector training estimates were recommended to be 5 percent of gross budget. Most libraries are not even close. Obviously, a substantial training program costs something. But how much should a library spend for training? How much is enough?[23]

A recent survey in the printing industry, which, like libraries, constitutes a knowledge business, reported that about 50 percent of all printing companies spent $250 or less annually to train each employee; 31 percent of the companies spent $251–$750 annually; and 18 percent spent over $1,000. In the same survey, 55 percent provided all training on company time, while 43 percent trained on a combination of paid and unpaid time.[24]

A December 2006 Society for Human Resource Management (SHRM) survey found that American businesses were finding training more important than previously because they believed that skills and abilities of their human capital would drive performance, and they were using generic training (84%), cross-functional training (80%), and leadership training (71%) to drive performance. Meanwhile, training costs were rising: "In 2004, the average annual expenditure per employee increased to $955 after remaining steady at $820 over the previous two years."[25]

One important part of determining costs is deciding what to include in the calculation. Andy Hubbard, a professional trainer in the banking industry, an information industry where employment and service models often resemble library organizations, writes: "[The] cost of training includes the purchase of research and development of training materials, instructor compensation, space allocation, capitalized equipment (PCs and audiovisual equipment), production of student materials, and other incidental materials."[26]

Hubbard says that two expenses ought to be excluded: "the cost of transportation to the class for remote participants and the compensation of participants while they are in class." In the operating budgets of most libraries, this allocation would mean that transport to convention or conference locations would be excluded, but the costs of seminar registration fees and materials would be included.

Using Hubbard's criteria, in FY 1996, when we gathered our first full compilation of St. Louis Public Library (SLPL) training costs, we were spending close to $150,000 for training. That amounted to about 2 percent of the institution's total salary line. In FY 1999, the total training figure moved well over $300,000 or something more than 4 percent of all SLPL salaries. In the same three-year period, the cost to train all full-time (and full-time equivalent) employees on annual average rose from about $585 each to over $1,100 each.

Training in private sector corporations over the last few years has soared, as companies having trouble hiring the staff they need at the salaries they want to pay have started large training programs. A 2014 *Forbes* article reported that training costs had grown 15 percent in the previous year, a huge jump given the size and the extent of training that the private sector already accomplished.[27]

We have checked out the 4–5 percent of salary-line figure with several directors of other large urban libraries. A number of such institutions, especially if they are in a period of technological transformation, are expending similar percentages of their budgets on training.

The problem with these training costs is that they don't advantage workers very much. That is because lower level workers in libraries, non-MLS, usually don't see their salaries increasing very fast; in fact, according to Federal estimates, they will only increase about as fast as the salaries of workers as a whole, that is, about 2 percent per year.[28]

STAFFING PATTERNS ARE CHANGING DRAMATICALLY

Complicating the staffing finance issue is the reality that staff titles and the work descriptions that go with them are changing rapidly. One significant aspect of this cost set is the intrusion of technology into the work equation. All technology-based work, and other types of library work as well, is moving or has the potential for moving off-site, away from buildings called library or even community meeting centers. Employers are recognizing this trend by making ever greater percentages of their workers working from their homes or offices of external organizations.[29] The author of the article writes, "As business grows they ramp back up to train new hires, sales people, and leaders. This is among the most discretionary of all corporate spending areas, so it is an excellent bell weather for business confidence." New private sector training is not only for leadership, but for many other areas as well, including specialized worker cross-training and technology training.

One university librarian, who has benefited from working at home, states that he regards telecommuting as a positive thing. He suggests that if a library has to cut salaries, the staff might negotiate for a half day each week working from home. The University of Washington has formal guidelines for allowing and administering telework, and they are used. On the other hand, the writer notes that[30]

Some kinds of tasks or positions are more suitable for telecommuting than others— generally tasks/positions that require little or no contact with the public, like cataloging, indexing, working on websites or the library's intranet, developing user aids, virtual reference, and writing reports. However, even reference librarians might have time scheduled off the desk, which could be used for telecommuting.

CONTROLLING STAFF EXPENSES

Thus, like other changes in library, telecommuting has variable impacts, with some employees winning flexible time away from the office setting and others being less available to all staff. Meanwhile, though, this dramatic change is shifting the tenets of expense management. In early 2014, Computerweekly.com, a British journal articulating problems similar to what US libraries are facing, posted an article that outlined the financial changes in staff management in industry that the shift would bring. This may give a glimpse at library futures, as well. Here is that brief document about the implications of off-site work specifically and technological changes in the workplace in general.

"Getting Expense Management Right"[31]

More and more employees are now carrying out business activities while out of the office. Many of these activities have costs—expenses—for which they will need to be reimbursed. The age of the spreadsheet should be long-gone, but it stubbornly refuses to die. Now is the time for an accurate, speedy and fully reportable expenses system.

Travel and expense management is complex. Spreadsheets or other manual systems are ill-fitted to today's travel and expense (T&E) management processes. Alongside the increasing need to allow access to T&E management systems from multiple devices while employees are mobile, there is a need to ensure compliance both with corporate policy and legal requirements.

A corporate T&E policy is required. Failing to put in place a corporate T&E policy will lead to the inability to adequately track and monitor expenses—with the result that organizations won't be able to optimize their overall expense costs. Look for systems that come with 'best practice' templates out of the box, and adapt these on an iterative basis to best serve the organization.

A shared, cloud-based system will serve better than an on-premise deployment. A software as a service (SaaS) T&E system is better positioned to support an organization. Hardware and management costs are shared; the technical costs of provisioning and updating systems are handed over to the SaaS provider. New functionality can be more easily introduced—and changes to the legal aspects of T&E management can be more rapidly reflected.

"Open booking" activity has to be captured and managed. Some employees are now by-passing the use of travel management companies (TMCs) in order to gain what they see as better deals with faster booking and a greater control over their choice of airline, hotel and other aspects of an expense. T&E expenses are often an organization's second largest controllable cost behind salaries. Without all travel and expense activities being captured at an early stage and brought in under corporate policy, an organization runs the risk of not having full visibility into this data.

The legal aspects of T&E cannot be overlooked. Even within a single country, the laws on what can be claimed as a valid expense can be complex. Once international travel is brought into the mix, the need to understand multiple VAT rates and rules, per diems, cross-border rules and so on makes this a minefield for both the expense claimant and those dealing with the claim. A fully managed system from a provider who understands the whole market will enable these legal aspects to be embedded in the system and kept up to date.

24x7 support is an important aspect. Travelers need to be able to know that they can gain access to full support no matter where they are. For international travelers, this may mean support outside the general working hours at their home base. It is important that a system is chosen that provides full 24x7, worldwide support for claimants and claims processors—along with the in-depth knowledge around T&E management that is required.

Domain expertise will ensure continuous compliance—and optimize tax recovery. Choosing a vendor who has a proven track record of fast and expert deployment is paramount in getting up and running and gaining business benefits quickly. Choose a vendor who will truly partner with your organization to get the best out of your service, ensuring continuous compliance and effective tax recovery.

Conclusions. The days of using spreadsheets to manage travel and expense claims should be long gone. However, Quocirca's research shows that organizations are leaving themselves open to problems: whether these are disagreements with employees over what is a valid claim or insufficient information and inadequate reporting systems to meet the requirements of government (HMRC) audits. Her Majesty's Revenue and Customs (HM Revenue and Customs or HMRC) is a non-ministerial department of the UK Government responsible for the collection of taxes, the payment of some forms of state support, and the administration of other regulatory regimes including the national minimum wage. Ensuring that data across the whole of the employee base is collected and analyzed effectively will enable organizations to identify where employees are spending too much or claiming outside of policy or legal compliance.

Survey data accompanies this report. The survey data is well worth the time to increase depth of understanding about why the software vendor reached the conclusions outlined in the summary.

Decades ago, when the two authors of this book were consulting heavily, our organizations would not provide us with credit cards to handle these kinds of expenses. So, each of us had to run an accounting system in which to record expenses and reimbursements and to extend no interest loans to the various organizations which we had to bill for reimbursements. Even less dependency on cash today with more employees working away from the institution suggests that even smaller places ought to have an electronic accounting system that was friendly to expense and reimbursement recording.

Whether all library staff work at the library or they telecommute or libraries partner to share work online among libraries, staff costs are significant. It is important to be vigilant in controlling staff costs and salaries without diminishing customer service. Because staff costs are significant in all libraries and likely to rise every year, it is one of the biggest financial management challenges for libraries.

NOTES

1. ALA Fact Sheet #4. Retrieved on August 15, 2015, from http://www.ala.org/tools/libfactsheets/alalibraryfactsheet04.
2. Holt, Glen. "Ten Years in the Director's Chair. A Guide to Management Longevity." *The Bottom Line: Managing Library Finances,* 10: 3 (1997), pp. 126–43.
3. Farmer, Lesley. Brace Yourself: *SLJ*'s school library spending survey shows the hard times aren't over, and better advocacy is needed." *SLJ* Website. Retrieved on August 15, 2015, from http://www.slj.com/2012/03/research/slj-spending-survey-2012/.
4. Maata, Stephanie L. "Placements and Salaries, 2014. Explore All the Data." *Library Journal*, October 16, 2014. Retrieved on June 16, 2015, from http://lj.libraryjournal.com/2014/10/placements-and-salaries/2014-survey/explore-all-the-data-2014/#table6.
5. Zettervall, Sara. "Public Libraries: Whole Person Librarianship." *Public Libraries Online*. May 5, 2015. Maata, Stephanie L. "Placements and Salaries, 2014. Explore All the Data." *Library Journal*, October 16, 2014. Retrieved on June 16, 2015, from http://publiclibrariesonline.org/2015/05/whole-person-librarianship/lj.libraryjournal.com/2014/10/placements-and-salaries/2014-survey/explore-all-the-data-2014/#table6.
6. Zettervall, Ibid.
7. *Compensatory Time, Workplace Fairness*. Retrieved on August 23, 2014, from https://www.workplacefairness.org/comp-time. This particular website is a very convenient summary of the issues in "comp time." It is a good place to start research on this issue.
8. Paychex is described at its website and briefly in *Wikipedia* at https://en.wikipedia.org/wiki/Paychex.
9. ADP is summarized at https://en.wikipedia.org/wiki/Automatic_Data_Processing.
10. The summary details included in this list are from electronic copies of documents issued by the firm of Rubin Brown, Certified Public Accountants and Business Consultants, a multistate firm which handles a large number of museums and libraries as its accounting and/or audit clients. See the Rubin Brown Payroll Tax Guide, February 2, 2015, at http://rubinbrown.com/Payroll-Tax-Guide.pdf, and the Rubin Brown Payroll & Benefits Tax Guide, 2012–2013, at http://rubinbrown.com/2012–13%20Payroll%20Tax%20Guide.pdf.

11. If you are not approved, try entering at https://www.google.com/webhp?sourceid= chrome-instant&rlz=1C1QJDB_enUS595US596&ion=1&espv=2&ie=UTF-8#q=penn sylvania%20public%20library%20accounting%20manual.

12. *Pennsylvania Public Library Accounting Manual* is at http://www.portal.state.pa.us/ portal/server.pt/community/library_resources/8722.

13. Office of the New York State Comptroller, Division of Local Government and School Accountability. *Baldwin Public Library Payroll. Report of Examination. Period Covered: July 1, 2011–June 30, 2013.*

14. AFSCME. *Library Workers.* Retrieved on August 23, 2015, from http://www.afsc me.org/union/jobs-we-do/library-workers. Recent AFSCME blog posts, the origins of some of the information in these two paragraphs, can be searched from this main reference at http://www.afscme.org/union/jobs-we-do/library-workers.

15. *Union Library Workers.* News about Union Activity in Libraries, Archives, and the Information Sector. Retrieved on August 23, 2015, from http://unionlibraryworkers .blogspot.com/.

16. "Union Librarian," January 29, 2007. Retrieved on August 23, 2015, from http:// unionlibrarian.blogspot.com/2007/01/king-county-wa-pl-supervisors-join.html.

17. Ibid.

18. Cited in *The School Library Media Specialist. Program Administration. Budget Management.* Retrieved on July 3, 2015, from http://eduscapes.com/sms/administration/ budget.html.

19. *Wikipedia.* Retrieved on August 21, 2015, from https://en.wikipedia.org/wiki/Green_ building.

20. *Wikipedia.* "Deskilling." Retrieved on July 10, 2015, from https://en.wikipedia.org/ wiki/Deskilling. Other work groups besides librarians experiencing deskilling include: Assembly line workers replacing artisans and craftsmen; automated machine tools replacing machinists; automatic espresso machines replacing baristas; health care providers replacing doctors; nurses replaced by licensed healthcare professionals; along with social workers and teachers all being replaced by electronic programs.

21. Kent, Allen, Harold Lancour, William Z. Nasri, and Jay Elwood Daily. "Technology and the Deskilling of Librarians." *Encyclopedia of Library and Information Science: Supplement 16. Volume 53 of Encyclopedia of Library and Information Science, Encyclopedia of Library and Information Science.* Dekker, 1968, pp. 182–199.

22. *Brainy Quotes.* Retrieved on July 4, 2015, from http://www.brainyquote.com/quotes/ quotes/b/billgates191252.html.

23. This section is based on Glen E. Holt, "Staff training: How much is enough." *The Bottom Line*, 9:1 (1996), pp. 43–44.

24. Ibid.

25. Training Cost per Employee. SHRM (Society for Human Resource Management). December 1, 2006. For more on training costs, see https://www.shrm.org/research/ articles/articles/pages/metricofthemonthtrainingcostperemployee.aspx#sthash.ry 0Vc8kv.dpuf.

26. Holt, pp. 43–44.

27. Bersin, John. "Spending on Corporate Training Soars: Employee Capabilities Now a Priority." *Forbes.* February 4, 2014. Retrieved on July 9, 2015, from http:// www.forbes.com/sites/joshbersin/2014/02/04/the-recovery-arrives-corporate- training-spend-skyrockets/.

28. U.S. Department of Labor. Bureau of Labor Statistics. *Occupational Outlook Handbook. Library Technicians and Assistants.* Washington: Department of Labor, 2012. Retrieved on June 28, 2015, from http://www.bls.gov/ooh/education-training-and-library/library-technicians-and-assistants.htm.

29. Chad. "Librarian perspectives on working from home, flexible work schedules, and telecommuting." *Library Voice.* Posted on December 16, 2013. Retrieved on June 28, 2015, from http://libraryvoice.com/work/librarian-perspectives-on-working-from-home-flexible-work-schedules-and-telecommuting.

30. Ibid.

31. Quocirca. "Getting Expense Management Right." *Computerweekly.com.* Posted January 2014. Retrieved on April 26, 2015, from http://www.bitpipe.com/fulfillment/1420563 355_719.

CHAPTER 21

Capital Expenses

Cheops' Law: Nothing ever gets built on schedule or within budget.
—Robert A. Heinlein, *Time Enough for Love*[1]

Capital projects include building construction and renovation, as well as such things as replacement of building systems (new heating and air conditioning, improved plumbing or electrical wiring, lighting, etc.). Interior decorating and upgrading furniture can also be a capital expense and, for most libraries, major computer or automation system upgrades are considered capital improvements. The replacement of pieces on broken chairs or adding memory to a server is usually considered maintenance, and it is planned for execution as part of the operating budget. Replacing all staff desk chairs or getting a new server would be considered a capital improvement.

For tax-supported libraries, there are often regulations governing what library projects "fit" into the capital budget and how funds get designated as capital funds. On one hand, citizens don't want the public library or university to tax for more than they need to operate the budget and set up funds that roll over from year to year. On the other hand, libraries and other public institutions need to be able to save or tax to accumulate funds for necessary major upgrades to buildings and systems.

FINANCIAL MANAGEMENT OF LIBRARY CONSTRUCTION

This section is about maximizing the impact of your funds and getting special funds to complete a new library. The improvement suggestions in this section are organized around terms used widely in construction contracting.

- **Design–Build** (DB) is a form of public–private partnership used by some libraries which have the money but do not have all the knowledge needed to construct a new library.
    - "With the design-build-finance (DBF) procurement model, one contract is awarded the design, construction, and full or partial financing of a facility. Responsibility for the long-term operation of the facility remains with the project sponsor" (i.e., the library). . . . "This approach takes advantage of the efficiencies of the design-build (DB) approach and also allows the project sponsor to completely or partially defer financing during the construction phase of the project."[2]
    - The key to using this tool is for library staff to be able to specify realistically what they expect from the architect and construction company or consortia proposing to DB their edifice for the system. A library currently using the DB tool is Ramsey County (Minnesota) Public Library as they set up the construction of a new branch for the Shoreview Community.[3]
    - DB requires discipline, including planning what you actually need by way of construction, the help you need to set up the DB proposal, and a determination to stay within budget no matter how much pressure there is to go over budget.
- **Change Order**. Changes are inevitable in a library construction project: The site may have an ecological hazard, the position of a wall has to be changed, or multiple electrical courses have to be moved or added. While change orders can sometimes decrease long-term costs, they are likely to add to construction cost. The changes often involve more work for subcontractors and involve additional expenses.

One construction law expert defines a change order in the following way:[4]

"Change Order" is just a technical term for an amendment to a construction contract. When you hear Change Order, think contract amendment. Why? Because a Change Order is a bilateral agreement between parties to the contract—an owner and prime contractor, prime contractor and subcontractor, two or more subcontractors—to change the contract. A Change Order represents the mutual consensus between the parties on a change to the work, the price, the schedule, or some other term of the contract. And, because it represents a mutual consensus, a Change Order is usually the best, and least controversial, way to make changes.

Change orders need to be negotiated by people who know what they are doing on both sides of the table. And they are integral to any library project, as for example, "a short-term loan used to finance the building of some real estate project." In this case, a library would take out a short-term loan to begin the project while it secures long-term funding. Since its payment is dependent on the longer and larger loan, its future is somewhat riskier than other kinds of loans; hence, it has a higher rate of interest.[5] Construction loans are a form of bridge loan. Construction loans also are used at the close of a project while final funding is being secured from long-term loans (usually in the form of bonds), grants, or gifts. The other advantage of the construction loan is that it usually does not require payment of principal, only interest, during the period it covers.

- **Tax-Exempt Loans**. Most libraries are tax exempt, and "tax-exempt financing" typically yields at a rate of interest below the for-profit corporate rate that banks charge. Therefore, "financing a facility with a low-interest loan may . . . enable a borrower to move to a larger or more efficient site than it would otherwise have been able to purchase outright, or to rent or finance at market rates."[6] Tax increment financing (TIF) is a way of financing library building improvements in "blighted" areas that abates property taxes to raise money for capital improvements from private investors. Some states have made TIF financing illegal, as it gives advantage to users but reduces tax income to public agencies who would have benefitted from the taxes on the properties included in the TIF district that get no benefits in return.

AMERICANS WITH DISABILITIES ACT STANDARDS FOR ACCESSIBLE DESIGN

The Americans with Disabilities Act (ADA) became federal law in 1990 and is intended to prevent discrimination against individuals with physical or mental impairments. The ADA Standards for Accessible Design began to be enforced in 2010. The intent is to require library buildings to serve staff and users who have a variety of impairments. This includes having aisles wide enough for wheel chairs, ramps, plus Braille signage, and many other machine accommodations that provide access to the information and entertainment materials that many different users want.[7]

Compliance with ADA in public buildings is mostly mandatory and almost always costly. ADA compliance is often a requirement to get a building permit. It is important that the architect and construction manager have ADA expertise and that they have experience working with local and state ADA enforcement agencies and that ADA compliance be a part of the capital projects budget.

GREEN LEADERSHIP IN ENERGY OR ENVIRONMENTAL DESIGN CERTIFIED LIBRARIES

Funding for a Leadership in Energy or Environmental Design (LEED) building usually does not come out of an amorphous philanthropic cloud, but because a specific individual or foundation donor or a specific government program offers the inspiration for such construction. Because of that reality, we have treated LEED issues as about the management of money, not about fundraising.

Wikipedia summarizes LEED in the following succinct introductory article:

A green library is designed to minimize negative impact on the natural environment and maximize indoor environmental quality by means of careful site selection, use of natural construction materials and biodegradable products, conservation of resources (water, energy, paper), and responsible waste disposal (recycling, etc.). In new construction and library renovation, sustainability is increasingly achieved through Leadership in Energy and Environmental Design (LEED) certification, a rating system developed and administered by the U.S. Green Building Council (USGBC).[8]

Examples of LEED-certified library buildings are the public libraries in Fayetteville (Arkansas), Seattle (Washington), Charlotte (North Carolina), Minneapolis (Minnesota), and the National Library of Singapore. The University of California, Merced, also has an LEED-certified library. In addition, *Green Libraries, A Website for Green and Sustainable Libraries* lists 42 specific library buildings as meeting qualifications.[9] This website also offers a useful citation to a couple of the essays from Antonelli, Monika, and McCullough, Mark, eds., *Greening Libraries.* Sacramento, CA: Library Juice Press, 2012. A mixed bag, but some scholarly essays balance the "How I Did It Best" narratives.

RULES FOR SUCCESS IN CAPITAL IMPROVEMENTS AND THE CONSTRUCTION ZONE

How do you become a successful library builder or manage a major capital project that has excellent results for the least amount of money? Here are our findings from lots of reading, multiple conversations with library builders, and our own construction experiences.

1. Train to Manage Construction. The greatest problem that librarians face when they rehab an old library or build a new one is a lack of experience and training for what goes into a building project, especially in highly visible places in which to make a huge mistake. And, most library buildings have that degree of visibility. Most librarians come to the construction cycle with a few do-it-yourself projects as their experience. So, they attend a seminar or two sponsored by ALA or a similar specialty library-related organization. That's a start, but there's more that needs to be known. Library construction is a giant set of trade-offs. Your greatest advantage is to find out all you can about building before you start, then learn and learn and learn because every mistake in planning or actual construction will cost money—usually lots of it.

2. Anticipate a Changed Future. The greatest mistake in current library design is that it too often replicates old libraries. A good question to begin with in building planning is: "What business will the library system be conducting in this building in 10 years?" Will 50 percent of the floor space be computers? Will community programming space needs increase? What percent of this library's business will be in book check out in the 10 years? Will there be more or less staff working in this building in 10 years? And what will the staff be doing by way of work assignments? Great retail stores almost always anticipate the future. They assume that retailing space will have to look different and function differently in a decade than it does now—and they make their interiors malleable. Building malleability always must be a design keynote in library buildings. Lack of flexibility will make needed changes in the future costly.

3. Form Follows Mission. Our first rule is that a library building and its various elements must do an efficient job of helping carry out our mission-driven activities in good taste and without costing a fortune. A good library building can be distinctive without being expensively monumental. If you can serve your community well with a less expensive building, do so—and spend more on the collections, computers, and staff that will provide library service that will delight your users.

4. Borrow and Adapt That Which Already Works. Borrow successful areas from other libraries, especially newer libraries. Borrowed ideas can include an efficient, adjustable-height service desk for a branch, good signage for another branch, pleasant restrooms not hidden away in secret (and insecure) corners, and computer tables and carrels that move wire management, desktop and laptop computer settings beyond the book age. And don't be afraid to borrow and adapt from good retail design no matter what the store sells. Because the idea is tested, adaptation is almost always better than experimentation with something that is groundbreakingly new.

While library vendors specialize in products that have been tested in library settings, it may be useful to look to furniture providers, lighting, and even shelving outside the library market. Hotels, hospitals, and museums may have more to choose from as they are larger markets, but have the same quality as traditional vendors. However, don't neglect local construction and manufacturing companies. Local carpenters may be able to build custom shelves or furniture for less cost than having vendors customize standard pieces for you.

5. Build the Best You Can Afford. Building effectively almost never means building as cheaply as possible. If you intend to use your new library building for longer than a few years, then higher quality and therefore more expensive components—doors, floors, windows, plumbing, millwork, and shelving—ought to be "built to take it" over the long haul. Cutting corners in any building means paying for it again and again, not just in floor space, but in the maintenance and upgrading of HVAC, lighting, wiring, restrooms, and doors.

6. Hire an Architect with Library Construction Experience. Every architect in every town or city wants to design at least one library before retiring, and boards almost always want to give as many local architects as possible a chance to work on a library project. The difficulty in hiring an architect with no library building experience is that you and I then have to pay for the architect's learning curve in order to build a library that works. If you think this bit of advice overly dramatic, here is a question: "Tell me once more, why do you want such a heavy load factor on the floors?" Or getting back engineering drawings that show an electrical outlet for the vacuum cleaner in the middle of the main run of the computer power cable. If it is possible for you to specify an architect with library design experience, do so. If not, be prepared to conduct classes in basic library design and to pay for the privilege.

7. Don't Assume You Know More About Buildings Than Any Architect or Engineering Professional. We hire architects (or electricians, interior decorators, or plumbers) for the same reason we turn to all professionals, to gain specialized knowledge. Once hired, your job is to work with those professionals so that your system gets the best library for the money. Of course, you should ask lots of questions and you should point out the necessities in floor loading, at least adequate: stack lighting, and how related functions need to nest together. You also should learn enough to check the details of construction drawings to help find the inevitable mistakes. And you should be willing to make financial compromises on some building elements to get the elements you really want in the new structure.

8. Know What You Want Ahead of Time. The more you know about what you want, the more detailed the specifications can be in the building program that you and your staff compose, the more your library will be able to control building costs. A good building process, and that includes the contacts between library construction staff and architects, almost always enriches a building program written by staff. That's because the consultation creates new possibilities that neither architect nor staff have considered previously.

Most change orders in construction come because staff change their minds about significant project elements.

9. Hire a Construction Manager. The more construction that a system is handling at once, the greater the need for professional construction management to handle day-to-day oversight of building activities. Construction managers come with different size staffs and with various kinds of expertise. They are worth considering for time management, quality control, and value engineering, to name only three of their most used specialties. It is a great mistake to believe that regular library staff can oversee complex construction projects without regular management tasks being left undone. The more construction, the more time staff has to spend on it, and the greater the need for professional coordination of the construction operations. If construction is handled in house, then a talented staff member needs to be designated as the construction supervisor to oversee the various projects. And that staff hole has to be filled to keep operations running smoothly.

10. Avoid Project Delays. Project delays are the most frequent reasons for escalated construction costs. Some, like a steel or a concrete strike, can't be avoided. Others, such as waiting around while library administrators and construction company managers fight over who will be responsible for the increased costs incurred in a change order because of problems in the original drawings, can be avoided by good planning and good communications. Starting a construction project at the right time also can avoid time slips, and it can avoid inflation in project costs and the extension of interest charges.

11. Involve as Few Staff as Possible in Project Planning. Building planning is a very specialized act. A lot of library staff, including many excellent librarians, do not have the ability and/or the knowledge to describe library operations in a way that contributes to a sound building program. Consultation needs to be on subjects that staff knows about. That usually involves workstation amenities, current (not expected) traffic flows, and how the old building's service areas function, especially as they affect current service. The best source of information about current and potential users is not only staff, but also demographic studies and focus groups and surveys of users and nonusers. Never build or rehab a facility without developing this demographic information and consulting with user focus groups.

12. Reuse the Buildings You Own. There are lots of good reasons to tear down or move out of old library buildings. Not enough parking and no room to build more is one. No realistic possibility of rehabbing because of poor condition or structural peculiarities is another. Location on an inconvenient or out-of-the-way site is a third. A "gut rehab" of an old building, however, may be lots cheaper than buying a new site and starting from scratch. The first place to begin thinking about new construction is with a facilities needs assessment to see if it will be cheaper to rehab than to start over.

13. Have Your Purchasing Life in Order. Erecting a new building adds work to staff who already have a lot to do. Nowhere is this observation clearer than in the library's purchasing unit, whether that function is handled by a few hours weekly from a single person or by multiple staff in a purchasing department. Construction almost always escalates purchasing staff workload. Depending on where you are in your construction projects, purchasing staff work escalates between 40 percent and 100 percent over regular buying. And just in case you don't get "it," a construction project is not the right time to redo your institutional purchasing requirements.

14. Get a Good Lawyer. Being sued or needing to sue someone, unfortunately, is a regular part of the construction business. A subcontractor doesn't get paid and decides that, in spite of all legal evidence to the contrary, a suit against the library is the quickest road to payment. A contractor becomes lethargic about completing the project "punch list" because he decides unilaterally that he needs to be paid more before he can finish the project. Or when a footing or wall is built in the wrong place, the contractor, the architect, and the engineer all yell at each other, then stand back and hold out their hands to the library "owner" for a "change order" that will make them all whole financially. A good construction attorney needs to be part of the library building team from the moment the institution begins to think about hiring a space planner and/or an architect.

15. Build in Preventative Maintenance. Our system operated a beautiful old Carnegie "palace" as its Central Library. That "palace" did not have a single janitor's closet on any of its floors. Floor refinishing, therefore, entailed lugging equipment from floor to floor. Lights were 42 feet in the air; the only way they can be changed is by renting a mechanical "cherry picker" that costs a month's pay for a branch manager just to bring it into the building. Many modern libraries have similar maintenance problems built into them: table tops with surfaces that require refinishing (rather than heavy buffing) to get rid of scratches, HVAC systems with filter replacement points that only a contortionist can access, or custodial closets that make building maintenance professionals shake their heads in disbelief. Selecting too many different kinds of lamps, especially those with ballasts, means that all will need to be replaced as soon as any pressure comes to save energy costs. Trying to reduce maintenance costs and conceptualizing a computerized preventative maintenance program when designing a new or rehabbed building can save enormously in long-term operating costs.[10]

Library facilities are important whether they are big, little, modern, or historic. Whether they are a room in a school, university, or city hall, all libraries should be functional, easily maintained, and with any luck, comfortable and delightful. Those outcomes are no small tasks for most librarians who might have little or no experience or interest in facilities. Since capital projects are a major expense in time and money, it is important to have the right team of people working to do the best by staff and users. Building projects will always be there, so it is worth the effort to get the skills needed to manage them. To conclude, library buildings are hardly ever finished—unless they are about to be put under the wrecking ball. Your library buildings must meet today's and, as far as possible, tomorrow's service needs as well. All these decisions have financial aspects.

NOTES

1. GoodReads. Retrieved on August 15, 2015, from http://www.goodreads.com/quotes/tag/building.
2. Federal Highway Administration. *Innovative Program Delivery. Public Private Partnerships. P-3 Defined*. Retrieved on July 4, 2015, from http://www.fhwa.dot.gov/ipd/p3/defined/design_build_finance.aspx. See also, Rodriguez, Juan. "Understanding Public Private Partnerships." *About Money*. Retrieved on July 4, 2015, from http://construction.about.com/od/Trends/tp/Understanding-Public-Private-Partnerships.htm.
3. Johnson, Brian. "Design-Build Team Sought for New Shoreview Library." [*Minnesota*] *Finance & Commerce*. March 23, 2015. Retrieved on July 4, 2015, from http://finance-commerce.com/2015/03/design-build-team-sought-for-new-shoreview-library/.
4. Glazov, Josh. "Construction Contracts: Top 10 Terms—Changes (Change Orders)." *Construction Law Today*. Posted on January 17, 2015. Retrieved on July 7, 2015,

from http://www.constructionlawtoday.com/2011/01/construction-contracts-top-10-terms-changes-change-orders/.

5. Construction Loan, *Free Library.* Retrieved on July 7, 2015, from http://financial-dictionary.thefreedictionary.com/construction+loan.

6. Newman, Richard A., and Arent Fox. *Tax Exempt Financing for Nonprofit Facilities.* Access National Bank. Retrieved on July 7, 2015, from http://www.accessnational bank.com/home/fiFiles/static/documents/taxexempt_financing_nonprofits_.pdf.

7. See the U.S. Justice Departments document "Guidance on the 2010 Standards for Accessible Design at http://www.ada.gov/regs2010/2010ADAStandards/Guidance 2010ADAstandards.htm for particulars.

8. Wikipedia. Retrieved on August 21, 2015, from https://en.wikipedia.org/wiki/Green_building.

9. "Green Libraries: A Website for Information About Green and Sustainable Libraries." Retrieved on July 9, 2015, from http://www.greenlibraries.org/.

10. Adapted from Holt, Glen E. "Rules for Survival in the Construction Zone." *The Bottom Line,* 12:1 (1999), pp. 34–37.

CHAPTER 22

Acquisition of Materials

If a book is worth reading, it is worth buying.

—John Ruskin[1]

In the introductory quote, John Ruskin assesses a book's worth. Unfortunately, locating, ordering, paying for, receiving, and processing library materials is often time consuming and expensive, because each acquisition also requires a good deal of accurate recordkeeping and logistical handling within the institution's financial systems.

Librarian Frances Wilkinson and her colleagues articulate the basic financial pressures in this system when they write, "A basic feature of acquisitions . . . is the ability to display the budget, show fund allocation, and track encumbrances and expenditures in as close to real time as possible."[2] In other words, a significant goal of acquisitions is keeping track of money available as well as funds spent.

Materials budgets are often complex guides since they can be divided by subject, format, and funding stream (annual budget, bequest, endowment, etc.). Most libraries manage acquisitions using an automated system, so data only has to be recorded once and both selectors—acquisitions staff and finance officers—have access to the same information in a timely fashion. For more detailed information on financial issues or acquisitions, see Rachel Kirk's *Balancing the Books: Accounting for Librarians*, which covers many more financial topics.[3]

VENDORS

In the simplest form, libraries need to buy books and other materials from some individual or firm. Librarians subscribe to serials. They contract for databases and eBook services. Even the smallest libraries in the United States find vendors who will give discounts and not charge taxes rather than buy at the local bookstore. Even the mighty Amazon will set up accounts for libraries with varying price discounts. Many librarians use vendors like the giants, Baker & Taylor or Ingram, or for the school trade, Follett. Likewise, librarians don't subscribe to serials and magazines individually, they use a vendor like EBSCO, ProQuest, or Gale. These companies also sell access to indexes and information databases.

Most librarians also contract for services that may include cataloging, special library binding, or book processing. In some cases, libraries have standing orders (send all the Pulitzer Prize books the day the winners are announced) or have vendors select books. Libraries often have vendors bid on a contract every few years, to make sure they are meeting their institution's legal requirements and to be sure they get the best prices possible.

It is also important to compare the cost of vendor services to the cost of doing the work in house. If library management is very efficient and can keep staff costs low, using a vendor to provide processing services will increase cost. It also may be that in-house operations are more accurate, more flexible, and faster than vendor services. Staff in each library needs to evaluate in-house operation and decide which mix of services works best for processing, cataloging, computer services, and public services staff. As with any purchases, vendor services need to be carefully planned, realistically costed, and monitored to ensure good results.

LIBRARY EXPENDITURES BY TYPE[4]

For a sense of magnitude, what follows is an overview of funding of collections by type of library.

Public Libraries

- In 2012, total expenditure for public libraries is back up to $11.5 billion: 84.5 percent from local sources, 6.9 percent from state sources, 0.5 percent from federal sources, and 8.2 percent from other sources, including earned income.
- Of the total, public libraries spent 67.6 percent for staff, 11.4 percent for collections, and 21 percent for other expenses, including the Internet equipment, contracts and consultants, auditors, architects, and attorneys.
- Of the money spent for collections, 63 percent went for print items, 16.7 percent for digital materials (eBooks, serials, scores, maps, pictures, etc.), and 20.4 percent to purchase old formats, like microfilm, and new formats, like DVD and electronic downloads.
- There was a huge variation in budget size, with 20.3 percent of public libraries with budgets of less than $50,000; 43.3 percent with operating budgets between $50,000 and 399,000, and 36.2 percent with annual expenditures over $400,000.

School Libraries

School libraries get most of their operating income from their parent institutions, but their collection figures are appallingly small. "During the 2010–11 school year, public school library media centers spent an average of $9,340 each for all information resources." Of that total, $6,010 was to purchase books and $490 for audiovisual materials. "The number of holdings in public school media centers per 100 students was 2,188 for book titles and 81 for audio/video materials at the end of the 2010–11 school year." Bureau of Indian Education schools spending was marginally higher.

School Library Journal (SLJ) reports similar values assembled in different ways. The report's author, Lauren Barack, writes,

> School librarians work with media budgets that average $6,970 a year—or a spending allowance of about $10.64 per student annually. . . . Elementary schools budgets are lower, with just $8.86 to spend on each student, with middle schools slightly higher, spending $9.55 on overall materials per student. High school budgets, however, are significantly better, at $13.47 per student.[5]

Academic Libraries

In many ways, academic libraries are quite different financially from the other two kinds of libraries. Here is a recent summary of their finances:

> Just over half of academic libraries, 2,023, had total expenditures of less than $500,000 in fiscal year 2012, while 1,104 academic libraries had total expenditures of $1,000,000 or higher. . . .
>
> During fiscal year 2012, academic libraries spent about $3.4 billion on salaries and wages, representing 49 percent of total library expenditures (Table 8).
>
> • Academic libraries spent a total of approximately $2.8 billion on information resources. . . . Of that, expenditures for electronic current serial subscriptions totaled about $1.4 billion.
> • During fiscal year 2012, academic libraries spent approximately $123.6 million for bibliographic utilities, networks, and consortia.[6]

COSTS

According to book wholesaler Baker & Taylor, the average book prices in 2015 are as follows:

Trade Hardcover Fiction	$26.67
Trade Hardcover Nonfiction	$28.02
Trade Paperback Fiction	$15.48
Trade Paperback Nonfiction	$20.02
Mass Market Paperback	$7.69[7]

No class of libraries has suffered from collection cost perils more than those at large universities. Two library professionals on the Chapel Hill campus of the University of

North Carolina, Judith Panitch and Sara Michalak, laid out the issues in a 2005 summary article.[8] The scholarly pair point out this financial reality:

> As the Consumer Price Index rose by 68% from 1998 to 2003, science, technology and math (STM) serial prices rose by 215%. Big commercial serial publishers could impose this increase because of the fixed nature of the STM refereed journal market, plus the increasing number of professional researchers attempting publication in high visibility journals in these fields.

The figures, of course, show that magazine and journal costs were then experiencing rampant inflation. The problem with these figures is that they did not abate.

Panitch and Michalak also provide an overall introduction to this financial problem. They write:

> The term "serials crisis" has become common shorthand for the runaway cost increases of many scholarly journals. The serials crisis has also come to be closely associated with the pricing practices of certain commercial publishers, particularly in the areas of science, technology, and medicine (STM). To an extent, this characterization is correct—prices for journals in certain areas from certain publishers have skyrocketed far beyond the capacity of most libraries or universities to keep up. But "serials crisis" is perhaps a bit misleading, implying that if we just got the fever to break—convinced publishers to be more reasonable—we could return to business as usual. That will not happen, and probably cannot, since the serials crisis is, more accurately, only the symptom of a larger crisis in the system of scholarly communications. It is upon this system that the proper functioning of the entire academic enterprise depends.

Rising serials costs affect the whole university:

- The STM (Science, Technology, Medicine) serials problem produces financial pressure on subscriptions in other disciplines. Looking everywhere for funds to pay the subscription costs of these prestigious private sector- or independent organization-published journals, university acquisition librarians are pressured to take money from their social sciences or humanities collections budgets, for both journals and monographs.
- The scholarly serials question is not just a library problem. Universities pay salaries and provide research facilities to professors who referee scholarly journals for free and who publish articles without expectation of honoraria or other direct payment for their work. Universities are complicit in this situation, by allowing their professors to participate in this system with its myriad subsidies for for-profit journal presses.
- Changes in subject matter studies complicate financial issues. Different disciplines, departments, and divisions have different criteria for material acquisition. If you are heading the acquisitions process for one or more of these groups, you need to find out this criterion, making them as explicit as possible for all involved. Research scientists, for example, may want more emphasis on current journals and databases rather than on books. Disciplinary shifts may change collection needs to new interdisciplinary science or science discipline research specialties and new area studies publications in the social sciences and humanities. Acquisitions also will be a different priority in the budget of a public library specializing in high circulations of recent and new books than for STM-oriented academic library or even a chemistry department specializing in the basic education of pre-meds.

- Publisher and/or distributor limit the number of simultaneous users. Moving from paper to electronic publications didn't always help meet heavy demand, because publishers' agreements frequently limit the number of simultaneous users or the length of time that users might retain access to electronic copies. It is a common mythology that electronic publications can be checked out to every user at once without a massive payment that allows a large number of multiple users.
- Older patterns of access to students and scholars in various disciplines are challenged by library adaptations to higher costs, because they narrow previous patterns of availability that have maintained relative stability for decades. Faculty disagreements over library policy increase.
- The enhanced ability to detect fraud is another complication. That is because the number of retractions of scholarly journal articles has increased, probably less from a growing tendency for authors to commit research fraud than a more sophisticated mechanism to ascertain if cited research was miscited or misinterpreted.[9] As part of the overall journal pricing issues, the value of a much-cited author's article probably increased.
- Book prices also have increased—faster than the cost of living. One author calls college textbooks "absurdly expensive," noting that their prices rose by 812 percent from 1978 through 2013, a higher rate than prices for new homes, medical services, and consumer prices.[10] Those prices are carried upward more by the ability of publishers to raise them for profitability than because of escalating ink and paper prices. In fact, paper publishing companies in 2011 were more concerned about rising postage prices than about raw material or manufacturing costs.[11] Prices for textbooks, especially in the sciences for college and high school students, rose rapidly and steadily.[12]

However, there are numerous solutions for expensive textbooks. Another reason that textbook prices have fallen is the expansion of the business of textbook rental from places like Campus Books, which offers you the opportunity to buy or rent textbooks, showing you price differences, including how much you will receive when you return the book you purchased.[13] Rob Berger, a regular *Forbes* columnist on consumer finance, recommends rentals rather than purchase, and generally favors Amazon as the source for college textbook rentals.[14]

Librarians often create alternatives to deal with rising collection prices. Academic librarians involved in acquisitions tend to work within the authority systems as they find them. Working within the traditional framework of the subscription journal and rising book costs, scholars, librarians, and publishers have sought to create new dissemination models and open-source publications to beat collection costs. With librarians involved or leading in all these examples, here are adaptations to higher material costs in U.S. universities and colleges.

- Librarians cancelled subscriptions. Tim Collins took over as president of EBSCO in 2014. As Collins took over at EBSCO, price increases had begun to slow. EBSCO projected that the increase for 2015 would be only 5–7 percent.[15] Collins noted:

    Libraries are . . . showing a willingness to solve their budget problems by moving to electronic content or canceling databases that contain duplicate content and negotiating multi-year deals with vendors that can provide full solutions. Some of those choices are impacting spending with increases being anticipated in individual eBooks, electronic journal subscriptions, eBook and e-journal packages and full-text databases.[16]
- Reacting to the posted increases, librarians were just saying no to high prices. The cancelled little used and nonused paper and/or electronic subscriptions no matter how

prestigious it was for a library to have them in their holdings. This is part of management of collection budgets rather than "just buying."

- Part of academic cost control was collaboration. In January 2004, the Provosts of UNC-Chapel Hill, Duke University, and North Carolina State University elected to terminate the Triangle Research Libraries Network joint license to Elsevier Science.[17] Meantime, Harvard, Cornell, and MIT, along with other schools in their consortium, refused to accept a contract from Reed-Elsevier. These actions brought an investment downgrade of Reed-Elsevier stock, demonstrating the wider economic issues involved in library serials.[18] Another collaborative solution was the Scholarly Publishing and Academic Resources Coalition (SPARC), an alliance of universities, research libraries, and organizations, created to identify and support alternatives to the traditional pathways of scholarly communications.[19]
- Academics started new electronic journals outside the purview of the publishers and professional associations which were escalating costs. Stanford University Library's High Wire Press uses online publications as a tool, keeping the sacrosanct peer review model but in an electronic setting to deal with scholarly content in STM.[20] SPARC, described in the previous paragraph, along with a purchasing consortium, cooperated with publishers of new journals to pledge fair pricing.
- Many of the new journals were open access; in effect, disallowing the for-profit capitalist costing models of many journals.
- Scholarly faculty took action. Faculty members, especially those who had already attained tenure, exercised the opportunity to say no by refusing to publish in, edit, or serve on the editorial boards of journals with predatory pricing practices and by exerting influence within their scholarly societies. Publishing in open access forums is another powerful statement. And some authors working with commercial publishers have had success modifying standard publication agreements in order to retain more rights in their own works. The problem with such suggestions is that authors and scholars often see them as contradicting their financial security and hindering their career lines to tenure.
- A few public libraries took their own swings at rising serial and book prices by saying that they would circulate other kinds of collections. One collection group was hand and garden tools. Tools had been around before, but not to the breadth of type or level of sophistication of the newer collections. Oakland Public Library, for example, has 3,500 nonbook items, like construction tools, to circulate to do-it-yourself homebuilders. Bakeware, Moog synthesizers, and human skeletons are among other "collections" that are being lent out. Needles are now lent along with books on how to knit at Ann Arbor Public Library, which launched its collection of objects three years ago with 30 telescopes. Encouraged by the telescopes' success, the library added tools, giant-sized games, musical instruments, art prints, and hundreds of other curiosities. During a recent week, 17 people were on a waiting list for a print of Gustav Klimt's "Forest of Beech Trees." Skokie (Illinois) Public Library circulates high-priced digital tools including GoPro cameras and portable computer hard drives, plus STEAM (Science, technology, engineering, arts, and math)—featuring digital microscopes, steel drums, and plastic human bodies with removable organs.[21]
- Academic, public and school libraries all started "Give a Book" campaigns. One regular holiday newsletter issue included the names of a variety of books with many different costs asking library users to buy them and make in-kind gifts of them to the library. The plea was made to reduce collection costs.[22]

- A quantitative collection pattern was substituted for the older system at Des Moines (Illinois) Public Library. The bottom line objective is to work within set collections acquisition budget, with the collection holdings modified by shelf age and amount of usage in that segment of the collections. This program was outlined in the following document in 2002.[23]

> The public library of Des Moines has addressed problems of a neglected materials collection and inadequate materials budget through a new and innovative collection plan based on quantifiable local standards. The library measures median collection age, and shelf availability of recently circulated items. The collection plan is based on a standard size determined for each library collection. Items added each year equal the number of items withdrawn. Collection budgets are calculated using formulas that will provide a five-year median age and at least 50 per cent availability in all types of materials. The library has succeeded in reducing the median age from 16 to eight years and has achieved 50 per cent availability in almost all collection areas.

- Moving users from certain kinds of collections to other collection areas. In the midst of these serial changes, inspired in large part by new electronic communications technology, many libraries set up communications programs with their constituents to tell them about alternative collections. For example, there are forms from the Non-Profit Information Center, IRS tax forms, newly scanned local ordinances and genealogy collections, publication of all types of business licenses, and special programs on home decoration, investing, and banking—with handouts furnished by the for-profit company. The message was simple: The library has services and sources of information that you should know about that do not involve expensive serial sets or high-priced books. In other words, if one kind of item is not available at your library, perhaps that library can furnish you with one just as useful or more useful and at less cost in time and out-of-pocket expense.

The facts of collections budgeting and buying are that it is the core of what librarians do. It is why many are attracted to the field of librarianship and why customers go to libraries. It is time consuming and expensive. It is also big business, so financial skill is truly required of all who buy, process, and weed collections.

NOTES

1. Dumb.com. Retrieved on August 17, 2015, from http://www.dumb.com/quotes/buying-quotes/.
2. Wilkinson, Frances C., Linda K. Lewis, and Rebecca L. Lubas. *The Complete Guide to Acquisitions Management*. Santa Barbara: Libraries Unlimited, 2015, p. 47.
3. Kirk, Rachel A. *Balancing the Books: Accounting for Librarians*. Santa Barbara, CA: Libraries Unlimited, 2013.
4. ALA. *Library Operating Expenditures: A Selected Annotated Bibliography. ALA Library Fact Sheet No. 4.* Retrieved on July 17, 2015, from http://www.ala.org/tools/libfactsheets/alalibraryfactsheet04.
5. *SLJ's Average Book Prices for 2015*. Retrieved on August 22, 2015, from http://www.slj.com/2015/03/research/sljs-average-book-prices-2015/.

6. ALA. *Library Operating Expenditures: A Selected Annotated Bibliography. ALA Library Fact Sheet No. 4.* Retrieved on July 17, 2015, from http://www.ala.org/tools/libfactsheets/alalibraryfactsheet04.

7. SLJ's Average Book Prices for 2015. Retrieved on August 22, 2015, from http://www.slj.com/2015/03/research/sljs-average-book-prices-2015/.

8. Panitch, Judith M. and Sarah Michalak. *The Serials Crisis. A White Paper for the UNC-Chapel Hill Scholarly Communications Convocation.* January, 2005. Retrieved on April 13, 2015, from http://www.unc.edu/scholcomdig/whitepapers/panitch-michalak.html.

9. "Scientific Retractions Are on The Rise, and That May Be a Good Thing." *priceonomics.* June 24, 2015. Retrieved on July 11, 2015, from http://priceonomics.com/scientific-retractions-are-on-the-rise-and-that/.

10. Weissman, Jordan. "Why Are College Textbooks So Absurdly Expensive?" *The Atlantic.* Posted January 3, 2013. Retrieved on April 15, 2015, from http://www.theatlantic.com/business/archive/2013/01/why-are-college-textbooks-so-absurdly-expensive/266801/.

11. Cardona, Mercedes. "Paper and Ink Prices Rise, but Industry Executives More Troubled by Postal Hike." *Direct Marketing News.* Posted May 1, 2011. Retrieved on April 15, 2015, from http://www.dmnews.com/paper-and-ink-prices-rise-but-industry-executives-more-troubled-by-postal-hike/article/201370/.

12. "Why Textbooks Cost So Much. It's Economics 101." *The Economist*, August 16, 2014, p. 24.

13. See how the pricing comparison works at Campusbooks.com at http://www.campusbooks.com/.

14. Burger, Rob. "Finding The Cheapest College Textbooks (A Case Study)." *Forbes*, August 2, 2015. Retrieved on August 4, 2015, from http://www.forbes.com/sites/robertberger/2015/08/02/finding-the-cheapest-college-textbooks-a-case-study/2/.

15. *EBSCO Information Services Releases Serials Price Projection for 2015.* Posted October 2, 2014. Retrieved on April 16, 2015, from https://www.ebsco.com/news-center/press-releases/ebsco-information-services-releases-serials-price-projection-for-2015.

16. Collins, Tim. *The Current Budget Environment and Its Impact on Libraries, Publishers and Vendors.* Retrieved on April 16, 2015, from https://www.ebscohost.com/uploads/general/current-budget-environment.pdf.

17. Retrieved on April 16, 2015, from http://www.lib.unc.edu/spotlight/provost.html.

18. "Fitch Downgrades Reed Elsevier to 'BBB+'; Outlook Stable." *Reuters.com.* Posted April 2, 2015. Retrieved on April 15, 2015, from http://www.reuters.com/article/2015/04/02/idUSFit918852820150402.

19. Retrieved on April 16, 2015, from www.arl.org/sparc/.

20. Retrieved on April 15, 2015, from highwire.stanford.edu.

21. Williamson, Warren. "Taking A Long-Overdue Sledgehammer To The Public Library." *Fast Company.* Retrieved on September 12, 2014, from http://www.fastcompany.com/3035406/innovation-agents/taking-a-long-overdue-sledgehammer-to-the-public-library.

22. Lynden, Frederick C. "Managing Rising Materials Costs." In Sul H. Lee, ed. *Acquisitions, Budgets and Material Costs: Issues and Approaches. Monographic Supplement #2 to Journal of Library Administration.* Routledge, 2013, p. 113ff.

23. Truck, Lorna. "Plain English Collection Budgets: A Collection Plan for Public Libraries." *The Bottom Line*, 15: 4 (2002), pp. 167–73.

CHAPTER 23

Other Expenses

Beware of a little expense. A small leak will sink a great ship.

—Benjamin Franklin[1]

Some "other" expenses are far from small, but large or small, they are a part of the library financial system and are important to manage effectively. Often, they are treated separately because they don't "fit" in to regular lines of the budget or they are governed by different rules. Or they are separated because it is important to track them to control expenditures. Here are some of the "other expenses," with suggestions from writers about how to handle those issues.

SPECIAL PROJECTS

Staff of many different kinds of libraries get drawn into budgeting when they are asked to develop a "project budget" or a "special project budget" for a particular effort. These could be one-time activities such as program and events to celebrate the centennial of the library's founding. Or special projects could be the cost of deep weeding the collection and shifting books on the shelves that is done once every 10 years. Or it could be a yearlong project to reach out and plan programs for new immigrants (or new businesses or new school curricula) in the library's service area.

For library administrators, the message is that keeping a little money in reserve for special projects and actually planning to raise money for a few special projects demonstrates administrative vision and responsiveness to staff articulation of program and service initiative efforts. ALA sets a model for this kind of behavior with its Grants and Awards Fund, an accounting point that keeps track of income available to provide grants to member organizations and to handle grants which come to the agency.[2]

LSTA presents special project budget options. The Missouri State Library, in recent years, has published a budget document that demonstrates how it uses special projects money to continue working on various projects, like retrospective cataloging, and initiate new projects, like Homework Help, using the Federal funds.[3] The special project designation is a significant demonstration of both legal and ethical use of federal money to achieve long-term goals of the state library and of many of the state's public libraries.

ENDOWMENTS AND BEQUESTS

As described in Chapter 16, a library may have endowments to support specific parts of the collection or to support a specific program or service. With endowments, the designated activities are usually funded with the income earned on the money in the endowment over many years. Bequests often are spent all at once as the donor has specified. Both endowments and bequests are kept in designated funds separate from the regular library budget to better assure that the terms of the gifts are met.

For example, a university library may have an endowment to support purchase of books and serials in a subject area or a particular language. The endowment would yield income each year for the collection specialist to spend over and above the library's regular collections budget. Or a public library might receive a bequest to promote programs for teens at a particular location over and above the library's annual program budget.

THE MOBILE LIBRARY FLEET

This includes bookmobiles and tech-mobiles as traveling library services; vans to pick up and deliver reserves and checkouts from one location to another; automobiles for programmers to move between distant locations; plus mileage for various staff assignments. Vehicles are purchased under contract and within the library's purchasing policy. Fuel supply also can be purchased under contract and mileage to staff is handled as part of library reimbursement policy. Universities and school districts may provide a central pool of vehicles for deliveries and travel, but the library may be charged for their use so there needs to be a budget line for transportation.

REAL ESTATE

For various reasons, the library may have buildings to sell or rent, or it may rent or lease space from a third party. Most of these transactions would be managed through standard real estate listings and frequently by using a licensed real estate agent.

SHORT TERM

The library may, from time to time, create a budget line in order to study how money is spent in a particular area. This kind of research helps library administration find ways to save money with the least disruption of service to library users and to have such decisions based on actual costs.

Materials storage is an example of a short-term budget line. Libraries of all kinds need places to store books and periodicals. A library might have a special storage budget when it wants to track the expenses associated with various kinds of shelving sites. Closed stacks have costs because the library needs to pay for retrieval. With open stacks, more people—including those who are careless about returning materials to appropriate shelf positions, so shelf management becomes more complex—and therefore more expensive. Off-site storage costs for rent and retrieval is more expensive and takes longer than most self-service schemes.

SECURITY

Security often is handled by contracts, either with a security service vendor, with security officers of the host agency or with "side-job" contracts with trained police officers. Libraries have to decide their priorities in high security officers: Is the first order of protection against theft or to protect persons? Also, be careful to ensure that officers protect staff as well as library visitors. The mandate of the officers—and their training—will determine a great deal about their costs. Be careful about hiring underqualified security persons, the level of weapons you want officers to carry, and standard methods they are to use to intervene in security situations. All these will affect training needs and costs. Often, security budgets include funds for open hours protection, after-hours security checks, an alarm service, and funds for security for special events, including programs and fundraisers.

BANKING/MONEY MANAGEMENT

Libraries have fees for banking and investment management. If the parent organization approves, a library may have an investment specialist who advises the library's financial officers about investments. The fee structure for such advice ordinarily is contracted. Libraries often are charged banking fees even if the actual services are contracted for by the university, city, or school district. This might include payroll, issuing checks, and account management. Some libraries also fund the independent audit from the money management fund.

BUILDING MAINTENANCE AND CLEANING SERVICES

Many libraries hire their own custodial and maintenance staff or use staff employed by the university, school, or city. Other libraries hire an outside service for day-to day cleaning and have a list of outside venders to maintain the library facility. It is important to hire (or require from an outside vender) good supervisors to supervise these services and the best qualified persons as workers. In the level of maintenance and cleaners, you will have to decide the level of literacy you want (for reading labels, safety codes, etc.) and the certification you want to include on staff (e.g., HVAC, electrician, etc.). Remember too that the more complex the building (e.g., number of different types of library fixtures, HVAC units, water and sewer systems, etc.), the higher your cleaning and maintenance costs. Also, a solid preventative maintenance program will save lots of money on library machinery and transport over the long months and years you will use them before replacement.

COMPUTERS AND INFORMATION SYSTEMS

Computers need to be purchased, installed, and maintained. Software needs to be upgraded and all library computers and automated systems need to be kept secure in an ever-changing world. Most libraries need easy access to trained (and helpful) IT staff to keep both public and staff computers functional, and to provide some hands-on training for occasional and new users or new staff.

Even more than on other kinds of technology, computers and ILS systems have to absorb an enormous amount of abuse—and their hardware and software age quickly. A good way to handle this expense is with planned replacement. Your ILS staff often will want to hold on to "a system that works" longer than your users want you to hold them. Modular and wearable technology makes this situation even more complex, as does the technology in makers' spaces. Plan technological obsolescence with appropriate replacements and through several years, and try to move money from contingency lines to technology in anticipation of these replacements. Disposal of nonused technology is another matter. We have been in some library systems where rooms full of old computers are a major storage feature. In every case, there has to be a better way than letting older but still workable technology sit in storage getting dustier and more out of date.

EMPLOYEE FUNDS

The library has a responsibility to monitor staff behavior. This could include making sure staff act appropriately on the libraries' computer and phones and/or video surveillance. In addition, the library may do random drug testing, particularly if the school, university, or city mandates it. In any case, the library has to have funds to cover this kind of specialized employment activity.

Monitoring will become more prevalent as technology is enhanced, and it is already far-reaching now.[4] "A 2005 survey by the American Management Association showed that more than half of the employers who responded use video surveillance at work to counter theft, violence, or sabotage. And 16% of the employers surveyed used video surveillance to monitor employee performance." Filming staff behavior may or may not be appropriate, depending on whether or not staff know that it's happening.[5] A good place to start focusing on this issue is the NOLO introductory bibliography on this subject.[6] A good substantial essay is a 2013 article on the legal and ethical issues in monitoring employees.[7]

Another fund may be set up to help staff in various ways, and might include reward and incentive programs, support for family leave or military deployment, or salaries while on jury duty.

CONTRACT SERVICES

The former director member of this library writing team used a variety of contract services. All operated on behalf of the library with fees recommended by staff and approved by the board. Contracted services included:

- **Legal Services**. Budgeted to help handle legal issues with users, staff, changing personnel laws, ADA standards. "Free" legal services will always be an attraction from a board member or friend. One of our director friends once noted acidly, "Free legal advice is worth what you pay for it." On balance, the more complicated the legal issue, the more you should consider obtaining proper legal opinion from someone who will stay with you through an issue that has potential courtroom time in it. Note, too, that the more prestigious your paid legal consultant, the less likely attorneys among friends, governance board, or advisory group are willing to provide free advice without regard for consequences.
- **Insurance Representation**. A high visibility insurance broker who represents more than one company is a great hire for a library with many different insurance issues.
- **Counseling and Mental Health**. Most libraries contract for mental health, family, and drug counseling programs for its employees. Some contact for the services or the library agrees to pay for the services used. Obviously, this is highly confidential; so, often the actual recipient of the service is not identified.
- **Researchers**. Occasionally, the library will need professional research done from outside contractors. There are not many librarians who have enough background econometric, demographic, or marketing/public opinion polling to do the kind of research the library needs. Demographic knowledge is an area worth contracting. Relating circulation to demography is another. Understanding how many kindergartners to expect next year is useful to both school and public libraries. And all libraries need help relating and updating census information about the populations served by the library. Commuting studies that highlight service areas can be helpful, especially in cities and universities with long journeys to work and complex commuting patterns. Hourly fees or contract fees are the way to pay for these services.

Survey Monkey and other do-it-yourself survey tools on the net are fine if your questions are simple and the answers you expect are simple, as well. But if you need indepth information about your users and those who do not use the library, professional research may be needed.

Each library has its own traditions for how accounts are set up and used. Smaller libraries usually have simpler budgets, but most libraries have an array of special fund lines to meet legal requirements, to be clear about how much particular service cost, and to ensure that the library budgets and funds necessary services to library needs to operate. Some of these accounts are simple and straightforward, some are not, but they are all important to keep the library afloat.

NOTES

1. "12 Famous Quotes about Expenses and Savings." Retrieved on August 17, 2015, from http://www.slideshare.net/Stu-TelInc/12-famous-quotes-about-expenses-and-savings.

2. ALA, *ALA Fund Structure. Grants and Awards Fund.* Retrieved on July 3, 2015, from http://www.ala.org/groups/mleader/budget/alafundstructure.

3. Missouri State Library. *LSTA State FY14. Project Plan.* Approved on May 21, 2013. "2 LSTA Grant Projects—Funding from Federal FY 2013." Retrieved on July 3, 2015, from http://s1.sos.mo.gov/cmsimages/LibraryGrantsTemp/FY14LSTAProjectPlan.pdf.

4. "The Rise of Workplace Spying." *The Week,* July 10, 2015, p. 11.

5. Guerin, Lisa. "Workplace Cameras and Surveillance: Rules for Employees." *NOLO.* Retrieved on July 19, 2015, from http://www.nolo.com/legal-encyclopedia/workplace-cameras-surveillance-employer-rules-35730.html.

6. "Your Employee's Right to Privacy." *NOLO.* Retrieved on July 19, 2015, from http://www.nolo.com/legal-encyclopedia/employee-privacy.

7. Yerby, Jonathan. "Legal and Ethical Issues of Employee Monitoring." *Online Journal of Applied Knowledge Management,* 1:2 (2013). Retrieved on July 19, 2015, from http://www.iiakm.org/ojakm/articles/2013/volume1_2/OJAKM_Volume1_2pp44–55.pdf.

SECTION VII

Assessment and Evaluation

CHAPTER 24

Evaluating the Budget

One of the great mistakes is to judge policies
and programs by their intentions rather
than their results.

—Milton Friedman[1]

IN-HOUSE BUDGET EVALUATION

In most libraries, someone is "watching over" income and expenses to make sure staff are spending as directed by the annual budget. In many libraries, managers get monthly or quarterly budget reports for the accounts for which they have responsibility. They are expected to check if there are errors, and then try to solve any problems. This might include items that have been charged to the wrong account, being overcharged by a vendor, or orders not being made in a timely fashion.

This ongoing attention to detail helps correct mistakes and discourage fraud. It can also allow library staff to alert administration to the need to spend more quickly or to retard purchases in specific lines of the budget, so adjustments can be made to meet unexpected expenses or credits. This constant attention makes it more likely that the budget will be balanced at the end of the budget period.

Libraries close the books annually and report how funds were actually spent. By comparing what was spent to what was budgeted, library administration, staff, and governance boards can evaluate how successful both the budget and the spending has been.

As mentioned in Chapter 8, library annual reports usually include a report on the budget and how it was spent and what was accomplished by spending the budget. Any variance in the budget, like overspending, fund reallocation (moving funds from one line of the budget to another), or underspending, whether accidental or intentional, is explained in budget notes.

Libraries receiving grant money are required to report budget updates annually, as well as to provide a report on spending at the end of the grant project. Public libraries report year-end budget information to the state library agency (which, in turn, is shared with IMLS). School and university libraries provide a year-end report to their parent organization and special libraries file reports as required by the organizations they serve.

The American Library Association (ALA) collects budget data in order to compile statistics about library budgets nationally. Alas, ALA takes so long to process much of this information that it is historical rather than current when it is issued years later as part of its laggardly reporting process. Your change model should be to drive currency in fiscal reporting. The true Information Age is an era in which financial currency is the rule, not the exception. That's as true for libraries as it is any other American business.

In simplest terms, the fiscal year annual report presents the approved budget and tells what actually happened to the library's funds. The library's business office or accountant will have receipts and other documents to verify this budget report. Many library administrators and governing boards use this kind of in-house budget assessment when planning future budgets, and to improve accounting practices, and evaluate vendor performance where there are problems.

THE AUDIT

Libraries, no matter their funding source, should have a regular audit. An audit is a "systematic and independent examination of books, accounts, documents and vouchers of an organization to ascertain how far the financial statements present a true and fair view of the concern. It also attempts to ensure that the books of accounts are properly maintained by the concern as required by law."[2] In other words, an accountant, not connected with the day-to-day operations, checks and balances to see that there is no fraud or gross inaccuracies in the library's bookkeeping, and that the library is in compliance with the law, and that the library uses appropriate accounting practice.

The exact circumstances of the audit will differ from library to library. Cities and states have elected auditors who make sure libraries (and other government agencies) conduct an appropriate and timely audit. Universities may have an internal auditor who will work with the library, or libraries may hire an outside accounting or auditing firm to conduct the audit. Auditors are certified public accountants who have training and extra certification in conducting impartial and thorough examinations of an organizations books. While the auditors work directly with the library's financial department, library staff may be asked to give more details about purchases and contracts or they may be questioned directly by the auditors. Obviously, it is important to be organized, have documentation when possible, and to be as honest as possible when responding to the auditors.

The result of an audit is a report sent to the library board, governing administration, or host institution. The best report is one that issues an "unqualified opinion." This means the auditor has no recommendation for improvement nor has the auditor any concerns about the financial compliance with the established checks and balances of the library. This is also called a clean opinion. Auditors also report "qualified opinions" when they find problems with the finances or the library. This report would have an explanatory paragraph that includes the problem or problems with suggestions on how to correct the problem. The auditor can also issue a disclaimer of opinion, which means the library could not or did not cooperate with the auditor.

While libraries always want to receive an unqualified opinion, it is not unusual for auditors to find issues that are reported for remediation. The audit is important to help improve the financial health of the library and to certify to taxpayers, governments, and donors that the library is free of fraud and that it uses its funds as they are intended.

ECONOMIC MEASURES OF LIBRARY SUCCESS

For-profit companies have several ways to measure their success, and some of these measurements may be useful in measuring library success as well. Return on Investment (ROI), economic impact, and cost–benefit analysis (CBA) all are ways to evaluate the financial success of an enterprise.

Of these three, economic impact is the least likely to be used for libraries. Economic impact measures the financial benefits to a community, university, school, or business of a specific venue or event. This is often used in context of the benefit of sports stadiums or sporting events to the community. Impact is measured by ascertaining additional employment, tax revenue, and spending on restaurants, hotels, and transportation that are generated by an event. For instance, Super Bowl XLIX generated $719 million in total economic impact for greater Phoenix, according to the Arizona State University's W.P. Carey School of Business. The numbers include direct spending by football fans, media, and tourists in town to watch the New England Patriots and Seattle Seahawks, as well as less direct "ripple effect" benefits such as travel and local transportation.[3] While some libraries may attract tourists or outsiders to the building (think Library of Congress), most libraries serve locals and don't aim to serve others in a way that generates tourist dollars.

The authors of this volume worked with two other professionals, one an academic economist and the second a successful long-term school administrator, to develop a CBA application for public libraries. This work started in 1994, and a decade later resulted in a ILMS-funded, ALA-published study laying out the ups and downs of using CBA methodology in 15 different public library systems in many different states.[4]

ROI is the measure of profit generated for an investment or company over a specific time period. For example, if you invested $100 in the Acme bookbinding company and after a year that investment was worth $110 dollars, your ROI would be 10 percent. Good for you, as this would be a high ROI. CBA is somewhat more nuanced. CBA estimates and totals up the equivalent money value of the benefits and costs to the community of projects to establish whether they are worthwhile. These projects may be dams and highways or can be training programs and health care systems.[5] Or libraries. CBA allows a library to find the relative value in dollars of services and programs and to distribute value over different users groups.

Again, libraries are cost centers and are not expected to make a profit; so, ROI or CBA has to be adapted to be appropriate for use in libraries. The adaptation is to calculate the dollar value of services provided per year (as opposed to using sales figures and profit and loss statements) and compare that to the tax investment or library budget. The results are stated as the value of services provided per tax dollar.

ROI is calculated for individuals by creating categories of services, asking users how much of the services they use, and multiplying this number by an assigned dollar value. If a library users reported using seven books from the library, the total value of book lending to this user would $105 (7 × 15 = $105). The calculator then adds all the values together and calculates the RIO. For the user above, the calculator figures the RIO like this: Your personal ROI is based on your responses and the typical annual tax contribution for your library. You see a returned value of $31.81 for every $1 invested.

The weakness of this approach is that the values are usually inflated so the results are inflated. For example, it might be argued that borrowing a book should not have the value of replacing the book, but rather a 10th of the cost of the book based on 10 circulations per book. So, instead of valuing a circulation at $15, it should be valued at $1.50. The value is that RIO is fairly easy to calculate and it is dramatic and positive.

CBA is similar to ROI, but the results are less likely to be inflated and it provides a richer data set to use when planning services. It is more elaborate and also costly to do. CBA also depends on users to assess what library services they use and what the replacement value of these services would be if they did not use the library. Typically, data is gathered by surveys given to library users. The surveys are meant to answer the following questions:

- What is the value to an individual to use the library resources?
- What is the value to the institution (university, community, school) of the library?
- What is the willingness to pay for a service?[6]

CBA also allows a library to calculate the ROI on dollars invested in facilities, equipment, and collections.

As with ROI, library staff create a list of possible services and give each a dollar value. Library users are asked how often and how much they use a service. They are also asked how much they would pay for the services if it were not available at the library. Users are also asked how much they would pay to replace the library if it were destroyed. Because users give there approximate household income, their willingness to pay for the library can be tempered by what they can afford. Using a mathematical formula values of the library are calculated.

In St. Louis, we wanted to know what value business put on the library and, because we spent a lot of energy and money serving youth, parents, and teachers, we were able to segment the population and customize the questions for each group.

Results of CBA can be stated as follows:

- For each dollar of local tax support to operate our library, members of our community received more than ___ dollars in benefits from library services.
- A dollar invested in our library facilities, equipment, and collection returns more than _____ percent per year in benefits to our community
- _____ cents of a dollar in community benefits from library services typically goes to households and families. The remaining ___ cents of a dollar of community benefits from library services comes from assistance to educators and students in our communities' schools and colleges.[7]

Libraries also gather nonmonetary data about how users value various services, particularly if the library uses open-ended questions (like "is there anything you would like to tell the library director?") or focus groups where users can discuss both the merits and drawbacks of library service.

Most libraries do not undertake either ROI or CBA without expert help in the form of an economist who specializes in this kind of methodology and a survey company that can conduct phone, electronic, or in-person interviews. The studies have to be carefully done to get reliable results.

Libraries might do these studies once a decade, but the results are tremendously helpful for the following reasons:

- Librarians understand their institution better and are better able to make positive changes in its operation.
- Results provide tangible results about the value of the library for boards, funders, and taxpayers.
- Study results help boost staff morale by demonstrating the value of the library to those it serves.
- Library staff can make better informed budget decisions.[8]

OUTCOME MEASUREMENT

Your library budget is only as good as what services it allows you to offer, so no budget evaluation is complete without looking at the outcome of spending the library's budget. In this sense, outcomes are the benefits or effects of library service on users. Most libraries see the budget as inputs—that is, what is spent and in input evaluation the focus is spending as planned. Traditionally, libraries have measured outputs—that is, the number of uses that result from spending the budget. This would include circulation, library visitation, program attendance/classes taught, and number of reference questions asked. Libraries have gone further to ask "so what?" and the taxpaying public has called for more accountability from all types of libraries.

According to IMLS, outcomes refer to changes in an individual's attitude, skill, knowledge, behavior, status, or life condition. An outcome is a benefit that occurs to participants of a program; when the benefits to many individuals are viewed together, they show the program's impact. Outcomes *always* focus on what participants will say, think, know, feel, or be.[9] The source on the effects or outcome of using the library comes from users. Outcomes are articulated as part of strategic planning before services or programs are offered or funded. See Figure 24.1 for an example of outcome evaluation (OE) planning.

Outcome data are collected by observation, testing, surveys, interviews, or focus groups. Often, an outside evaluator organizes and carries out data gathering to make sure it is systematic, complete, and accurate. This evaluator can be a library staff member who is not responsible for providing the program. In this way, you can find out what works best for most of your users, have data to use to change and improve your services, and have facts on how best to use the libraries resources, including budgets, to provide the best services and programs possible.

Outcome	Definitions: • Intended Impact	Examples: • Students will have basic Internet skills
Indicator	• Observable and measurable behaviors and condition	• The number and percentage of participating students who can bring up an Internet search engine, enter a topic in the search function, and bring up one example of the information being sought within 15 minutes
Data source	• Sources of information about conditions being measured	• Searching exercise, trainer observation
Applied to	• The specific group within an audience to be measured (all or a subset)	• Sixth graders who complete the workshop
Data interval	• When data will be collected	• At end of workshop
Target (Goal)	• The amount of impact desired	• Eighty-five percent of approximately 125 participants

Figure 24.1   Outcome Evaluation Model

Source: Adapted from "Frequently Asked OBE Questions," Institute for Museum and Library Services at IMLS.gov.

OE provides the following:

- OE helps staff work smart by providing a system to measure success and specific information to use to adapt or change programs and services.
- OE strengthens library planning and budget allocation.
- OE allows library staff to understand and describe the impact of its program and services on its users. OE enables communication amongst staff and between library departments, including administration. OE enhances communication with the community, donors, and program partners.[10]

OE provides accountability for public agencies, including libraries. OE is required by the federal government and will be increasingly required by agencies using state and local funds. OE may be required by private donors as well.

EVALUATION IMPLEMENTATION

Whether you are using OE, output or statistical evaluation, or some evaluation plan unique to your library, you should be careful to ensure that you have a plan at the beginning of the budget cycle, and that you carry out the evaluation as planned, and that the data collected is as accurate and unbiased as possible. Getting help from a statistician or survey design group may be necessary to do your evaluation. While this will add to the expense of the evaluation, it is important to get solid information from the evaluation.

There are some basic principles to follow:

- The links between the activities or services and the expected outcomes of the library must be clear and explicit in the evaluation design. For example, 80 percent of students who asked reference questions will be satisfied or very satisfied with the information they were given.
- The actual level or amount of service provided can influence outcomes. For instance, are users better able to use the library catalog with a direction sheet or after an online instructional workshop? Or is it more important that users look at the catalog on a regular basis?
- Negative findings can be just as important as positive results. If the online catalog workshop did not help users, why not? Are there better instructional techniques suggested?
- Qualitative data (interviews, focus groups, surveys) can be as useful as qualitative data.[11] Used together, the effectiveness of a service or program will be more clear.

CONCLUSION

It is always the goal to spend library funds as indicated by the approved budget.

This involves knowing how much you have to spend and keeping track on what you spend over the fiscal year and being sure you spend it as intended. Even in small libraries with slim budgets, this takes the commitment and time to do. Large libraries have systems and staff to ensure budget compliance.

Many libraries are pressured to demonstrate that the taxpayers and other funders are getting benefits from the library and that the finances of the library are operated for the demonstrable good of those served. Libraries may choose to use economic measures to show not only how the money is spent, but also the value the users receive. Or libraries may undertake OE to show the good uses the libraries funds are put to.

In any case, the key to evaluating budget effectiveness is to find out not what was intended, but to show the results of library funding.

NOTES

1. "Owl Re Wise Research and Evaluation." Retrieved on August 27, 2015, from http://www.owlre.com/wordpress/wp-content/uploads/2008/01/factsheet_owlre_quotes.pdf.
2. *Wikipedia.* Retrieved on August 27, 2015, from https://en.wikipedia.org/wiki/Audit.
3. *Phoenix Business Journal*, "Super Bowl XLIX generated $295M in direct spending, $719M in overall impact," June 24, 2015. Retrieved on August 28, 2015, from http://www.bizjournals.com/phoenix/news/2015/06/23/super-bowl-xlix-generated-719m-in-direct-ripple.html.
4. Elliott, Donald S., Glen E. Holt, Sterling W. Hayden, and Leslie Edmonds Holt. *Measuring Your Libraries Value: How to Do a Cost-Benefit Analysis of Your Public Library*. Chicago: American Library Association, 2007, passim.
5. San Jose State Department of Economics, *An Introduction to Cost Benefit Analysis*, Retrieved on August 298, 2015, from http://www.sjsu.edu/faculty/watkins/cba.htm.
6. Kingma, Bruce. *The Economics of Libraries, Cost-Benefit Analysis, and Return on Investment*. Retrieved on August 28, 2015, from http://libvalue.cci.utk.edu/sites/default/files/kingma_libvalueworkshop.pdf.
7. Elliott, Donald S., Glen E. Holt, Sterling W. Hayden, and Leslie Edmonds Holt. *Measuring Your Libraries Value: How to do a Cost-Benefit Analysis of Your Public Library*. Chicago: American Library Association, 2007, p. 110.
8. Ibid., p. 118.
9. IMLS. "Frequently Asked OBE Questions", Institute for Museum and Library Services at IMLS.gov. Retrieved on August 30, 2015.
10. Fasick, Adele, and Leslie Edmonds Holt. *Managing Youth Services in Libraries*. Santa Barbara: Libraries Unlimited, 2012, p. 42.
11. Karsh, Ellen, and Arlen Sue Fox. *The Only Grant-Writing Book You'll Ever Need*. New York: Basic Books, 2014, p. 195.

SECTION VIII

Communication about Money

CHAPTER 25

Communicating Library Financial Principles

A popular government, without popular information,
or the means of acquiring it, is but a prologue to a farce or a tragedy; or, perhaps both.
                                                                —James Madison, 1832[1]

If "everything is about money" in the library business, then librarians ought to be communicating about money with all of their constituencies every chance they get. That admonition is true for messages to staff, users, taxpayers, corporate officials, and civic leaders, all of whom have an impact on the future of the library. Such a communications program needs to be systematic and ongoing, highlighting the positive impact and benefits which flow to users and the greater community because of the work the library does on behalf of the community.

As pointed out in previous chapters, the congeries of circumstance, including the law, institutional policies, and regular communications with constituencies provide a smorgasbord of opportunities for communicating about the library's monetary policies, and how they serve to benefit their users and the community generally. Library spokespersons need to be trained to set even minor "feel good" stories into the context of a financially well-operated organization that gives back more than it gets in individual and community services.

Even if they are not very interested in institutional finances, professional librarians need to help make the monetary case for their organizations. Below, we have summarized the financial principles which ought to be told and retold to library constituents as part of developing long-term communication relationships.

THE LIBRARY IS ACCOUNTABLE

The library, through its staff, is accountable to its funders, to its users, and to agencies and organizations that are set up to govern or regulate its operations. When library staff act like they are not accountable, trouble usually develops quickly—sometimes just for one or a few employees, sometimes for the institution as a whole.[2] Here are a couple of examples:

As an ACRL report points out, libraries can play "a crucial role in helping the whole university demonstrate its accountability because it connects students, faculty and administration in a unique way." And accountability is a repeated theme in a 2012 publication outlining 30+ pages of specific standards for quality school libraries in the State of South Carolina. Standards for details of the physical setting, collections, and staff of school libraries in the state are stated specifically and in some detail. Both of these publications show the continuing importance of accountability as an ongoing principle in library operations.

THE LIBRARY OPERATES USING PROFESSIONAL ACCOUNTING STANDARDS

Along with accountability, the library staff should be professional in financial operations. A "shot across the bow" of library's nonprofessionalism in finance shows up in a UC-Davis Internship/Career Center publication, which touts the good and the bad of various career options. One advantage of library work, according to the guide: "Exciting work; an opportunity to feel that your work makes a difference." Then, there are the disadvantages: "Low pay; never being sure that what you did has definite outcomes because there is no bottom line to financial accountability measures."[3] This last assertion, of course, is untrue, but the Career Center carries forward the incorrect observation anyway.

If you work in a library large enough to have its own finance office, this group of specialists likely will include one or more Certified Public Accountants. Financial specialists often are the first to spot operational problems because of the way that library money is handled or reported. As well as being watch dogs, financial professionals engender confidence that everything is above board and mistakes get corrected. If you work in a small library or for some other reasons are doing the library financial management yourself, there are several options to get accounting help. Many state libraries have a consultant who can help set up accounting systems. Often, the local United Way or other community agency offers education or advice or the help of an accountant to small nonprofit organizations to help them meet the legal and ethical financial obligations. Local colleges or universities may offer accountancy and other financial professional interns to help library workers in small libraries have high standards.

THE LIBRARY BUDGET IS NOT MYSTERIOUS BUT PUBLIC

Budgets are often calendared, planned, and passed in a public process open to staff members and the public generally. And, of course, the approved budget is a public document. Lots of library professionals of every stripe would prefer not to discuss money publicly, because such discussions often lead to opening up conflicts over institutional resource allocation.

In almost every library in the United States, financial records are public, and they must be kept (and available) on site at all times in the business office of the library. Electronic recordkeeping has shifted some financial records storage issues, but has not obviated holding and access requirements. Usually, library staff follow public information access laws issued by federal, state, and local governments and/or the public information policy of the host institution.

LIBRARY INCOME AND SPENDING REPORTED AT SCHEDULED TIMES

Advisory committees, governance boards, and related friends and foundations often receive regular monthly or quarterly reports on the process of the library's finances throughout each fiscal year. If a budget shortfall is expected, library administrators ought to announce how the library is preparing for it, when the cuts are being (or will be) implemented, and any remedies the library is taking to hold services when cuts have to be made.

Do not announce that the institution is "doing more with less," which leads easily to the question, "Then why weren't you doing more? Or, why weren't you spending less?" Instead, use the regular communications opportunity to announce that the library staff works hard to be an accurate communicator of its financial situation and makes best use of its financial resources.

Many, even most, libraries offer monthly financial reports. Normally, such reports show opening balance, transactions, and ending balance for each fund; show actual expenditures versus budget for each month and track year-to-date spending; and include a balance sheet for an overall portrait of the library's finances. Monthly reports should also include notes to comment on or explain items as needed. Make these regular financial reports available to staff groups, including unions, as they are to other constituent individuals and groups.

LIBRARIES OPERATE FINANCIALLY WITHIN PUBLIC LAWS AND POLICIES, INCLUDING THE ANNUAL AUDIT

These laws and policies include the annual audit. These legal requirements and policies, covering investments, banking relationships, purchasing, and contracting guidelines, are all reviewed in earlier chapters. They should be public documents to the fullest extent of the law.

It is that reality that provides a communications framework for publicizing the library audit. The audit brings outside professional expertise and advice to library finance. Beginning in 2009 for the 2008 fiscal year, all nonprofit agencies were required to file an IRS Form 990 tax return to maintain their status. If your library has $25,000 annual income, it must have a certified audit.[4]

How the library staff presents the audit is important. Auditors and their written "Report Audited Findings" is a good portrayal of how your library is doing in handling its finances. The independent auditor completes the report of the facts that have been researched against the audit criteria (the standards, procedures, and objectives) against which practices will be measured. For example, does every expense over $50 get checked by two different staff members in the library finance office?

The auditors usually will present an audit opinion that is unqualified, qualified, or adverse. Unqualified means that no exceptions to stated control procedures were found, qualified means that some were found, and adverse means that finance probably is ready for some new staff or a new head. No library official who is worth anything fools around with a qualified or adverse audit opinion.[5] Because library audits can be long and technical, librarians often report the results in summary but make the audit letter available on request.

THE LIBRARY INVESTS MONEY WITHIN A PUBLIC INVESTMENT POLICY

This policy sets the parameters of how an institution handles its financial surpluses. All investment policies began with an overview statement. We thought the relatively simple investment policy used by Hinsdale Public Library (http://www.hinsdalelibrary.info/wp-content/uploads/2009/04/Investment-Policy-2012.pdf) could be used by libraries of many different sizes. Here is the introduction to that document:[6]

> Policy: It is the policy of the Hinsdale Public Library (the Library) to invest idle public funds in relatively risk-averse assets which will provide the highest return possible while meeting the cash flow demands of the Library and conforming to all State Statutes governing the investment of public funds.
>
> Scope: This investment policy applies to all cash and investments held for each of the funds maintained by the Library including, but not limited to, the operating and capital reserve funds. Monies from individual Library funds may be commingled for investment purposes.

After original approval, the investment policy is revised as the library staff sees shifts in the investment climate and the financial condition of the library.

CONFLICT OF INTEREST POLICY

Like the Investment Policy, a library's conflict of interest policy is a way to avoid ethical entanglement of staff, governance officials, and so forth with for-profit companies. The added importance of this policy is that it lays out how the possible conflict is to be communicated and to whom that communication needs to be made. The American Library Association (ALA) suggests use of a conflict of interest policy similar to the following:[7]

> No Board member or committee member of the. . . . Library shall derive any personal profit or gain, directly or indirectly, by reason of his or her participation on the Board. Other than compensation, no employee shall derive any personal profit or gain, directly or indirectly, by reason of his or her employment by the. . . . Library except through activities that may facilitate professional advancement or contribute to the profession such as publications and professional service and have been fully disclosed to the Board.

This document requires board members to disclose personal interests in issues before the board and to decline to participate in any decisions on the matter. And the ALA document includes a probation of board members and staff to use patron records for their benefit. Board members and staff should sign a document stating they understand conflict of interest and will follow the library's rules regarding conflict of interest. The issues connected with conflict of interest concern these issues. Who should sign it? What conflicts should be clarified? What is a violation? Who implements it if a breach appears to have occurred or seems likely to occur.

THE LIBRARY PRACTICES ETHICAL HIRING AND PROMOTION POLICIES WITHIN THE CONTEXT OF AFFIRMATIVE ACTION LAWS

The library's hiring process, including its job announcements and selection procedures, ought to be an open book. If recruitment of minorities is a significant issue, then the library should make a point of doing all it can to hire, train, and retrain minorities so they can retain their jobs and/or move up in the library hierarchy. This latter point is especially important because the library profession generally is both older and whiter than it ought to be to match up with the demographics of those whom libraries generally serve. The main point here is the difficult task of conveying that within the library's strategic plan and its available budget, staff is being paid at appropriate levels of compensation, and everything possible is being done to recruit wanted staff from all demographic categories.

PUBLIC LOBBYING IS LEGAL AND APPROPRIATE FOR LIBRARY OFFICIALS

Many library professionals engage in legitimate political work on behalf of the library's finance, including individual and group lobbying with staff from other libraries. There are laws about who can lobby and about what lobbying can be done, both in terms of paying staff and advertising on issues. At the heart of the lobbying issues are financial issues: who pays for what and when? If there is doubt about lobbying, be conservative in terms of the money used (private sector, not public), who lobbies, and if the staff member(s) are being paid by the library when they are lobbying.

A great place to begin acquiring information on lobbying is an ALA electronic page titled *Tax Status and Lobbying*. This information-packed page is a compilation of synoptic reports from organizational "chapters," which are defined by the ALA constitution as "any legally constituted state, provincial, regional or territorial library association" (ALA Constitution, Article X, section 3).[8]

Reporting on his findings associated with this compilation, Arizona State LIS Professor Tom Wilding, president of the Arizona Library Association, in his summary of lobbying legislation, even notes the significance of the type of 501 IRS status particular organizations have in terms of their lobbying objectives.[9] You'll learn a lot about lobbying in your state and other states by starting here.

YOUR LIBRARY ADDS VALUE

Your professional staff contributes to company projects by their research and by saving users' time. Americans are timebound and time conscious. If you want to see the importance of saving time as a value added, compare the messages from Amazon.com, which operates almost entirely online, and your local library, which sends a message, then goes silent. The library neither follows up, and often it does not initiate communication; it is almost never proactive.

Meanwhile, every day Amazon.com suggests several Kindle books that it thinks we might like to download and read, plus weekly and monthly lists of materials profiled from our previous orders. Providing options to users which they did not know they had is one way of adding value.

Another way is by getting grants from philanthropies and government to be used by the library to improve the lives of the people of this community. And, then telling users about those grants and how they will benefit from them. Take a look on the net at the annual reports of the Tulsa Public Library or that of the Magic House Children's Museum in St. Louis, both of which make superb use of annual reports to their constituents.

USE IMAGES TO HELP USERS AND SUPPORTERS SEE THE LIBRARY IN NEW WAYS

Museums are much more conscientious about using photographs and graphics of all kinds than libraries. Libraries are very graphic places and becoming more so all the time as communications—both fiction and real life—become more graphic. It is sad that library image presentations are dominated by architectural views. Constituents would rather see images of libraries with persons than the mausoleums which are so often portrayed in library publications.

Look at examples of what has happened to novels, graphic novels, and nonfiction books generally to see how graphics are becoming ever more important in reading and information inquiry. Your library is a memorable, visual place. *Kill Shakespeare*, a graphic novel, which has five creators and appears to be on its way to creating a series, is one of the new products doing well in libraries.[10] Have staff record the changing images and use them in library publications.

USE ELECTRONIC COMMUNICATION TO RELATE TO LIBRARY USERS AND SUPPORTERS

Consider the full communications realm: from Facebook on electronic iPhones and their ilk to whatever communications device or social media innovation that currently is being used by the library's users when this book is read and used. As with all other kinds of communication, these have clusters of users who regularly examine their search, travel, study, and free time options using these forms of communication.

These trends are now sufficiently far along that librarian authors have begun to spell out options. Karen Calhoun,[11] Nicole Henning,[12] Paula Watson-Lakamp,[13] and Walt Crawford[14] all have assessed the new technologies and found the myriad technologies which library professionals can use as part of their applications. Librarians must keep up with the groups using these devices. They mark out the principal direction of current technology change as it marks out innovative pathways for users and the libraries that want their patronage.

To conclude, the principles of good financial practice articulated here ought to be the foundation blocks on which library financial communication is based. Everyone who works at the library as a salaried employee or volunteer ought to know enough about library finances to communicate the basics to all users no matter what the context. Remember that the intent of financial communication is relationship building. And your library ought to be building relationships all of the time.

NOTES

1. Government Secrecy and Openness Quotes. Retrieved on August 31, 2015, https://fipa.bc.ca/library/Public_Education/foiquotes.htm.
2. Howard, Jennifer. "Libraries Have a Key Role in Academic Accountability." *The Chronicle of Higher Education.* June 5, 2012. Retrieved on August 27, 2015, from http://chronicle.com/blogs/wiredcampus/libraries-have-a-key-role-in-academic-accountability/36497.
3. UC Davis. Internship and Career Center. *[Comparison of] Business and Non-Profits.* Retrieved on August 27, 2014, from https://icc.ucdavis.edu/lab/business/Differ ences.htm.
4. Internal Revenue Service. *Charity and Non-Profit Audits.* Retrieved on September 24, 2015, from http://www.irs.gov/Charities-&-Non-Profits/Exempt-Organizations-Audit-Process. This website is the main entry point for nonprofit audits. It has a huge number of subject listings with very clear, and well-worked out commentary on a non-profit's audit responsibilities.
5. Russell, J.P. "Generating Audit Findings and Conclusions." *Quality Progress*, December 2006. Retrieved on July 12, 2015, from http://asq.org/quality-progress/2006/12/standards-outlook/generating-audit-findings-and-conclusions.html.
6. Hinsdale (IL) Public Library Policy Investment Policy, 2000. Revised 2008, 2012. Retrieved on August 26, 2015, from http://www.hinsdalelibrary.info/wp-content/uploads/2009/04/Investment-Policy-2012.pdf.
7. American Library Association. *Sample Board Of Trustees and Library Employee Conflict of Interest Policy [for] Officers, Board Members and Employees.* Retrieved on July 12, 2015, from https://www.google.com/webhp?sourceid=chrome-instant&rlz=1C1QJDB_enUS595US596&ion=1&espv=2&ie=UTF-8#q=american+library+associ ation,+Sample+board+of+trustees+and+library+conflict+of+interest+policy.
8. ALA. *Tax Status and Lobbying.* Retrieved on August 30, 2015, from http://www.ala.org/groups/tax-status-and-lobbying.
9. Ibid.
10. Facebook, *Kill Shakespeare.* Retrieved on September 29, 2015, from https://www.facebook.com/killshakespeare.

11. Calhoun, Karen. *Exploring Digital Libraries: Foundations, Practice and Prospects.* Chicago: ALA, Neal Schumann, 2014.
12. Hennig, Nicole. *Apps for Librarians: Using the Best Mobile Technology to Educate, Create and Engage.* Santa Barbara, CA: Libraries Unlimited, 2014.
13. Watson-Lakamp, Paula. *Marketing Moxie for Librarians: Fresh Ideas, Proven Techniques and Innovative Approaches.* Santa Barbara, CA: Libraries Unlimited, 2014.
14. Crawford, Walt. *Successful Social Networking in Public Libraries.* Chicago: ALA, 2014.

GLOSSARY

Accounting Policies. The specific policies used by a library to prepare its financial statements. Accounting policies differ from accounting principles, in that the principles are the rules and the policies are a company's way of adhering to the rules.

Accounts Payable. Bill sent from a firm or individual requesting payment for a service or product purchased. Receipt of such a bill starts the payment process in a library.

Accounts Receivable. Bill sent *from* the library to a firm or individual requesting payment for services, products, or fines.

AFSCME. *American Federation of State, County and Municipal Employees*, a national union that represents library workers.

Aliteracy. Aliteracy (sometimes spelled alliteracy) is different from illiteracy. Most library finance is not advanced math, and many librarians seem to prefer financial aliteracy.

Allocation. Dividing a category of costs among different cost centers, as materials for children, teens, and adults all on one invoice.

Amazon Style. Personalized book/audio/video recommendation schemes that are based on prior patron usage. A user desire for library service customization matching that to be found in the private sector.

Americans with Disabilities Act (ADA). A set of Federal mandates on how persons with disabilities must be treated in public buildings, including libraries. Aisle width, seating, tables, restrooms, stair access all are governed by federal ADA standards.

Annual Report. A good communications document to help promote the work of the library and a good place to start thinking about next year's budget plan.

Assets. All that is owned by the library, including cash, accounts receivable, buildings, vehicles, and investments.

Audit. Review carried out by external accountants (certified auditors) to ensure that library funds have been spent according to legal requirements, agency regulations, and professional and institutional standards. The principal feature of this report is a judgment as to whether the audit is issued on a "qualified" or "unqualified" basis. An "unqualified" report is like getting an A+ for the course.

Authorized Budget. Budgets move from a "proposed" or "tentative" category to "official" or "authorized" by appropriate approval of a legislature, governance board, CEO, and so on. The "authorized" budget is the chief financial action document for the forthcoming and current fiscal year.

Balance Sheet. The financial statement that describes the resources under a library's control on a specified date. It consists of three major sections: **assets** (valuable rights owned by the company), **liabilities** (funds provided by outside lenders and other creditors), and the owners' **equity**. On the balance sheet, total assets must always equal total liabilities plus total owners' equity.

Banking Relationship. Involves selection and flexibility of relationship with the financial institution that holds the library's assets. The banking relationship includes financial advice within the framework specified by the library.

Benefits. Insurance, family leave, and vacation benefits that often adds a significant amount to stated annual salary. Benefits always need to be included in library staffing costs.

Bequest. Gift of personal property donated to a library on the death of the wealth holder. Bequests often are spent all at once as the donor has specified. Both endowments and bequests are kept in designated funds separate from the regular library budget to better assure that the terms of the gifts are met.

Bid Specifications. The library's first offer to a vendor indicating types, quantities, and agreed prices for products or services, that is, terms or bid specifications to which it will usually agree, a seller bids on the option. Bid specifications cause trouble for many libraries, because librarians often find themselves plowing new ground when trying to work through specialized specifications that meet the standards of engineers, space planners, binderies, or technology specialists.

Bonus. A salary device that sometimes is proposed as a way around stated public salary limits. Librarians need to find out if bonuses are legal in their work circumstances, and if so, in what form.

Bottom-Up Budgeting. The budgeting process where managers are asked to draft a full-scale operational program for the upcoming fiscal year. Budgets are then "rolled up" and adjusted to create the whole library budget.

Budget Adjustment. Libraries that operate as departments often receive budget adjustments up or down from their host organization because of changed income or unforeseen expenses.

Budget Authorization. (See Authorization of Budget).

Budget Categories. Categorization by type of expenditure (e.g., staff) or activity (special YA project). It is a way that fiscal specialists organize resources and expenses by fund and within funds.

Budget Preparation Calendar. Key dates within the current fiscal year at which the prior year's budget is closed, various aspects of the future budget year are deadlined, and the new FY Budget is adopted.

Cafeteria Benefits Plan. A selection of benefits from which a library staff member may choose, as, for example, a particular kind of medical insurance.

Capital Budget. A budget category or type of budget that contains the designated funds for capital expenditures, which in modern libraries usually includes not only buildings, but major forms of technology as well.

Cash Flow Statement. Exactly what its title indicates, but usually does not appear in library annual reports because of the minimal nature of cash income sources that fuel the library

Cash or Credit Sales. In the private sector annual reports, sales often are further broken down into cash and credit, a very important distinction if the business depends upon cash sales to pay its expense.

Change Order. A general term because a contract between the library and a vendor or contractor must be changed because of a "breach of contract," that is, a necessary change. A shift in the scope of work to be accomplished by a builder, usually at an increase in price or over a longer time.

Check Request. A standard way to pay. Also called a purchase requisition form. This form and most other business forms used in libraries are available at Biztree.com. Related documents are included, as well.

Checks and Balances. The various records systems in place from policies and procedures to maintain appropriate demonstrable controls in the library's financial systems.

Collections Budget. A budget category with funds designated to purchase or rent collections. Electronic collection access only recently has found its way into collections budgets in some libraries.

Comp (Compensation) Time. This involves giving certain staff paid time off—as if they were working regular hours—when they are not present rather than paying them at overtime salary rates. Comp time schemes start in libraries usually with the best of intentions but can cause endless amounts of compensation trouble, including being illegal in some institutions.

Compliance Terms. Category of terms usually related to how staff obtain reimbursement for expenses they have incurred on behalf of the library. Or, "terms" appears on an invoice stating how the payment is to be made.

Construction Manager. Libraries often hire a construction firm to act as the library's agent in all aspects of a library's erection or rehabilitation. This situation works best if there is congruence between the CM and the library's representatives to stay on top of project work and cost.

Contract. An agreement to buy or sell.

Contract Formation. Establishing the terms for a contract.

Contract Services. Services furnished by cleaning companies, maintenance specialists, cataloging specialists, and other service staff who are not on a library payroll. The roles of contract workers associated with libraries generally have increased in recent years.

Control. Public agencies like libraries have to demonstrate that all their funds are under control, including formal requests for payment, payment under stated terms, with audited statement of what occurred. Running out of money is regarded as the height of library mismanagement.

Cost–Benefit Analysis. The estimated monetary benefits that have accrued because of public investment. For example, "For every dollar invested in x library, it generates $3 in measurable benefits to the people and businesses of the community where it operates." CBA is an econometric exercise that deserves the attention of a qualified economist to work with library staff in setting up the terms of the various equations.

Criteria. The requirements which library vendors must fit to meet institutional requirements.

Critical Path Budgeting. This technique lays out the time and cost variables in a particular project. Literally, how much will the library spend, for what, when, to complete this project. It is a cousin to Gantt Chart planning, which estimates the timing of project start and finish dates in order to publicize the need for expenditures at certain times to keep a much-wanted project going and completed on time.

Debt. Money owed to a creditor.

Debt Service Fund. An allocation (set aside) to pay the interest on particular loans, often used to handle the interest on a construction loan which is of sufficient magnitude that it cannot be handled out of regular income flows. Therefore, an accounting fund is created to hold the money as it is accumulated until it has to be paid.

Deferred Compensation. Most frequently, we have encountered deferred compensation in the accumulation of combinations of sick and vacation days which have to be paid by the library in cash, usually when the staff member leaves the institution. Increasingly, libraries are instituting "use it or lose it" provisions to keep these pots of deferred compensation from accumulating.

Depreciation. Reduction in the value of a capital asset like a building or computer. Depreciation in libraries is one way of portraying when capital items need refurbishment or replacement.

Design–Build is a form of public–private partnership used by some libraries which have the money but do not have all the knowledge needed to construct a new library building. The library, therefore, specifies in general terms what it wants in the building, and contracts with a construction company that handles all the details to produce the finished building—receiving a fee for its services.

Directors and Officers (D&O) Insurance. D&O indemnifies library directors and officers against losses suffered because of legal action brought for alleged wrongful acts in their capacity as directors and officers, including defense costs over both criminal and regulatory charges.

Dividends. What libraries earn from their investments. A form of income that libraries apply to the expense of various operations.

Doing More with Less. Whenever the economy fades, some library leaders proclaim that this or that library knows how to do more with less. This notion continues to be anathema to all kinds of library professionals who recognize that this assertion carries with it the notion that the library could have been doing more than it did with the resources at hand. One library professional has written that the more correct version of this story is how library staff during budget cuts "did less with less."

Double-Entry Bookkeeping. Double-entry bookkeeping entries are recorded by debiting (subtracting an amount from) one or more accounts and crediting (adding the same amount to) . . . one or more accounts with the same total amount. The total amount debited and the total amount credited should always be equal, thereby ensuring that the accounting equation is maintained (i.e., balanced).

Earned Income. Funds which a library earns by selling services or products to various constituents, including training classes for private sector corporations, custom research for specific companies, food services, book sales, and gift shop items.

Educational Assistance. Library scholarship assistance for staff working to advance their education—to get their GED, BA, MLIS, or some special certification that makes them more valuable to handle library work. Terms of such grants have to be approved as legitimate forms of contracting, sometimes involving the nature of the money funding the educational efforts.

Electronic Records Management. Computers and off-site electronic records storage have shifted the rules of how libraries save their own business records, but auditors and the library's legal counsel may have more to say about what gets saved and how than do even high-level library staff members.

Employee Business Expenses. The big issues here are how the expense will be made, how will the expense be recorded, and how long reimbursement or payment will take. Cell phones, credit cards, and tablet computers all are involved in this changing expense category.

Encumbrance. An amount due (i.e., a burden) carried forward for payment at a current or future time. Libraries typically use it to move a financial commitment from one FY to another.

Endowment. An endowment is a donation of money or property to a nonprofit organization for the ongoing support of that organization. Usually, the endowment is structured so that the principal amount is kept intact while the investment income is available for use, or part of the principal is released each year.

E-Rate. E-Rate is the commonly used name for the Schools and Libraries Program of the Universal Service Fund, which is administered by the Universal Service Administrative Company (USAC) under the direction of the Federal Communications Commission (FCC). The E-Rate program provides funds for telecommunications and Internet access for libraries that serve low-income communities. E-Rate reduces communications costs through grants to individual libraries.

Expense Categories. The break out of expenses by type as in rent, insurance, utilities, supplies, and wages.

FASB Standards. Financial Accounting Standards Board (FASB) pronouncements consist of rules and guidelines for preparing, presenting, and reporting financial statements according to generally accepted accounting principles ("GAAP") in the United States of America.

Financial Illiteracy. A lack of financial knowledge that makes it difficult for many U.S. citizens to maintain a realistic view of their personal and the public's financial situation.

Financial Myths About Libraries. Chapter 18 in this book has multiple illustrations of the mythologies that pervade perceptions of libraries in all different kinds of constituencies. Libraries with well-prepared communication programs are able to respond to these myths in frank, informed ways, rather than providing graceless "no comments" when someone asks a question about the library that involves an assertion based on one of them.

Financial Statements. The income statement, balance sheet, and cash flow statement offer related information, but with different perspectives on performance.

Fiscal Year. The start up and end dates for the annual budget are set by the organization's by-laws, authorization by law, or enactment by board decision as the board acts under its legislative authority. Fiscal years in libraries often do not coincide with calendar years.

Fund Accounting. An accounting system emphasizing accountability rather than profitability, used by nonprofit organizations and governments like libraries.

GASB Standards. "The Governmental Accounting Standards Board (GASB) Statements are issued by GASB to set generally accepted accounting principles (GAAP) for state and local governments in the United States of America. These statements are the most authoritative source for governmental GAAP and for the work of certified accountants. Other business entities follow statements issued by Financial Accounting Standards Board (FASB)."

Gates Foundation Grants. Starting in 1997, the Bill and Melinda Gates Foundation gave millions of dollars to U.S. libraries, paying for the modernization of technology in many different libraries. Federal E-Rate funds have helped replace some of those inspired gifts.

General Ledger. Contains the chart of accounts, both debits and credits.

Government Performance and Results Act of 1993. Required libraries that received federal funds to measure the impact of those expenditures. With this change, a professional group that historically had focused on "outputs" now had to pay attention to "outcomes," "impacts," and "benefits".

Government Program and Results Act Modernization Act (GPRAMA). On January 4, 2011, President Obama signed H.R. 2142, the GPRA Modernization Act of 2010 (GPRAMA), into law. Section 10 requires agencies to publish their strategic and performance plans and reports in machine-readable formats.

Grants. Funds from individuals, philanthropies, or government agencies to improve some aspect(s) of the library. One of the ways that libraries add value to their operations is by obtaining grants to increase the funding for critical activities.

Green (LEED) Certified Libraries. A green library is designed to minimize negative impact on the natural environment and maximize indoor environmental quality by means of careful site selection, use of natural construction materials and biodegradable products, conservation of resources (water, energy, paper), and responsible waste disposal (recycling, etc.). In new construction and library renovation, sustainability is increasingly achieved through LEED, a rating system developed and administered by the U.S. Green Building Council (USGBC).

Income, Allocated or Earned. Library income often is from a single source, as a budget allocation from a university, college, city, country or state, or a financial office which has collected taxes authorized for the library, thereby sourcing a major revenue stream. Special libraries often receive their money from an organizational entity like a medical school, a legal firm, or a corporate budget. See also **Earned Income**.

Income and Expense. Income and expense are the two principal monetary categories in budgets, monthly financial statements, and annual reports.

Income Statement. Reports the library's revenue and expenses over a specific time period.

Invoice and Packing Slip. A noun or verb, an invoice is an itemized bill for goods sold or services provided containing individual prices, the total charge, and the terms of payment due. The packing slip is packed with boxes shipped to fulfill an order. It is a record of what has been shipped, not a billing invoice.

IRS 501 (C)(3) Internal Revenue Service Classification. Most libraries either have or are eligible to have status as an IRS Section 501(C)(3), which "is the public benefit category, and permitted purposes for organizations in this category which includes: charitable, educational, and literary." Under this category, libraries may engage in education and promotion of literacy and literature, including administrative and training costs, including most aspects of operating a library.

IRS 509 Classification. A few libraries, usually older ones, are classified as charitable government agencies under the IRS 509 code. That status usually has been given to older libraries, like large public libraries, which operate almost entirely with "government funds." Different operational requirements and differing rates of tax benefits for donors mean that most large public libraries would prefer to be designated as 501 (C)(3).

IRS Form 990A. Form 990 is an annual reporting return that certain federally tax-exempt organizations must file with the IRS. It provides information on the filing organization's mission, programs, and finances. Depending on the nature of their charter and/or operational authority, all academic, public, and school libraries have to file an IRS 990A statement each fiscal year to keep their not-for-profit tax status secure. Special libraries may be viewed as part of their corporation's for-profit structure, in which case they would not file a 990A.

IRS Form 1099. Miscellaneous income statement to contractors. Also, some library employees may receive IRS 1099 notification for some part of their income.

Journal of Accounts. A record of financial transactions in order by date, with an appropriate amount of detail to explain the transaction. It is the basic accounting document from which others flow.

Liabilities. The financial claims against the library's assets. What the institution owes.

Library Credit Cards. In modern libraries, using a credit card for a purchase is one way to purchase an item that is needed by the library. For example, a library maintenance person needs a specific kind of elbow joint to make a plumbing repair. The person uses a credit card the maintenance person carries to make the purchase. The library is billed monthly for such purchases.

Library Services Act of 1956. Federal funds could be used to bring isolated rural communities into modernity by planting or upgrading libraries (Chapter 4).

Library Services Act of 1964. Added federal funding for library construction and rehabilitation in urban as well as rural places.

Library Services and Technology Act of 1996. Federal funds could be used to help libraries fund new technology to match the rapid changes in a new age dominated by technology.

Lump Sum Budget. This type of grant designates a total amount to be given to the library, with the discretion for establishing the budget lines left to institutional or project managers.

Measurement. (See assessment, benefits and impact.)

Membership Fees. Another method of paying for library operation expense, viewed by many library professionals as the antithesis of "the free library movement." Those who are determined to be non-members of a library user community (e.g., nonresidents, not students of this college, etc.) often are allowed to use particular libraries by paying membership fees.

Mission Statement. Articulates the purpose(s) of the organization in the simplest and most powerful way possible.

Mobile Library Fleet. Vehicles used by the library to conduct its business, including bookmobiles, technology buses, pickup and delivery vans and automobiles used for outreach. This fleet can be miniscule or sizeable, but its expense has to be budgeted on some budget line.

Notes to the Financial Statements. Notes to financial statements contain all kinds of disparate information. In understanding financial statements, think of notes as explanatory footnotes.

Number Phobes. Those who fear numbers. This book encourages librarians not to love numbers or statistics but to learn how to use numerical measurement tools effectively.

Operational and Financial Review. The review ties major operational problems and/or achievements into finances. The review can highlight great successes or special large problems that are going to cause financial problems in the year(s) ahead.

Outcome Measurement. According to IMLS, outcomes refer to changes in an individual's attitude, skill, knowledge, behavior, status, or life condition. An outcome is a benefit that occurs to participants of a program; when the benefits to many individuals are viewed together, they show the program's impact. Outcomes always focus on what participants will say, think, know, feel, or be.

Partnership. Partnerships are a useful tool to pool resources with another complementary agency. An example would be where a neighborhood settlement house has a large number of potential library users as constituents and a library wants to increase the size of its reading program in that neighborhood without lots of new staffing.

Payroll Services. For-profit companies like ADP (Automatic Data Processing) and Paychex that handle multiple not-for-profit payroll accounts, including many libraries.

Performance/Function Budget. A budget reflecting resource input and services output for each organizational unit. Frequently used by libraries to link funding with services provided.

Petty Cash. Typically, in a library, the petty cash fund takes two forms: the amount of cash kept at the desk to accept fine payments and to make change for fines, small sales in the library store, and so on; or the amount of cash kept on hand in the finance office to pay to employees who make small purchases while working.

Planned Giving. Planned giving is a promise of a future gift. By definition, it is any major gift of value whether promised in the "lifetime or at death as part of a donor's overall financial and/or estate planning."

Planning. The allocation of resources in a timely way to reach a desired goal.

Profit and Loss Account. The profit and loss statement is a wonderful tool to ascertain the amount of financial variances among the various organizational units within the library. It is seldom seen in library financial documents because libraries are more about increasing community value and accountability.

Program Budgeting. Provides a detailed breakdown of all expenses in each program, the idea being to control activity by the amount of budget detail.

Property, Plant and Equipment. A balance sheet line that reports the capital assets of the library.

Public Library Inquiry. An attempt by leaders of the library profession to legitimize librarianship, raising it from its marginalized professional status while improving the public image of the institution, thus increasing patronage and federal financial support, between 1947 and the mid-1950s.

Purchase Orders. When a library issues a purchase order, and it is accepted by a vendor, those actions establish the terms of a contract. The same thing occurs when the library is a seller and accepts a purchase order; that establishes a contract. Modern libraries have other means of purchasing goods and services, but the purchase order is still very important in most libraries.

Purchasing/Procurement. Except for salaries, a vast majority of library expenses are covered by purchasing or procurement orders, two different names for the same buying process.

Real Estate. As libraries change their work character, they add, sell, or renovate various pieces of real estate. This category includes fees associated with buying, selling, and construction and rehab. Real property may have its own funding line in the budget.

Redbox Style. Lending machines or kiosks located throughout the community where people can check out books, movies, or music without having to go to the library itself. Redboxes reflect user desire for library convenience.

Referendum. An election for a library that has taxing authority to increase the maximum tax rate that a library can obtain directly from the community's taxpayers'.

Reimbursement. As in reimbursement request or reimbursement claim for a payback of money owed, usually to staff.

Retirement Programs. A major financial benefit in public sector agencies like libraries, now controversial because some retirement liabilities have gotten so large that taxpayers see no way of paying them off at full value.

Return on Investment. The gains or losses incurred from invested funds

Revenue. A line in the income statement that reveals the amount of revenue the library has received in the current fiscal period, frequently broken down by income type.

Risk Assessment. As changes occur in staff composition, it is well for libraries to spend time with risk assessment experts from the insurance industry. Health education and disability insurance riders are two cost components of staffing that deserve some attention. Risk assessment is a tool to determine or control costs of insurance. A second kind of risk asssessment is usually done under contract with a security firm, usually to check for building safety hazards.

Sarbanes–Oxley Act of 2002. Set new or enhanced standards for all U.S. public company boards, management, and public accounting firms.

Serials Crisis. Shorthand term for rapidly escalating costs in scholarly journals, particularly in the areas of science, technology, and medicine.

Sick Leave. Library benefit so that a staff member is not penalized financially by simple illnesses.

Social Security and Medicare Tax. A staff cost mandated to be paid by Federal law.

Special Project. Library staff often get drawn into budgeting by working in special projects organized by the administration or other staff. Libraries tend to be project oriented, eliciting project language and a project budget for any recognizable change that is to be made in the library.

Special Project Budget. A budget that connects financial data and activities in a unified implementation strategy.

Staff Budget. Budget category for most staff-related expenditures, but with lots of institutional exceptions because different libraries include or exclude some staff-related items. For example, does the staff budget include funds to pay for contracting with auditors, fundraising counsel, and so on?

Supplier Credit Accounts. Many libraries make their financial lives easier by setting up supplier credit accounts. For example, maintenance staff are authorized to buy parts and supplies at various hardware stores rather than maintain a huge central storehouse. Another example is to have nearly all office supplies purchased and delivered by a business supply company. Buying online has extended this kind of activity by quantum leaps. Not having these kinds of supplies in library stocks lessens theft opportunities.

SWOT Analysis. A simple but often useful form of planning analysis, which focuses on assessment of strengths, weaknesses, opportunities, and threats, which the library is facing.

Tagline. A memorable phrase that summarizes the work of the library. Chapter 9 has a discussion of taglines.

Tax-Exempt Loans. Most libraries are tax exempt, and therefore eligible for tax-exempt financing, which typically yields a rate of interest below the for-profit corporate rate that banks charge. Therefore, financing a facility with a low-interest loan may enable a borrower to move to a larger or more efficient site than it would otherwise have been able to purchase outright, or to rent or finance at market rates."

Tax-Exempt Status. See IRS entries in this Glossary for discussion of types of library not-for-profit status.

Tax Increment Financing (TIF). A way of financing library building improvements in "blighted" areas that abates property taxes to raise money for capital improvements from private investors.

Tax Withholding. Withholding of a portion of staff salary to match requirements of federal, state, and local taxing authorities. This figure is subject to changes by the library and the individual staff member, and great care must be taken to avoid accounting errors.

Third-Party Rights and Benefits. Terms in the contract that specify the "set aside terms" by which women, disabled, minorities, and unions are to be given specific benefits in the terms of the contract.

Top-Down Budgeting. Budgeting in which top-level managers work out the financial parameters in which library departments or other work units will work within the coming fiscal year.

Unfunded Mandate. An unfunded mandate occurs when the national, state, or local government legally requires another government agency or set of individuals to perform certain actions, but provides no funding to carry out the action. An example would be where U.S. Congress would designate computer education programs for citizens to be carried out by college and public library systems without providing any funding sources to start such projects.

Uniform Allowances. A library staffing expense when the guard force, maintenance, custodians, and other service staff are required to wear uniforms at work.

Vision Statement. The vision statement articulates the hopes for the organization.

Zero-Based Budget. A budget that starts at zero rather than relying on previous library budget experience.

SELECTED BIBLIOGRAPHY

Bakke, David. "The Top 17 Investing Quotes of All time." *Investopedia.* May 16, 2011. Retrieved on August 3, 2015, from http://www.investopedia.com/financial-edge/0511/the-top-17-investing-quotes-of-all-time.aspx#ixzz3hndFpCcv.

Barak, Lauren. "SLJ's 2014 Spending Survey: Savvy Librarians Are Doing More with Less." *School Library Journal.* April 15, 2014. Retrieved on July 26, 2015, from http://www.slj.com/2014/04/budgets-funding/sljs-2014-spending-survey-savvy-librarians-are-doing-more-with-less/#_.

Becker, Samantha, Michael D. Crandall, Karen E. Fisher, Rebecca Blakewood, Bo Kinney, and Cadi Russell-Sauve. *Opportunity for All: How The American Public Benefits from Internet Access at U.S. Libraries. The U.S. IMPACT Study A Research Initiative Examining The Impact of Free Access to Computers and The Internet in Public Libraries.* Washington, DC: Institute for Museum And Library Services, 2010.

Bera, Sophia. *The Scary State of Financial Literacy in America.* Posted April 18, 2014. Retrieved on January 5, 2015, from http://www.dailyfinance.com/2014/04/18/the-scary-state-of-financial-literacy-in-america/.

Brandon Gaille. *List of 37 Catchy Slogans and Taglines.* Posted September 8, 2013. Retrieved on January 19, 2015, from http://brandongaille.com/list-37-catchy-library-slogans-and-taglines/]a somewhat different purpose, that of marketing an image in very synoptic form.

Burger, Robert H. "Financial Management of Libraries and Information Centers." (Currently GSLIS 590FM). Fall, 2010. In possession of author.

Daubert, Madeline J. "Fundamentals of Accounting." *Financial Management for Small and Medium-Sized Libraries.* Chicago: ALA, 1993. pp. 36–52. (Available as pdf on course website.)

Dervitsiotis, Kostas N. *Critical Path Budgeting: A Synthesis of Budgeting and Critical Path Scheduling.* Corvallis: Oregon State University, Scholar's Archive MA in Mechanical and Industrial Engineering, 1965.

Dobler, Donald W., and David N. Burt. *Purchasing and Supply Management, Text and Cases*, Sixth Edition. Singapore: McGraw-Hill, 1996.

Dossett, Judith. "Budgets and Management in Special Libraries." CLIS 724. "Special Libraries and Information Science." Dr. Robert Williams. April 28, 2004. In Williams, Dr. Robert C. *Special Libraries Management Handbook.* University of South Carolina: College of Library and Information Science, 1993–2004, 2007. Retrieved on June 19, 2015, from http://faculty.libsci.sc.edu/bob/class/clis724/SpecialLibrariesHandbook/INDEX.htm.

Doucett, Elizabeth. *What They Don't Teach You in Library School.* Chicago: ALA, 2011.

Evans, Edward G., Margaret Zarnosky Saponaro, Holland Christie, and Carol Sinwell. *Library Programs and Services. The Fundamentals.* Santa Barbara, CA: Libraries Unlimited, 2015, Chapter 18.

Foundation Center. *Grant Space. Knowledge Base: How Long Should Nonprofit Organizations Retain Business-Related Records?* Retrieved on April 9, 2014, from http://grantspace.org/tools/knowledge-base/Nonprofit-Management/Accountability/record-retention.

Fridson, Martin S., and Fernando Alvarez. *Financial Statement Analysis: A Practitioner's Guide.* 4th Edition. Hoboken, NJ: Wiley, 2011.

Gorman, Michael. *Our Enduring Values Revisited. Librarianship in An Ever-Changing World.* Chicago: ALA, 2015.

Greene, Edward F., Leslie N. Silverman, and David M. Becker. *The Sarbanes-Oxley Act: Analysis and Practice.* New York: Aspen, 2003.

Gross, Malvern J., John H. McCarthy, and Nancy E. Shelmon. *Financial and Accounting Guide for Not-for Profit Organizations.* 8th Edition. Hoboken, NJ: Wiley, 2013.

Hallam, Arlita W., and Teresa R. Dalston. *Managing Budgets and Finances. A How-To-Do-It Manual for Librarians, Number 138*. New York: Neal Schuman Publishers, 2005. p. 12.

Hartsook, Robert, and Suzanne Walters. *Resource Development for Libraries*. Wichita, KS, and Denver, CO: By the authors, 1992, p. 9. Typescript. Copy in authors' possession.

Harvard Business Review. *Finance Basics. Decode the Jargon; Navigate Key Statements, Gauge Performance*. Boston: Harvard Business Review Press, 2014.

Jones, Gwyneth. *The Daring Librarian. Blog post*. Retrieved on August 3, 2015, from http://www.the daringlibrarian.com/2013/04/who-needs-librarian-when-you-have-google.html.

Kirk, Rachel A. *Balancing the Books: Accounting for Librarians*. Santa Barbara, CA: Libraries Unlimited, 2011.

Library Operating Expenditures: A Selected Annotated Bibliography. ALA Library Fact Sheet 4. Retrieved on September 14, 2015, from http://www.ala.org/tools/libfactsheets/alalibraryfact sheet04. Includes a listing of recent electronically available articles from Net sources.

Lusardi, Annamaria. "Financial Savvy Key to a Secure Retirement." *Financial Literacy and Ignorance*. Retrieved on July 28, 2015, from http://annalusardi.blogspot.com/. This article also is on her *Forbes* blog at http://www.forbes.com/sites/pensionresearchcouncil/2015/04/17/financial-savvy-key-to-a-secure-retirement/. Paragraph breaks have been inserted to make easier the recognition of the separate findings.

Matthews, Joseph R. *Measuring for Results: The Dimension of Public Library Effectiveness*. Santa Barbara, CA: Libraries Unlimited, 2003.

Matthews, Joseph R. *The Bottom Line: Measuring the Value of the Special Library or Information Center*. Englewood, CO: Libraries Unlimited, 2002.

Newman, Bobbi. "You Can Not Do More With Less—Less for Libraries Means Less For Our Communities and They Deserve More." *Librarian by Day*. July 18, 2012. Retrieved on July 26, 2015, from http://librarianbyday.net/2012/07/18/less-for-libraries-means-less-for-our-communities-and-they-deserve-more/.

Parikh, Neel, Clifford Jo, Georgia Lomax, and Sally Porter Smith. "Making the Case for Budget Reductions: Pierce County Library's FY 2013 Budget." *Public Library Quarterly* 33, no. 1, 2014.

Polevol, Lee. "5 Tips for Choosing the Right Bank for Your Business." *Intuit Quick Books*. December 2, 2014. Retrieved on August 30, 2015, from http://quickbooks.intuit.com/r/banking/5-tips-for-choosing-the-right-bank-for-your-business.

Roberts, Brenda. "We Build Communities Through Knowledge: Demonstrating the Value of the Professional Public Librarian." In *Defending Professionalism: A Resource for Librarians, Information specialists, Knowledge Managers, and Archivists*, edited by Bill Crowley, 45–46. Santa Barbara, CA: Libraries Unlimited, 2012.

Smallwood, Carol. (p. 264) *The Complete Guide to Using Google in Libraries: Research, User Applications, and Networking. v. 2*. Lanham, England, and Plymouth, UK: Rowan and Littlefield, 2015.

Smallwood, Carol. *Librarians as Community Partners: An Outreach Handbook*. Chicago: American Library Association, 2010.

Smith, Arnott, and Kristin R. Eschenfelder. *Public Libraries As Financial Literacy Supports*. The School of Library and Information Studies, University of Wisconsin, Madison, December 2011, Center for Financial Security, Family Financial Security, Webinar Series, December 13, 2011. Sponsored by a grant from the UW-Madison School of Human Ecology Beckner Endowment. Retrieved on July 27, 2015, from http://cfs.wisc.edu/presentations/Eschenfelder2011_PublicWebinarPR.pdf.

Smith, G. Stevenson. *Cost Control for Nonprofits in Crisis*. Chicago: ALA, 2011.

Steele, Victoria, and Stephen D. Elder. *Becoming a Fundraiser: Principles and Practice of Library Development*. Chicago: American Library Association, 2000.

Turner, Anne M. *Managing Money: A Guide for Librarians*. Jefferson, NC: McFarland, 2007.

University of Minnesota. University Policy Library. Using the University Procurement Card. 1996. Retrieved on June 15, 2015, from http://policy.umn.edu/finance/procurementcard.

U.S. Government, Internal Revenue Services. *Compliance Guide for Tax-Exempt Organizations (Other than 501(c)(3) Public Charities and Private Foundations)*. Washington, DC: IRS, 2015 edition. Retrieved on August 2, 2015, from http://www.irs.gov/pub/irs-pdf/p4221nc.pdf.

Walther, Larry M. *Principles of Accounting*. 2015 Edition. Chapter 21. "Planning for Success, [Section on] Budget Periods and Adjustments." Retrieved on August 2, 2015, from http://www.principles ofaccounting.com/.

INDEX

ABOUT THE AUTHORS

Glen E. Holt, PhD, holds master's and doctorate degrees in history and urban studies from the University of Chicago. He taught at Washington University in St. Louis for 13 years, then became executive director of the St. Louis Public Library for 17 years. Holt's administrative expertise has won him a variety of awards, including the 2002 Charlie Robinson Award by PLA. He has articles in *Library Trends, Public Libraries, Library Journal*, and *The Bottom Line*, where he wrote a quarterly column on the economics of librarianship for 10 years.

Leslie Edmonds Holt, PhD, consults with libraries, schools, and child-serving agencies. She worked at the St. Louis Public Library as Director of Youth Services from 1990 through 2004. Holt is past president of the Association of Library Service for Children (ALSC) and has been active for many years in ALA, PLA, ALSC, and other state and regional library associations. She is coauthor of *Success with Volunteers* and *Managing Children's Services*.